Play Between Worlds

Play Between Worlds

Exploring Online Game Culture

T. L. Taylor

The MIT Press
Cambridge, Massachusetts
London, England

First MIT Press paperback edition, 2009
© 2006 T. L. Taylor

In addition to conference proceedings, portions of this book previously appeared in the following publications: chapter 3 (in Danish), "Power Gamers Just Wanna Have Fun" ("Spil Som Håndværk i en Online Verden"), in *Digitale Verdener,* Ida Engholm and Lisbeth Klastrup (eds.), Copenhagen: Gyldendal, 2004; chapter 4, "Multiple Pleasures: Women and Online Gaming," *Convergence* 9: (1) 21–46, Spring 2003. In addition, with permission of Mikael Jakobsson, some of my contributions to our coauthored article appear here in the section on guilds (2003), "The Sopranos meets *EverQuest:* Socialization Processes in Massively Multi-user games." Fine Art Forum 17 (8).

Habitat © LucasArts Inc.
Ultima Online © 2005 Electronic Arts Inc., All Rights Reserved.
EverQuest is a registered trademark of Sony Computer Entertainment America Inc. in the U.S. and/or other countries. © 1999–2005 Sony Computer Entertainment America Inc. Images used with permission from Sony Online Entertainment Inc. All rights reserved.

MIT Press books may be purchased at special quantity discounts for business or sales promotional use. For information, please email special_sales@mitpress.mit.edu.

This book was set in Stone Sans and Stone Serif by Graphic Composition, Inc. and was printed and bound in the United States of America.

Library of Congress Cataloging-in-Publication Data

Taylor, T. L.
Play between worlds : exploring online game culture / T. L. Taylor.
   p.   cm.
Includes bibliographical references and index.
ISBN 978-0-262-20163-6 (hc. : alk. paper)—978-0-262-51262-6 (pb. : alk. paper)
1. Internet games—Social aspects. 2. Fantasy games—Social aspects. 3. Role playing—Social aspects. I. Title.

GV1469.17.S63T38 2006   794.8—dc22   2005058010

10 9 8 7 6

Contents

Acknowledgments

Much like how the game of *EverQuest* is possible only through a constellation of actors, knowledges, and practices, so too is this book. I am deeply indebted to all the players and designers who have let me peek into their worlds and have talked about (and often debated) various topics with me. Their generosity is the foundation on which this work is built. My thinking on the variety of issues I raise here is also deeply informed by not only the written work of fellow researchers, but the conversations and sharing I have been lucky enough to have with so many interesting and thoughtful friends, colleagues, and students. Over the years this research also has been able to find a home (through conferences, journals, and colleagues) within several multidisciplinary communities (AoIR, 4S, and game studies) and for that I am very thankful. To be able to inhabit a space that supports work that crosses traditional borders is a real privilege.

Of course, there are always those few who do a kind of double-duty—reading drafts, letting me extensively pitch ideas at them, cooking me a meal and getting me through the final push. Kelly Joyce has been an incredible source of support to me for years now, always encouraging me, reading (last minute) drafts, and giving excellent critical advice. I am also especially grateful to Mikael Jakobsson, who not only has made daily life more bearable in the face of this project, but has deeply informed my thinking about the game and always helped me keep a handle on the movable object that is *EverQuest*.

While whatever errors in this book of course remain my own, it could not have been produced without the fortunate assistance of a very extended network of help, conversations, and feedback.

1 Finding New Worlds

Taking It Offline

I am returning to Boston for a convention after having moved away a few years earlier. When I lived in the area during the 1990s, I several times found myself making my way to a downtown hotel—for a twenty-fifth Internet anniversary celebration, a popular regional science fiction convention, or a virtual reality (VR) show. This time I am heading to the Park Plaza Hotel for an event that seems to link these previous forays together. I am going to an *EverQuest* convention. *EverQuest* (*EQ*) is a massively multiplayer online game (MMOG), which launched commercially in March 1999 and hosts hundreds of thousands of players who participate in a virtual game world in real time using the Internet. Using avatars of Gnomes, Elves, and a variety of other fantasy-inspired characters, players move through a vast 3-D landscape and battle mythical creatures with magic and virtual swords. Within a block of the hotel I begin seeing people wearing nametags—typical enough for a convention—but I quickly notice something different. The names written on them are odd sounding and seem to contain arcane information. From this small detail alone I know I am at the right place. I slip on my own badge declaring my game character name, my server, and my (by then defunct) guild. Now identified as "Iona, Bailerbents, Hidden Lore," I quickly feel the silent shift from outsider to fellow gamer.[1] I had not thought about myself much in those terms before this project, but I am struck by how oddly familiar this identity now feels.[2] This event, a "Fan Faire," presents some unique experiences in blurring the boundaries between game and nongame space, off- and online lives, avatars and "real" identities and bodies. The longer I have spent with *EQ* the more I have come to believe that this boundary work is at the heart of massively multiplayer games, and indeed Internet life in general.

There is a tradition within Internet communities for online friends and gaming partners to get together for face-to-face meetings. Sometimes these events are called "bashes," sometimes "cons" (as in convention), but generally they involve people flying or driving to a location and spending a weekend just hanging out with each other. In the course of my fieldwork in Sony Online Entertainment's *EverQuest* I had not yet attended one of the game's formal offline gatherings, so when I saw the announcement for one in Boston I decided it was time to go. At the time I had spent the past three years interviewing users, playing alongside them, joining "guilds," and generally participating in the life of the game. For this event I wanted to see how the players handled meeting each other offline and how people integrated their gaming lives with their "real" ones.

I arrive early on Friday evening and the big opening reception has not yet started, so I kill nearly an hour wandering the upstairs balcony, alternating my attention between the various merchandise tables (where you can buy a sword or ring that looks vaguely like *EQ* fantasy objects and very much like stuff you would see at a Renaissance faire) and looking out down onto the ground floor of the hotel where more and more Fan Faire participants turn up and mill about. Since many people do not know in advance what their game friends look like, there is a lot of scanning going on, looking for familiar names on the badges we all wear. I wait in a long line for my free Fan Faire shirt, basically a promotional item for the upcoming expansion to the game, *Planes of Power*. A simple cheap white t-shirt, the kind I never wear, but it also sports a small Boston Fan Faire logo. For some odd reason I am happy to have it when I see this. Suddenly I have something material on which to hang my participation in not just this event, but the game more generally. After getting the shirt I look at my watch and realize I still have nearly 45 minutes to pass before the doors open to the main ballroom. My own social nervousness creeps up on me as it always does, which feels like a nasty personal failing for an ethnographer. I resist my impulse to pull out a book and just find a quiet reading spot and instead end up walking around the balcony at least six more times. There are a group of people huddled around a small table very intently playing the soon-to-be-released paper version of *EQ*. Off in another room are machines installed with *EQ* so that Fan Faire participants can still play the game while away from home. I keep catching different server names on the tags everyone has hanging around their necks. It is the one word on the badge readable in a quick glance. Suddenly at one point a guy with brush-cut hair walks over and introduces himself. He is from my server, Bailerbents, and I instantly feel more a part of the crowd. I belong. He is wondering, as I am, where our fellow server players might be but, unlike me, he has guildmates who are supposed to turn up, so he says goodbye to go look for them. By this point the lobby and upstairs are truly packed and I am marveling at how many people have actually come. I have been to my share of offline meetings for other virtual worlds, but those had all been organized by the participants themselves. While a few gatherings reached around fifty participants or so, most were smaller affairs involving a handful of people coming together for a weekend. But this event is quite different. It is run by Sony Online Entertainment (SOE), the current developers and publishers of the game, and all those attending here have paid an $85 registration fee, not to mention hotel and airfare costs for some. As I look around the space what I have noticed in the game becomes more apparent. *EQ* draws a more diverse fan base than often is imagined. While few people of color are present, there are men and women, teens, the twenty-something contingent, and a fairly decent number over thirty.

Finally eight o'clock rolls around and I line up with all the others to enter the main ballroom for the kickoff event. There is a rush in and we all find that the large grand ballroom is filled with round tables of varying sizes with the server names on them. The edges of the room are set up with low-end snack foods (fresh vegetables, cheese, and crackers) and quite a few cash bar stations. The organizers of the event have done a smart thing by encouraging server members to sit together—if you do not know anyone when you arrive at the Fan Faire, you gain an instant community through identification with a server. *EQ* players do not play in one world but are scattered amongst duplicate versions of the game that reside on separate servers, now totaling forty-seven, each of which has its own name and often develops its own culture.[3] This table setup kicks off a kind of battle of server pride, something I have certainly never experienced before around the game, and I am struck by how much the structure of the event fosters these group identities. I never really thought of myself as specifically a "Bailerbents player" until this moment where, in a huge hall filled with people, it becomes a shared identity and easy point of connection. As with the game itself, the social connections quickly become a focal point of the experience. To my surprise I find that the server identities run strong and quickly people are chanting server names, as well as playfully taunting and teasing each other across tables. I spot the Bailerbents table and my heart sinks a little—the table is very small and completely un-occupied. I had been reading one of the server message boards and had the impression a fair number of people were coming, but we clearly are outnum-bered by other servers. Across the room I see moments of recognition spark-ing where people are meeting each other for the first time, face to face. Several people start holding up the server signs from the table and waving people over. There is an amazing amount of easygoing friendliness already, and much laughing and cheering.

The guy I met earlier spots our table and sits down with me. I think we are both a bit nervous about what the table size means. He is still scanning the room and I, honestly, am ready to pretend I am from another server just to hang out with more people. Eventually my anxieties are proven unnecessary as more people show up, including several couples. I wonder, as I have in the past, why that singular image of the male teenage isolate hanging out and gaming online holds so strong in the face of real players. The demographic truth is much more mundane. My servermates turn out to be incredibly nice people and, for those of us who have never met before (in-game or offline), we begin to exchange information. The procedure seems to be to either hold up your badge or look down at it, then back up at the person, in answer to the question "Who are you?" It's a familiar routine where everyone easily as-sumes what is meant by "you." Lori Kendall, in her wonderful ethnography of a text-based virtual world, describes attending an offline gathering hav-ing made her own nametag in advance to include both her online and offline name. She arrived at the party only to find everyone was using their online names, even when they sometimes knew each other's "real" ones (Kendall, 2002). The vibe is much the same at this event, where even the couples refer to each other by their in-game names. At some level it feels a bit taboo to pre-sume you could ask about people's "real" names. Indeed, I think I only men-tion mine once in name exchange, somewhat awkwardly.

I buy an overpriced drink and continue to chitchat about the game, which is the main topic of conversation. We discuss particular monsters and "zones" (areas of the game) and begin to recount sometimes funny stores about mis-adventures. One of the guys talks about having sold a character on eBay and, though he thought he would not mind it, found it disconcerting to log in one day and see, as he put it, "someone else using my avatar." Finally around 10 p.m. I decide to call it a night and head back to Cambridge where I am stay-ing with a friend. I am fairly tired from the overwhelming amount of activity and new people to process. I make my way through the crowded ballroom, amazed at how many people have turned up for this event. As I walk down Bolyston to the number 1 bus, I think about how my early Internet experiences seem to have led me here, to this moment when Internet, fantasy worlds, and VR collide.

On Saturday I arrive in time to participate in one of the popular events, the Live Quest. I do not know much about how it will work but am familiar with quests in the game, which usually involve solving puzzles and collecting artifacts to turn in for a special item. Sure enough, the offline version is much the same. The SOE representatives running the event organize us into groups according to our servers again and I meet more Bailerbents people. Many more turn up to this event and I hear about the various parties from the night before. The ballroom has been rearranged into rows of seats, and as our server gathers together to wait for things to kick off a man shows up and starts handing out roses. I assume he is selling them or simply giving them out to his friends, but he quickly makes clear all Bailerbents women will get one. He tells us that he is known for handing out "virtual flowers" in the game and I notice how he is mimicking his online identity and actions, how he is performing a kind of offline incarnation of his online persona. Sometimes, it seems, it is the real that imitates the virtual. I wonder if, when I meet him in the game next time, we will draw this offline experience into that space. How will I compare this real flower to his virtual one? Should I? These larger questions become a bit muted when I realize I am now stuck with carrying around a long-stemmed rose which will make participating in the event a bit awkward. My ambivalence about the gender implications of the whole "all the women get flowers" issue reminds me of the ways that as researchers we can hold complicated relationships to the cultures we explore. I strike an internal compromise and, out of some respect for the gesture and also to not cause "trouble," I keep the rose but break it in half and stick it in my backpack. Tucking away a virtual flower online is certainly much easier, I think.

The hall is completely full and people once again are cheering and teasing those from other servers. The woman in charge, Cindy Bowens (a community manager for the game at the time), runs through some welcome information and tells us how the day will proceed. Before we are to begin, though, she remarks that a large promotional *EQ* sign has been taken from the lobby overnight. She says, in a joking but clearly serious way, that if it is returned within an hour there will be no questions asked but after that hotel security tapes will be reviewed and when the guilty parties are found out their characters will be banned. There is a kind of knowing nervous laugh across the room as people seem to acknowledge that, more than anything, the threat of being banned from the game carries huge weight. Sure enough, the banner is returned before she is done speaking, a potent reminder of the power of not only the game, but the company that runs it. Once announcements are over the Live Quest event starts.

The Bailerbents group splits into two teams, and I am with most of the people I met the night before over drinks. While I have never encountered any of them in the game I now know bits and pieces about them—both from their anecdotes about online adventures as well as stories about their families and jobs and where they live. Several of the team members have done Live Quests at other Fan Faires so they draw on that experience to direct us. I take a role as one of the runners—the part of the team that makes mad dashes gathering clues. Much as when I research the game itself, I find myself playing too, which brings with it affectivity and unguardedness. This method of participation puts the researcher in the interesting methodological position of being, both in practice and emotionally, deeply embedded in their world of study.

As the Live Quest gets underway the somewhat upscale hotel is transformed, and I smile at how a kind of properness gets up-ended. The entire hotel lobby and its public spaces have now not only been entirely taken over by players but by *EQ* company representatives dressed up as game characters. They wander around providing puzzles, clues, and rewards. Off in a corner or along a hallway I see someone in a cape, someone dressed as a wizard, someone wearing a kilt as Barbarians in the game do. People quickly dart across the room, up stairs, into the various ballrooms, all in a run to win. Regular hotel guests wander into the lobby and instantly look confused. Normal public behavior gets thrown out the window as it collides with the hotel's transformation into game space.

The conventions of the computer game are followed and even though this quest is "live" and offline, it unfolds much like the online "virtual" version. People line up to "hail" actors who are actually imitating artificial intelligence characters from the game. The loop of having a simulated person in the form of a game character now being imitated by an actual person in the hotel lobby is quite a twist on the real/virtual distinction.[4] The participants speak words as surely as if they had typed them in the game online (Hail, Sir Gandry) and everyone runs around—I run around—trying to find all the characters we need and catch them as quickly as we can. My fellow runner and I dash up stairs, wind our way around balconies, wander halls below the ground floor. We get puzzles that we then take back to the table where the rest of the group, consulting *EQ* reference books, complete them. Our group falls into place fairly easily—from playing the game we all know how to step into required roles—and game knowledge and skills are transferred to this space without anyone thinking twice. The clues in the Live Quest relate to the online game's locales, monster names, or procedures for completing tasks, and each participant jumps in with answers based on their play experience. In reward we get some slips of paper that have on them the image of the game currency—platinum, gold, silver, and copper—simple paper drawings signifying virtual coins which themselves refer to offline precious metals.

The Live Quest lasts a couple of hours and we are playing right to the end. We are running around, working hard, but clearly we are not nearly as on top of things as many of the teams. We are not supposed to cheat, of course, but several of us cannot help feeling some teams have an edge. Indeed, some part of me thinks that next time I should bring some walkie talkies. Even though we come nowhere close to winning, the process of playing got us all engaged with each other and was fun. I am not even sure we quite knew what it would take to win the Live Quest, but we played nonetheless.

After the event some people decide to go get lunch but I stay to hear some of the scheduled talks. The other big events at the Fan Faire are sessions where players can hear directly from, and ask questions of, the developers and artists involved with the game. These events serve as a kind of "real time" community forum, not entirely unlike those on online message board systems where people post comments and sometimes a developer pops in and replies. One of the sessions is a developers' forum. It is held in a large and very full room. Participants clearly are anxious to hear about plans for the game, as well as to voice their opinions and raise concerns they have. A panel of *EQ* developers proceeds to field questions from the audience about all aspects of game play and I am struck by the way many users ask quite precise questions about it. The developers are queried on specific things to improve (sometimes met with boos or clapping from audience members) and the developers reply equally attentively. It is an instrumental discussion—no meta questions that so often occupy academics such as intellectual-property concerns or questions about freedom of speech. The session is recorded so it can be posted on the *EQ* boards later, which produces a feeling that while this is a local conversation, the questioners in some ways stand for, are representatives of, the much larger *EQ* community. Indeed, on a message board I frequent I later read people expressing disappointment that particular questions had not been raised. Some felt the questioners might have done a better job in putting the developers' "feet to the fire" to address some tough gameplay issues. These forums thus extend the boundaries of not only the event space, but the roles of those who participate.

After the developer sessions we lined up again, this time for dinner. As I entered the hall I was quickly waved to one of the Bailerbents tables, a contrast to my experience of somewhat aimless wandering just twenty-four hours earlier. Some people from our server have gone in and quickly grabbed two tables next to each other near the front of the hall for us all to sit together. I end up at a table of people I have spent most of the day with. The dinner itself is fairly uneventful and is followed by a series of raffles for some good items such as computer speakers and membership to *Allakhazam,* a popular third-party Web site. By this point people at our table have grown familiar with each other, now having played, talked, and just hung out for hours. As with the game, the Live Quest became a powerful shared experience and dinner that evening was easy and congenial because of it. Though we all continue to adhere to the unspoken norm in which we only call each other by our "game names" we have a new bond built around not only our server identity but through several hours of working together through play. In the same way online game experiences are recounted and used as a way of building community, we now talk about the Live Quest. From there the conversation traverses, fairly seamlessly, across stories about people's lives—both real and virtual. We chat about where we are from, what we do for a living, how we all started playing, and who we play the game with. I find out that one of the couples is, in fact, sister and brother-in-law to one of my in-game friends. We all move back and forth through our offline identities and our in-game ones. As "Iona" I am able to live in that complex space of participant observer. While the power of play puts me, as a researcher, into new and sometimes unfamiliar, risky territory it also gives me a powerful way to connect to the community I study. Though SOE is throwing another party that night, most people at our table are unsure whether or not they are going. It costs extra to attend and many of them have already spent a large amount of money to participate thus far. In the end many of us say our goodnights, always with comments about contacting each other back in the game once we are home. While I do not become friends with everyone I met from my server, I definitely leave feeling I have made a few new connections with people I genuinely like and would be happy to see more of, even if just in our shared virtual world.

The next night, back home in North Carolina, I log in and test the waters. I send a message to one of my Live Quest teammates—Hey there. This is Iona, we met in Boston:)—and wait. Across my screen I see, Hi!! Was great to have met you! Looking for a group? And so we group up again, in this instance as avatars online, and head off to quest—virtually.

This experience of the Fan Faire, while on the one hand quite unique as a phenomenon all its own, also epitomizes for me some of the things that have long captured my attention with *EverQuest*. Much like the game, it weaves together the offline and online, the real and the virtual, as well as muddying the formal boundaries of "game" and "not game." The transmission of information about the event to those not present, the Live Quest money simulating in-game money which itself simulates real world currency, people bringing in their online identities, networks, and experiences to these kinds of offline events, or the ways the convention presents moments and connections that feed back into the online play experience itself—the Fan Faire, much like the game, is a kind of in-between site.

As also became quickly apparent to me, social connections, collective knowledge, and group action are central to the individual's experience. Both at the Fan Faire and within the game, solitary players quickly find themselves immersed in much larger structures that are crucial to their enjoyment of the space. The social is not just an add-on. Much like my experience of the Live Quest, it is in the moment of play in which the social and the formal game intersects that the more familiar connections are created. Shared action becomes a basis for social interaction, which in turn shapes the play. At the Fan Faire, of course, while there is a common object everyone is gathered around, there are interesting variations in how people talk about the game and describe their play. There is no single-typed *EQ* player, nor any single way to play the game. Similarly, people evoke different forms of *EQ* through their play (not unlike how, for some, the Fan Faire was a guild meet while for others it was a chance to talk to the developers). Some refer their play around Web sites or particular guilds they rely on, others construct their interaction with the game through specific family relations. In much the same way that there is a multiplicity of play, we might also imagine a multiplicity to the artifact of *EQ*.

This book is in some sense a collection of what I think of as border stories. It is not, for example, a story of everything that has happened in *EverQuest* since its launch. I anticipate such a story would only be told successfully through the studies of a variety of researchers approaching the subject from different angles. My work has focused on players or issues that typically are not seen as central in retellings of these games. I am interested in gaps or boundary work in that such locations can be the place in which definitions become problematized or previously hidden practices are accounted for. This book takes up, for example, the notion that games like *EverQuest* are fundamentally social spaces. While the creators of MMOGs have actively designed for sociability, this aspect of them does not commonly filter out into how the public understands what it means to play a computer game. Examining player life allows us to problematize the all-too-common formulations about computer games as an isolating and alienating activity. By looking at the areas of gaming normally neglected, I hope to suggest that we can learn something useful about both the games themselves and also about the broader culture in which they are embedded. I also turn my attention to power gamers, gamers who play in ways that seem to outside observers as "work." Rather than saying these players are overly invested, playing the game wrong, or ruining the experience for others by being too focused on what they do, I use their style as a way of examining our underlying notions of what constitutes play. Power gamers help us understand the limits of using terms like "fun" and give us ways to talk about how play sometimes feels like work, and may even be painful, repetitive, or boring. Power gamers reside between the worlds of play and work, illuminating for us assumptions and properties of both. In much the same way I take up the seemingly "fringe" category of power gamer players, I explore women players in the game and suggest that the games industry continues to ignore the active engagement of women to the detriment of both commercial potential and the experience of the actual players. Researchers often have over generalized what exactly women want from computer games, formulating a fairly narrow stereotype about femininity and the kinds of play women engage in. By looking at women who play *EverQuest*, I suggest we can broaden our understanding not only of women gamers, but interrogate underlying notions of femininity. The final area I explore revolves around questions of ownership of game space. In a world where much of our life is embedded in commercial systems and corporate "publics" games like *EQ,* which is owned by the major corporation Sony Online Entertainment, offer us an interesting opportunity to analyze what happens when emergent cultures confront privatized systems.

Ultimately I believe this case study of *EverQuest* can provide not only a useful snapshot of the larger multiplayer culture that is emerging in the world of gaming, but some more fundamental insights into issues that are independent of games—the relationship between work and play, gender identities, the use of technology in our lives, and our complicated relationship with commercial culture.

On Becoming a Gnome . . . and a Researcher

When I first began *EverQuest* I did not have in mind that I was launching a new ethnographic project that would lead me to spend the next four-plus years of my life engaged with the world and its players. I began not unlike many others—the game was meant to be a distraction for me from the "real" work at hand. Almost immediately, however, I began to see a space not unconnected from what I had been investigating previously. There were avatars, people communicating, a shared persistent virtual space, and items and objects that filled the world with artifacts. As my new character, a small Gnome Necromancer, began to engage in the world, killing rats and meeting other players, I found myself captivated.

I should note that this was after several weeks of motion sickness. It is always fascinating when our corporeal bodies conspire against or play catch-up to our digital ones, and having most of my screen experience grounded in text or lower-end graphical worlds, I was not quite prepared for the experience of embodiment and motion the game produced in me. *EverQuest*'s high resolution, three-dimensional nature—one that allows you to shift from first to third person perspective—took some adjustment. I had to acclimate to the new experiences, the new visions the technology afforded me. It did not help, of course, that I picked a type of character, a Gnome, who starts out in underground caverns (to this day it takes me some time to get used to indoor game locales). But in retrospect I think even this early experience in negotiating the dual spaces—running around in caverns on my screen and sitting upright in a chair at a desk in my apartment—signaled my overriding impression of engagement with these spaces. When we enter into places like *EverQuest,* we are indeed playing between worlds.

As I think back about this initial choice of character, one made not with an eye toward future research, I can see ways I both benefited and was hindered by it. As is always the case with shared virtual environments, how you choose to represent yourself has meaningful implications psychologically and socially. In my past work on social virtual worlds this was certainly the case. Users often spoke of the ways their avatar shaped the kinds of conversations or interactions they had. Meg, one participant of an early social graphical world, said, for example, "I have a favorite human [avatar] that I use the most now. [The] cat and lion [avatars] are more for playful moods. I seem to connect more with people as a human, and people open up more. Whereas as an animal . . . it's more of a surface thing. Lots of fun . . . but not all that much depth" (Taylor 2002, 52). Another member of the world commented on the ways avatars shape our sense of ourselves: "But I have [been] experimenting quite a bit, and the one thing that I've found most interesting is that people treat you based on how you present yourself, and, if you pay attention, you'll notice that *you* change depending on how you present yourself" (ibid. 56).

When I began *EQ* I faced the same choice all new players do: what gender, race, and class should I play? This language can be somewhat confusing to those unfamiliar with these games and more use to popular or social-science discourse in which terms such as "race" and "class" indicate very specific (and sometimes problematic) variables around identities. In *EQ* they both refer to something quite different and yet something that has similarly profound effects (though I will take this issue up a bit more critically in chapter 4). In the game players choose from "races" that probably are best thought of as species types. This language, and even the kinds of choices available, go back to pen-and-paper role-playing games. For example, when I started *EQ* players had to choose to be a Barbarian, Gnome, Troll, Halfling, Ogre, Erudite, High Elf, Half Elf, Dark Elf, Wood Elf, Dwarf, or Human.

The races have a range of strengths and weaknesses. Barbarians, for example, are quite strong but not as intelligent as Elves, who are more intelligent but also weaker. These capacities are rendered via points, also known as statistics (again another convention going back to tabletop gaming). The Barbarian, for example, begins with 60 intelligence points and 103 in strength while the High Elf starts with 102 and 55 respectively. The quantification of capacities, abilities, and skills through these stats is the underlying foundation of the game. Indeed the focus on stats makes up a large part of the game, especially at the high end, given how integral they are to the characters' abilities. The choice of race is, both theoretically and practically, tied to the class the player picks as some combinations simply are not allowed. Classes might be best thought of as ability sets or vocations. The original group of choices I had was Bard, Wizard, Ranger, Necromancer, Druid, Monk, Shadowknight, Magician, Enchanter, Paladin, Rogue, Cleric, Shaman, and Warrior. Wizards, for example, damage monsters and opponents by casting magical spells while Warriors engage in direct combat using weapons.

The instruction manual that came with the game gave some basic ideas about how races and classes combine to make characters, but just as important for me was the character-creation screen which allows experimentation with which combinations worked and what different characters looked like. Eventually I found many Web pages dedicated to player-generated tables, overviews, and character-planning guides outlining the pros and cons of various permutations. When I created other characters it was to these I would turn to more fully understand my options. I should also note that character-building choices require an alignment with forces of evil (as in the Necromancer, whose specialty is commanding the undead or wielding plague and disease) or good (as in the High Elf Cleric, whose main job is the healing of other players or bestowing protections). There has always been a somewhat dizzying amount of information at this stage of the game and many players simply do not bother with some of the arcana in the choices (often because they do not fully understand the underlying workings of the game mechanics). As I discuss later, the complexity of the game has continued to increase, but suffice to say that when I began my time in *EQ* I made some very basic calculations in my character creation that had a lasting impact on me both as a player and, I discovered, as a researcher.

My first character was a female Gnome Necromancer.[5] While I admittedly did not give much thought to which gender category to choose (typically I represent myself as a woman online, as I am in "real life"), I quite consciously chose both other categories—Gnome as the race and Necromancer as the class—based on several factors. When I looked at the choices of female avatars available I found what many women I have talked to over the years report: an assortment of fairly stereotypical sexualized bodies. Female avatars in *EQ*, especially those derived from a basic human form, wear very little clothing and often have large chests and significant cleavage. I am particularly sympathetic to the kinds of tensions Lori Kendall (2002) recounts in her work on MUDs where she found herself, as a feminist researcher, dealing with "partly compatible" settings in which her values were not always aligned with that of either the space she was involved with or the participants in her project. In many ways this is exactly how I felt when confronted with the avatars of the *EQ* world. Both the Gnome and the default Human were a bit better in that their clothing was a little less revealing. Having a human character did not appeal to my more experimental side, so I picked the Gnome avatar as it was the clearest path I could see out of a particular kind of gendered representation.[6] In part, by virtue of not looking too much like a "normal human" it seemed to present a nice option for breaking away from the typical form femininity takes in these games. My hunch about the Gnome proved quite on target over time. I believe I received many fewer "hey baby" comments than I would have had I chosen one of the more common female characters (something I confirmed with later experimentations with character creation). As a researcher I also think that the Gnome was so unassuming, so nonaggressive (compared to, say, a Barbarian), and indeed often seen quite playfully, that it facilitated spontaneous interaction and communication with players of both genders—something invaluable to me as a researcher.

When I decided to be a Necromancer I was relying much more on the information that was provided by the game, which was very little. By comparison, players starting the game now are given much more grounding. The original game manual, however, included no detailed descriptions of the classes and races available—the pros and cons of each—as there are now. Interestingly, the original manual opened with an eight page narrative on the history of the world and the gods, ending with the now infamous *EQ* tagline, "You're in our world now!" Such a backstory would be seen as an indulgence now to be sure. But by reading these stories one could hazily intuit what it might mean to choose to become a Dwarf ("Brell claimed the bowels of the planet and created the Dwarves, stout and strong, deep beneath the mountains of Norrath") or Elf ("And on the surface of Norrath did Tunare create the Elves, creatures of limitless grace and beauty"). Of course, my sensibility toward the more shadowed and idiosyncratic led me to pick a Gnome ("consumed with tinkering their devices") and while I did not know much about Necromancers, my nightowl-ish tendencies made me think it would be fitting. In this way I was using the game as an opportunity to experiment, but my choices also were shaped by some reflection of what might be "more me" or what might feel right. Of course, what is so striking now is how much my lack of knowledge of traditional tabletop gaming limited those initial choices. My early MUD (multiuser dungeon, a text-based virtual world) experiences were primarily around postapocalyptic storylines, so the fantasy world of *EQ* remained a bit of a mystery to me. I had no real sense of the various issues that arise from different types of characters, which in turn meant I did not configure my character optimally but instead went with what I liked. At the time I had no real idea of what kinds of people I would meet in the game, or the kinds of group activities I would become involved in. Much like my offline personality, I was more inclined to pick a character that would let me hang back in the shadows and be somewhat self-sufficient, at least until I got a lay of the land.

While I do not want to suggest a researcher can make inherently good or bad choices in terms of thinking about how representation and game structures will affect their experience and data, I do think understanding how avatars and play choices are inextricably tied to the research process is important. In this regard, my choice of Necromancer was probably not the most ideal, at least initially. Necromancers are able to play alone or "solo" for a much longer time over the course of a character's life than many other classes. For this reason my experience grouping with others in any kind of regular way came a bit later than, in retrospect from a methodological perspective, I would have liked. I did group with others from a very early stage, but I did not rely on having to do so in the same way I would have if I had been a Warrior, for example, who would need another player to heal her as she fought. Nor was I particularly valued in groups as a Cleric would be. My choice certainly fit my personality and in that regard probably kept me playing, but it did have downsides. I learned good team skills much later in my game life than others, and at times it took a bit more work for my participation to be seen as valuable (again, the best comparison is with a Cleric or Druid, who rarely are unable to find a spot in a group given their very useful skills).

On the other hand, in part because of the nature of my play as a Necromancer I found a fairly rich world of "external" *EQ* spaces. This came about in a couple ways. I ran into relatively few other Necromancers, so I relied heavily on a fan-run Web site and bulletin board to assist me. The site provided not only forums where other Necromancers would chat but an enormous number of databases around spells, playing strategies, and the like. The choice of Necromancer also structured my game play sessions. When soloing I often had a lot of "downtime"—time in which the character is sitting around regaining health or mana (a depletable and renewable element used to cast spells) between fights. I typically played the game on one machine and would have a second computer running alongside for browsing message boards, looking up maps, and basically extending my playspace well outside the confines of the formal game. Had I been a Warrior regularly grouped who got healed by others and therefore had little downtime, my experience of an *EQ* play session would have been vastly different.

I should note here that a couple years into my playing the game I did try a different character and indeed experienced a very different world. I opted for a Barbarian Warrior that was the exact opposite of my Gnome Necromancer in both looks and skills. Though the Warrior often fought in the same locations (known as "zones") my previous character had, even fighting the exact same mobs, the experience was quite different as I was much more reliant from the earliest stages on the help of others and the ability to get groups together. I found myself much more often in a leadership role as "tanks" (characters that deal out and take direct, close-up damage from a monster) often take charge of initiating battles and coordinating the actions of others by deciding what they should attack and when. I rarely found myself with downtime to browse Web sites while I played and in many ways felt a much stronger sense of duty and responsibility for the people in my group. Since I was the character who was supposed to be able to "take the hits," when a teammate came under fire—and, in the worst case, died—it was hard to not feel more pressure to improve my skills to prevent such a thing from happening again. I found this dramatically contrasted to my experience playing a Necromancer, in which as a spell-caster I would hang back in a group situation, watching with a kind of distance and often multitasking amid battles.

With these characters I came to inhabit the world and game alongside fellow players. Through the course of that time I moved through several guilds, saw sets of people and friends leave the game (and a few come back), and eventually found myself outpaced by a game that grew and changed in some fundamental ways from the one I started in 1999. This work is a product of that engagement, a product of a qualitative approach in which the researcher immerses herself in a culture and lives, talks, and works with and among the community members for a stretch of time. I want to make a strong case for the role of this method, and of ethnography, participant observation, and interviewing, in understanding the richness of spaces like *EverQuest*. As Christine

Hine describes it, the goal of this kind of work "is to make explicit the taken-for-granted and often tacit ways in which people make sense of their lives. The ethnographer inhabits a kind of in-between world, simultaneously native and stranger" (2000, 5). The game I began playing is not the same game that exists now. The experiences I had that first week, month, even year, were only a slice of what life was like in the space over the long run. Deep qualitative approaches methodologically foster this kind of layered understanding. As Mikael Jakobsson remarked on his own experience, "I myself have several times thought that I had reached a status quo where the gaming experience would not change dramatically again—only to be proven wrong by continued play. The understanding of the properties of the game world goes hand in hand with a more developed experience of the game as a player" (forthcoming, 14). Of course, I do not want to say short-term or quantitative work can tell us nothing about life in virtual worlds. Certainly it can, and throughout this book I make use of work done by scholars whose methods are quite different from my own. But the account that follows, my account, is deeply informed by my choice of method.

In a very grounded sense, then, this work is based on numerous player hours logged in the game (over several characters and several years), membership in guilds and a variety of social networks, reading and participation on player-run bulletin boards, meeting in-game people offline, attending a Fan Faire, and fairly active reading and keeping up-to-date with map sites, databases, comics, as well as formal and informal conversations with players. My research practice is that of bricolage, pulling from a variety of techniques, tools, and methods to understand a mix of practices, representations, structures, rhetorics, and technologies (Becker 1998; Denzin and Lincoln 2003). It is worth noting how many of these items fall into "extra-game" activities, and this should be an early signal about the meaning of the title of this book. Playing *EQ* is about playing between worlds—playing, back and forth, across the boundaries of the game and the game world, and the "real" or nonliteral game space. It is about the moves we make between the corporeal and the "virtual." This book is deeply concerned with understanding the nuanced border relationship that exists between MMOG players and the (game) worlds they inhabit. The stories that follow do not simply contain themselves to phenomena "within the game" as it is narrowly defined via the system's rules or structure, but instead tries to tackle the ways these game worlds are interwoven with activities, lives, practices, and structures typically seen as "outside" of, or secondary to, the game. My hope is to show that the very notion of being able to bound off what is game and not game is not a particularly fruitful way of understanding these spaces—either as games or via their status as a cultural space.

If the history of MMOGs should be told with an eye on both text-based worlds and social graphical environments, we might similarly turn to Internet studies to help us make sense of this blurred boundary life. That field has grown almost in tandem with my time researching *EverQuest*. While many of us had been researching Internet phenomenon since the early 1990s, the first official Association of Internet Researchers conference was held in 2000. Some of the best work to come out of nongame virtual spaces has revolved around an exploration of the ways online and offline life are interwoven together in complicated ways.

A good deal of Internet research in the 1990s focused on what might be seen as a hard line between the on- and offline worlds—epitomized by the now infamous cartoon in *The New Yorker* of a dog boasting to another that "On the Internet, nobody knows you're a dog" (Steiner 1993). The second wave of Net studies took a more critical approach and elaborated ways in which the online world was not a tidy, self-contained environment but one with deep ties to value systems, forms of identity, and social networks, and always informed by the technological structures in which it was embedded. This is not to say that experimentations do not exist online (such as gender-swapping) but that how people make sense of and experience who they are online is not inherently separate from who they are and what they do offline. What seems more to be the case is that people have a much messier relationship with their off- and online personas and social contexts. That people can slip into and out of complex social networks that cross not only online and offline space, but genres within the online world is a fact often under-acknowledged. The journalistic anecdotes that circulate, of identity deceptions for example, hide a much less sensational, even mundane, integration of technology into people's everyday lives. People are very adept at moving back and forth between on- and offline spaces and relationships, even while being ambivalent or unsure of how to frame the experience online life produces. These nuanced practices of negotiation, of flexibility in the face of emerging technology, are quite different than early rhetoric, which mostly framed online life as a bounded-off zone of experimentation. While online life certainly has experimental qualities, it simultaneously has a broader context in everyday offline lives and practices.

Similarly, we also might complicate the earlier formulations that saw online life as simply always referring back to the offline. My call to attend to the interweaving of these spheres is not that we need to reground in the offline so that we can attribute meaning or significance to online lives. It is not, for example, that online worlds are spaces in which we simply work out offline issues and once sorted, happily leave. That story over-privileges the offline in ways that are not particularly useful. It is instead the case that we have phenomena that are unique to both spheres and also occupy spaces of overlap. What happens in virtual worlds often is just as real, just as meaningful, to participants. A friend can be a friend online, even if you never meet them face to face. It is, of course, much simpler when we bound off both spaces and try and come up with tidy categories for each, but what I find in my work (and see in many others') is that people live much more in the gaps between the two and negotiate that experience in fascinating ways. This research then takes as an instructive jumping off point the work done in critical studies of online environments and technologies. Its departure point is one in which not only the design of the game is looked at, but the actual use and practices that circulate around it are considered. And rather than simply taking *EQ* at face value, so to speak, this book tries to understand the ways not only the artifact of the game, but the production of play within it, are multiply constituted by a variety of actors located in particular social contexts. In much the same way we now see the relationship between on- and offline life as not a bounded one, in many ways a game/not-game dichotomy does not hold.

2   Gaming Lifeworlds: Social Play in Persistent Environments

After years in the making and millions of dollars in development costs *EverQuest,* one of the most popular MMOGs, purports a subscriber base of around 420,000, with peak play periods hosting 100,000 simultaneous gamers and generating sizable revenues each year (Asher 2001; Humble 2004; Marks 2003; Morrison 2001; Tedeschi 2001; Woodcock 2005).[1] Measured against the 2000 U.S. Census, the population of "*EverQuest* would be the 35th largest city in the U.S., between Long Beach, Calif., and Albuquerque, New Mexico" (Humble 2004, 25). Since being launched, 2.5 million copies of the game and its expansions have been sold and the game continues to have a team of about 50 people working with it daily, with some additional support staff in India.

Despite the seeming novelty of this game, *EverQuest* (and MMOGs in general) can be traced back to several older traditions both in gaming and virtual multiuser spaces. Tabletop gaming, most notably *Dungeons and Dragons* (*D&D*), provides some of the basic structure and underpinning of many multiuser fantasy-genre games. In *D&D,* players create characters by building from a palette of attribute types (like charisma and dexterity) and then, using dice rolls, are assigned various amounts of points to these and other skills. Character sheets detailing all the abilities of each character are used as players adventure together through scenarios laid out by a fellow player, a game master (GM, or DM for dungeon master within *D&D*). This emphasis on adventuring, group action, and characters built out of a combination of statistics and equipment was carried over to computer gaming with the creation of MUDs.

MUDs (multiuser dungeons) form a second thread in the history of *EverQuest* in that they heavily informed not only the designers of the game, but the entire genre that has emerged in MMOGs. MUDs are text-based virtual environments hosted on a computer that allows users to log in and participate in the world. Using Telnet (or any of the client programs designed specifically for MUDding),[2] the players connect to a remote computer via the Internet. The host computer can be located anywhere. Once in the space, players are given a textual description of where they are. The first MUD (known as *MUD1*), for example, began like this:

Narrow road between lands.
You are stood on a narrow road between The Land and whence you came. To the north and south are the small foothills of a pair of majestic mountains, with a large wall running round. To the west the road continues, where in the distance you can see a thatched cottage opposite an ancient cemetery. The way out is to the east, where a shroud of mist covers the secret pass by which you entered The Land.[3]

The player types commands such as look, say, get, north, east, and various emotive commands to interact with the game's world. They can move around in the space and, depending on the type of MUD it is, proceed on adventure-like quests, kill monsters, walk along virtual streets and shops, go into clubs, socialize, and a wide variety of other activities the various worlds might offer. The genre dates back to 1979 when, by spring of that year MUD was being developed by the team of Richard Bartle and Roy Trubshaw, both of Essex University.[4] As Bartle describes it, "The game was originally little more than a series of interconnected locations where you could move and chat" (Bartle 1990a). This version was rewritten several times with Bartle developing the system into *MUD1,* a "fantasy environment, i.e. a vaguely medieval world where magic works and dragons are real" (Bartle 1990b). Bartle notes that, "Most of the first generation of lookalike games stayed in the genre, partly because the authors liked that kind of game (or they wouldn't have played *MUD1*), and partly because *MUD1* could be used as a source of ideas for commands, spells, monsters and so forth" (ibid.). Indeed, what remains quite striking is how many MMOGs continue to operate in this fantasy genre and remain based in the preferences and play styles favored by the designers themselves.

Spring 1980 brought a handful of external players to MUD to test it out given the good fortune that Essex University was a part of an early packet-switching system and was connected to the ARPANet. Bartle writes, "The game was initially populated primarily by students at Essex, but as time wore on and we got more external lines to the DEC-10, outsiders joined in. Soon, the machine was swamped by games-players, but the University authorities were kind enough to allow people to log in from the outside solely to play MUD, so long as they did so between 2 am and 6 am in the morning (or 10 pm to 10 am weekends). Even at those hours, the game was always full to capacity. Thus, MUD became a popular pastime throughout the modem-using computer hobbyists of Britain. I also sent copies of the code to Norway, Sweden, Australia and the USA" (Bartle 1990a). Brad King and John Borland note in *Dungeons and Dreamers,* a fascinating account of some of the more biographical and nitty-gritty details in the computer game developer scene, "In Bartle's MUD, the people he knew were the game, and these people became one of the first communities to bond wholly inside the context of the game world" (2003, 54). The popularity of the game signaled a new turn in which multiuser spaces were to become one of the more innovative developments within Internet technologies and certainly a genre that excited many computer users. The importance of Trubshaw and Bartle's early work is not just its contribution as a game system but that it also marks the beginning of development within a broader genre—multiuser virtual worlds. The early ethic of public source-code release with the MUD development community, and the fact that it intersected with an audience often largely based in universities (who had ready access to the Internet and technology) spawned many adoptions and variations in the scene, helping fuel the growth of multiplayers in general.

In a move away from a strict gaming theme, in 1989 a Carnegie Mellon student by the name of James Aspnes built a somewhat different kind of server which he named TinyMUD. TinyMUD was a space in which the prime activity was not slaying dragons, but world building and socializing with other people (Bruckman 1999; Keegan 1997). Keegan argues that "TinyMUD revolutionised mudding, replacing combat and competition with socialisation and world building. Made such a giant leap away from (then) conventional that some didn't even consider it a 'game.'"[5] Beyond breaking the game-oriented formula of MUDs, it also served as an important precursor to MOO, yet another "flavor" of text-based world.

MOO (MUD, object-oriented) proved to be a significant development in early multiuser worlds. Released in 1990 by Stephen White, its emphasis on object-oriented classes and object creation was an important addition to the kinds of spaces available at the time. MOOs quickly became highly user-extendable environments, often geared toward social, professional, and educational themes. The ability of users to learn the language relatively easily and create objects of their own made them particularly popular. While the worlds of You are in a dark corridor are still around and gaming spaces continue to develop a sophistication all their own, the social worlds fostered by

MOO, or TinyMUSH, or any of the other variants now available, mark a turning point in online virtual spaces. No longer just a playground for gamers, MUDs in the 1990s established themselves as suitable for a variety of activities, experiences, and users (for some excellent work on MUDs and graphical worlds see Cherny 1999, Dibbell 1998, Jakobsson 2002, Kolko 2000, LeValley 1999, Mortensen 2003, Pargman 2000, Reid 1996, Schaap 2002, Schroeder 2002, Schroeder, Heather, and Lee 1998, Suler 1996, Sundén 2003, and Turkle 1995). Though originally grounded in a *D&D* gameplay style, as they developed they began to more explicitly orient toward a kind of virtual "worldness" and, as such, prefigure the kinds of spaces we see in *EverQuest*-like games.

While MUDs typically figure into the histories that are told around MMOGs (indeed many of the most prominent designers of the genre come from MUD-ding backgrounds) it is also important to consider the ways the history of graphical social worlds intersect the story. In 1985, four years before the creation of the socially oriented TinyMUD platform, Lucasfilm Games in association with Quantum Computer Services created *Habitat,* an online graphical virtual environment for multiple users (figure 2.1).[6] Using a home computer and modem, a person could dial into the QuantumLink computer system and access this world. Once logged on, they would see cartoon-like graphics rep-

Figure 2.1
Scene from *Habitat,* 1986

resenting the world and others in the space. Users could roam around the world, meeting others who were also logged in at the same time. They could walk, talk, and interact with people and objects in the world—much like in some MUDs, but without extensibility by users as with the MOO platform. Chip Morningstar and Randall Farmer, lead designers on the project and longtime developers of virtual worlds, describe their intent in an important early essay entitled "The Lessons of Lucasfilm's *Habitat*":

Habitat, however, was deliberately open-ended and pluralistic. The idea behind our world was precisely that it did not come with a fixed set of objectives for its inhabitants, but rather provided a broad palette of possible activities from which the players could choose, driven by their own internal inclinations. It was our intention to provide a variety of possible experiences, ranging from events with established rules and goals (a treasure hunt, for example) to activities propelled by the players' personal motivations (starting a business, running the newspaper) to completely free-form, purely existential activities (hanging out with friends and conversing). (Morningstar and Farmer 1991, 287)

This system was a significant development in networked virtual worlds. It was one of the first online graphical spaces in which average computer users could fashion for themselves avatars and undertake living in a virtual world. While games did exist in the space, its sense of emergent "worldness" was foregrounded. The original *Habitat* closed it doors in the United States in 1990 though the technology was then licensed to Fujitsu-Japan and a Japanese version of the Habitat world called *Populopolis* was born. The technology eventually made its way back to the U.S. (now under the name *Vzones*) and has been up and running in various forms (with the *Dreamscape* world being the oldest) since 1995. These worlds operate as an environment in which users can play games, role-play, visit with friends, decorate personal homes known as "turfs," and participate in a social world. With an economy, housing system, lively social life, and emergent player culture it is an artifact that anticipates the mass virtual worlds of games like *EverQuest*.

Though *Habitat* and the later *Dreamscape* were 2-D worlds using third-person perspective,[7] they spurned the development of a range of spaces. In 1995, the company Worlds, Inc. released *AlphaWorld,* the first 3-D world-building platform for multiuser environments to generate a sizable community. The first version of the product had only one avatar (the somewhat infamous "Cy," a very generic-looking faceless male) and allowed the user to assume first-or third-person perspective. People could log into the server, interact with others and, nearly as central, build homes and various structures. Users registered for "immigration numbers" and then became official "citizens" of the world, allowing them full access to building locations and objects in the space.

The mid-90s saw a boom in graphical virtual worlds with everything from the 3-D world of *Onlive! Traveler,* with its voice-enhanced talking heads, to *The Palace,* a somewhat cartoon-like space where players could create and run their own unique worlds complete with avatars, objects, and games.[8] This period was also the time of ambitious, though ultimately failed, ventures like VRML (virtual reality markup language) and standards for "universal avatars."[9] Often inspired by Vernor Vinge's influential story "True Names" and Neal Stephenson's book *Snow Crash,* many early world designers thought about and debated the possibilities for a "metaverse" in which large-scale vibrant virtual worlds, filled with numerous avatars, would coexist.

Around this period the graphical multiuser game world emerged. These spaces mixed together the long tradition of online multiplayer games (à la MUDs) with the cultures and "world" focus reminiscent of what we see in graphical social spaces. Games like 3DO Company/Near Death Studios's *Meridien59* (1996)[10] and Blizzard's *Diablo* (1996) offered players the chance to enter into a graphical space and play with others in real time. *Ultima Online* (1997) is often seen as the breakthrough game of the genre because of its popularity, world focus, and lively player culture (figure 2.2). It fairly quickly reached the 100,000 subscriber mark, far surpassing the kinds of player populations seen in MUDs and the handful of other graphical worlds.

As Elizabeth Kolbert described it in her 2001 *New Yorker* article about the game, "*Ultima Online* is also extraordinary detailed, down to its most banal features. Players can design clothes for their avatars; they can have pets and train them to do tricks; and they can construct elaborate houses, which, if they have the wherewithal, they can decorate with paintings and rugs and candelabra and tchotchkes" (Kolbert 2001). *Ultima Online* has become notable in the history of MMOGs not only for the ways it revolutionized multiplayer gaming, but for being a frontrunner on issues still under heavy debate. It was one of the first games to confront mass player protest, not to mention the sale of virtual items for real world currency. The development and support team (a number of whom have continued to build the MMOG genre) ultimately had to tackle one of the biggest challenges to these games, mass community management.

Figure 2.2
Ultima Online, 1997

The intent here is not to provide a complete history of these virtual worlds (which itself deserves an entire book) but to sketch out what I see as the historical context in which a game like *EverQuest* could arise. When the game launched in 1999 Internet use was continuing to accelerate and broadband services were reaching many major cities in the United States. Internet users were increasingly familiar with the notion of spending leisure time online (be it via chatrooms or surfing the Web) and combined with the popularity of gaming, *EQ* hit a fortunate window of opportunity. It piggybacked on the old culture of MUDding and tabletop gaming, as well as drawing on advances in graphics and multiuser virtual worlds.

The threads I am pulling together here are certainly not the only way to retell the history of these spaces. Indeed, they reflect my own research biography and the paths that lead me to *EQ.* I came to the game in November of 1999 when I was in the final stages of a large project on MUDs and social graphical worlds. I had spent a number of years researching embodiment in virtual environments and was tapering off that project. It was then that I began to hear about "this game, *EverQuest.*" As anyone who has spent time in virtual worlds can tell you, users of such spaces are often an inquisitive bunch when it comes to new places to explore. I was constantly tossed new leads on worlds to check out, and it was in this last half of 1999 that the word *EverQuest* began to appear more frequently in conversations. At the time the game had just hit somewhere around 150,000 subscribers, far more than I had ever seen in a multiuser space. I should note that the primary virtual world I was investigating at the time was not a gaming space and, not surprisingly, much of the way *EQ* was framed for me early on was as a world versus a game.

The relationship between these two categories is a fascinating one and something explored more and more by those interested in multiuser spaces. On the one hand *EverQuest* has many of the characteristics of a game: hunting monsters, pursuing quests (also for experience points), advancing a character through levels and achievements, and competing (sometimes directly, sometimes not) against fellow players. On the other hand, there is no winner. There is no obvious finish line, no point of completion, where it is clear the game has been won. While there are levels to progress through, which mark achievement, they have only a partial connection to any sense of completion. Indeed, the numerous players who continue in the game even after hitting the highest level (which the developers are always raising—from the original 50 levels to 70 at the time of this writing) are a testament to the way the game does not support closure. The game's old tagline, "You're in our world now," evokes the feeling that what you do in *EQ* is immerse yourself in a space. People create identities for themselves, have a variety of social networks, take on roles and obligations, build histories and communities. People live and through that living, play. Certainly MUDs have a history of this kind of rich social milieu and early graphical worlds had their fair share of gaming (typically player-driven), so this is not meant to be a story of two forms marrying to produce a new genre entirely. *EverQuest* instead popularized what had been brewing on a smaller scale for a number of years—the notion of shared persistent world environments full of both instrumental and free action.

The World of EverQuest

Like many games in the massively multiplayer genre, *EverQuest* is made up of a fantastical land covering several continents, planets, and "planes" inhab-

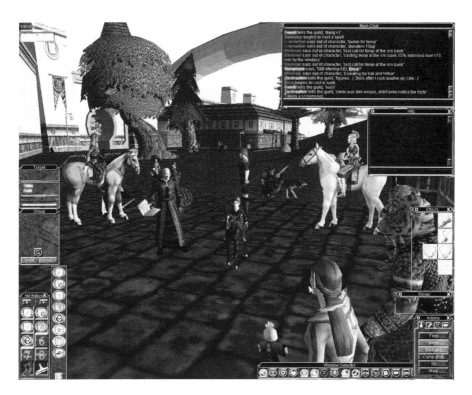

Figure 2.3
EverQuest's Plane of Knowledge

ited by numerous creatures and people, some "real" and some driven by fairly
basic artificial intelligence systems. The world of *EQ* is rendered in high-
resolution three-dimensional graphics complete with accompanying sound-
track (figure 2.3).

By purchasing the game and paying a monthly fee, users are able to connect
to *EverQuest* through a client program that communicates with the game
servers run by Sony Online Entertainment.[11] The world of *EverQuest* exists as
a persistent world environment players can connect to 24 hours a day and
game together.

As I describe in chapter 1, the first step for all players is to create a character based on a variety of choices that will inform their gameplay. Once the
character is created, they then enter the world and begin the process of
gaining levels to progress through the game. There are currently 70 levels a
player can attain, and with each level comes new skills, powers, and abilities.

Players gain experience (also known as "leveling" or "gaining XP," experience points) by killing monsters (known as "mobs") that represent a challenge to them, or through quests. By working either on their own or in a group with others, players wander the virtual landscape constantly looking for new challenges.

While some servers allow for players to kill other players (termed "player versus player" or "PvP"), the majority of *EQ* users spend time on player versus environment servers (PvE) and only kill nonplayer-character (NPC) mobs, creatures not played by any live person but instead animated through the internal artificial intelligence of the game system.[12] As players progress through the levels of the game and become powerful, they are able to travel more freely throughout the fairly large world that makes up the game. The landscape of the world consists of mountain regions, oceans and lakes, grassy plains, fortresses, and dark twisty dungeons. Most zones in the world (now totaling well over 200) have an associated level, meaning that players are likely to encounter monsters of a particular strength in specific areas. There are areas for new players, known as "newbie" zones, with creatures of very low strength (though certainly still a challenge to the new level-1 character) and higher-end areas where a single monster can take upwards of 55 people to kill. As a player becomes more powerful, creatures that once threatened them may no longer do so or, if they do attack, are killed easily. Because of the growth of the player's character over time the world of *EverQuest* is notably dynamic in a way many other computer games are not. The experience of the environment, monsters, other players, and even oneself changes over the course of a character's development. Monsters that were once quite formidable become easily killed and areas that were dangerous, or completely inaccessible, become neutral territory.

Although the game, with its world of magic and mythical creatures, seems to suggest a role-playing genre, players rarely employ any kind of formal RP orientation outside of special circumstances or the one server dedicated to the play style. The lack of role-playing in the game, however, does not mean that there is no interaction or social life among the players. One of the most notable things about games like *EQ* are the ways they are deeply social. While much of what we hear about gaming in the popular press evokes images of alienation and isolation, it is often a grave misunderstanding of (or sometimes a willful bias against) the nature of these games. The sociality of the space is not simply a matter of players talking to each other but a web of networks and relationships—sometimes weaving between on- and offline life, in-game and out-game—developing, and disintegrating, over time.

Despite my first character being one that could play alone ("solo") fairly easily, I was inducted quickly into the social worlds of the game. All new players typically start out having to spend a fair amount of time in the newbie zone with other low-level characters and monsters. It is here that players learn the initial skills required for the game and the ways to coordinate with others. When I first began *EverQuest,* travel across the regions was much more difficult than it is now. Given that I did not understand how to travel the world, not to mention my character being too poor and my not knowing how the "port" system worked (instantaneous magic transport from a player who is a Druid or a Wizard), I spent quite a few levels in the Steamfont Mountains, a newbie zone outside of my "home city," the underground caverns of kingdom of the Gnomes, Ak'Anon (figure 2.4).

Figure 2.4
Steamfont's guards outside the entrance to Ak'Anon

During those first few weeks of play I got to know the area very well. When I venture back now I still remember the valleys and hills, the location points of many monsters I killed . . . or was killed by. Returning is not unlike going back to a real-life hometown, with all the memories the landscape and architecture evoke. It was also here that I met my first fellow players, also typically Gnomes, who, like me, were very new to the game and running around trying to figure things out themselves.[13] Despite having spent a fair amount of time in MUDs, the text-based adventure worlds that prefigure MMOGs, and having some familiarity with the genre and even game commands, the world called "Norrath" certainly captured my imagination. When I began *EQ* in November 1999, most of the people I encountered found it all as new as I did.

Becoming a Player

While we sometimes imagine games as contained spaces and experiences in which a player sits down, examines the rules, and begins play, those like *EverQuest* seem to suggest a more complicated engagement. In large measure because of the multiplayer nature of the game, participants undergo a socialization process and over time learn what it means to play far beyond what the manual or strict rules articulate. To twist de Beauvoir's classic phrase, one is not born an *EverQuest* player but becomes one.[14] Constance Steinkuehler shows in her research on the MMOG *Lineage* how individual players are embedded in a "community of practice" and that through these communities they come to "understand the world (and themselves)" (Steinkuehler 2004).[15] There are then at least two levels—constantly interlinked and redefining each other—that work to acculturate players into the world and the gameplay: the structure of the game itself, and the culture and practices that have emerged in and around it. These form a much broader game apparatus, a sociotechnical one, that goes well beyond the artifact contained within the off-the-shelf box the game purchaser first encounters.

Interdependence is built into the very heart of the game, and from the onset players can see the benefits of cooperation. While I spent more time than some soloing when I began, it was still often the case that as newbies we would help out each other with tips, supplies (the game requires always having some food and drink in the character's inventory), or assistance in killing a monster before being killed by it. Avoiding death is particularly important both because experience points are taken away each time the character dies and "respawns," or restarts, at the last "home" point ("bind point") in the game. Depending on where the character dies, this can result in a fairly long run back to the corpse, where all the previously accumulated items are waiting to be picked up again. The "corpse run" can be one of the most harrowing, frustrating parts of the game because it is typically performed without the benefit of any weapons or armor (which reside on the now inert corpse back at the fighting area) and often involves dangerous travel. In newbie areas nonplayer-character guards are posted to help. They will typically kill any roaming monsters, so that running to guards, generally with monsters following quickly behind, and reaching them before being killed saves the character from death. Quite often, however, the protection of city guards is too far away, and this is where a game command for assistance comes in handy. When a player types /yell (or /y), it automatically broadcasts to those nearby that help is needed. Built into the system is a very fundamental affordance for social interaction. Since gaining experience by killing challenging monsters creates often precarious situations, this command becomes an important signal for someone to jump in and lend a hand. It is not without cost however. If another player assists and does more damage to the monster than your character did, you will not gain any experience points nor be able to "loot" the creature for items.[16]

The use of the yell command to receive help is one basic building block in supporting cooperation within the game. When I began, it was not unusual to find helpful higher-level players standing on the sidelines, so to speak, watching over lower-level characters in case the trusty /y command was issued and their help needed. Even among lower-level characters it was typical for groups of people to jump in to help out a struggling player, though often only after watching at a respectful distance either until the help command was called out or it was clear the player was in serious trouble. While the underlying narrative of the game suggests that players may actually be opponents (Dark Elves, for example, are supposed to be the sworn enemy of High Elves), I have only seen a request for help turned down a handful of times.[17] Whether for altruistic reasons or to demonstrate power, players typically help out each other as much as possible in these kinds of situations.

While the /y command represents a built-in social facilitator, there are numerous examples of emergent norms around the issue of combat help and assistance that reflect the ways communities creatively negotiate social action. The player who is running to a guard for help (or to a zoneline where they cross over into another area of the game and thereby escape trouble) is typically expected to use the "shout" channel, which is heard by all in the zone, to call out that there is trouble headed that way. This is not something mentioned in detail in the game manual nor in any rule set, yet over time the player community has found ways to negotiate the collective management of danger. In places like dungeons, for example, players will shout "train" as a way of signaling that a line of monsters is following close on their heels as they run to escape (figure 2.5). For those resting near an exit, this is invaluable. Without these kinds of informal norms many players can find themselves suddenly in the midst of a huge mob of monsters that might quickly slaughter them.

Around the issue of combat we can see a formalized mechanism for dealing with assistance (/y) and an informal norm (shouting "train"). But there is also

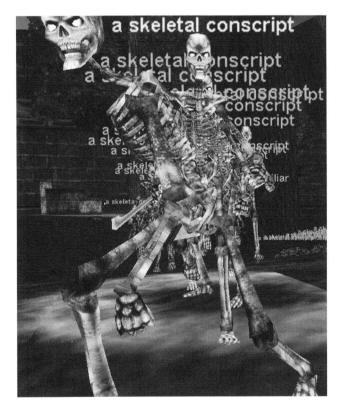

Figure 2.5
A train of skeletons

a third layer entailing an interpretative and symbolic appropriation of such events. Truth be told, players regularly still do find themselves in these sticky positions. Trains are such a common part of life that they actually form a point of nostalgia for many. People often exchange screenshots of particularly "good" trains (ones that are very large) or nostalgically recount starting or getting caught in one. No matter what the level of the player, trains seem to form a kind of universal connection point. But the fact that there are norms regarding what to do in a train situation also gives the community methods for evaluating the player who caused the problem.

Starting trains is a not infrequent method of "griefing" other players (causing havoc), and groups of players often decide fairly quickly, sometimes through public debate, whether or not a train was unintentional but excusable, unintentional but "dumb" (caused by poor judgment and probably avoidable), or intentional and therefore a grievance. Giving other players advance warning of any trouble you have caused is certainly one point that weighs in favor of the player in the court of public opinion. A humor page on trains, for example, provides a comical "grading" table and plays on the expected norms around the situation. Instead of awarding points for the best handling of the situation, the grading is based on how spectacular, how over the top, the train you created was. The player thus gets points for things like warning *after* the train hits (+50) and loses points for "no confirmed deaths" (−200).[18]

In many ways learning how to use the /y command, and more significantly learning to call out "train," point to the socialization that occurs in a game like *EQ*. As Jackie, a woman who has played the game since its launch, told me, it has changed somewhat from its earlier emphasis on role-playing to a more formalized normative environment. As she puts it,

A more rigid expected social structure has developed in *EverQuest* to the point now, I think a lot of people who come in they're more assimilated into the social structure. They learn the rules, how to behave and how to act in *EverQuest*. What's acceptable and what's not in the *EverQuest* society and it's less every individual defining for themselves what *EverQuest* is going to mean for them socially and asserting themselves socially.

While the game manual provides some of these basic guidelines, it is only the barest of frameworks for how to actually play the game. As Jackie suggests, new players are acculturated into the game and essentially taught not only how to play, but how to *be*. The manual can, for example, tell the player about the different kinds of "buffs"—spells that enhance or protect a player—available but it says nothing about the process of getting and giving them. There is, however, an emergent culture in the game that has, over time, formulated norms around social behavior, how favors are given out, how killing is handled, and how help is requested. One of the most important lessons a new player learns is that there is an entire culture within the game that they must accommodate. Players are socialized into the space and over time learn what it means to become a good *EQ* player.

Of course, there are certainly people who play the game with no real regard for others, who consider themselves "outlaws" and not beholden to their fellow players in anyway. But these are not the norm and, in fact, succeeding in a game like *EQ* absolutely requires adapting to all kinds of social practices and relationships that go well beyond, and sometimes in opposition to, any formal game rules. Those players who continue to cause trouble in the player community often find themselves ostracized. Players sometimes keep lists of those they have found troublesome and very frequently such information is shared by word of mouth not only across guild chat channels, but on message forums and e-mail lists. Bad players can acquire a reputation that has serious effects on their ability to get groups, be invited into a guild, and by extension advance in the game. Given the deep reliance on social networks to progress, sustained bad player behavior, while it does occur, carries significant costs and is typically weeded out.

The Necessity of Social Networks

MMOGs are by their very nature social ventures in that they involve numerous players gaming together in real time in a shared virtual environment. It is worth noting, however, the varying configurations of networks that occur and how they can change over time through the life of the game. While many players on the low- or mid-range side of the game modulate between playing alone and joining with others in small groups, at the high-end game participation in groups and collectives generally becomes the only way to gain experience and advance. Logging in for simply an hour can be quite difficult given the necessity of finding people to play with and a location to hunt in.[19] It is not uncommon for people to spend upwards of 3 hours, and in some situations 8 or more, playing the game. Instead of just blackboxing the "social," we might think of structures in the game via a kind of building block model so that you have:

The Player

Solo	The single character on its own.

several of whom make up . . .

A Group

Groups are formal teams that cooperate to kill monsters and share experience and items gained from the kills. They can range in size from 2 to 6.

Pairs	Players on a simple team consisting of the self and one other, typically a friend or complimentary class (for example, Warrior and Cleric).
Pickup groups	A collection of players who do not know each other (or not very well) who have found each other by either using the game's "looking for group" tool or have advertised in the public-zone channel for additional group members.
Friend groups	A collection of players who know each other fairly well—either solely within the game or outside of it—and do not share any formal alliance (via guild membership) but are actively grouped together.
Guild and ally groups	A subset of players drawn from their larger guild group or any ally guilds they are aligned with.
Hybrid groups	Mix of several of the other forms—groups made up of friends and strangers, guildmates and friends, etc.

several of which together constitute . . .

The Raid

Raids are complex, multigroup formations required to kill some of the higher-level, more menacing monsters in the game. The current raid tool limits a single formal raid group of 72 though often dual raids are run to increase the numbers.

Guild raids	Given many guilds have memberships ranging from 10 (the minimum required to be formally recognized) to hundreds, they are often able to generate enough participants to handle more difficult areas or monsters that cannot be handled by one group of 6 alone.
Ally raids	Many guilds have "ally" or friend guilds that share public allegiances to each other. Guilds may sometimes join with their allies to undertake large raids.

Pickup raids	These are raids formed around impromptu organization through chat channels or word-of-mouth in the game. While they may operate with some regularity, they do not require any advance sign-up and typically consist of members of a variety of guilds or those who are unguilded.
Scheduled (sign-up) raids	Somewhat less popular now that most players do not rely on third-party calendars (schedules hosted at non-SOE Web sites), there still remain some raids that require advance sign-up for participation (sometimes with qualification requirements) and are typically made up of people of a variety of guild affiliations.

While *EverQuest* certainly can be played alone, the solo game is only a partially realized experience. Indeed, the high-end game (where characters achieve levels 65 and higher) can in large part only be achieved via the help of others. This reliance on social networks, or communities, is an intentional aspect of the game design. As Brad McQuaid, original producer/codesigner of *EQ* and now president/CEO of Sigil Games, puts it:

Community is relationships between players, whether it be friendly or adversarial, symbiotic or competitive. It's also a form of persistence, which is key to massively multiplayer games. Without community, you simply have a bunch of independent players running around the same environment. Players won't be drawn in and there won't be anything there to bind them. The key to creating community, therefore, is interdependence. In *EverQuest,* we forced interdependence in several ways and although we've been criticized for it, I think it's one of a couple of reasons behind our success and current lead. By creating a class-based system, players NEED each other. By creating an environment often too challenging for a solo player, people are compelled to group and even to form large guilds and alliances. All of this builds community, and it all keeps players coming back for more and more. (Aihoshi 2002)

Supporting Networks through Structure

To this end it is possible to identify specific mechanisms within the structure of the game that facilitate various forms of social interaction and interdependence.[20] The importance of linking design with the social life of a game cannot be overemphasized. Mulligan and Patrovsky (2003) highlight, in very concrete ways, that the role-playing tools for communication or community building form an integral part of the game and suggest that designers must be attuned to creating robust systems that support this activity. In *EverQuest* each of the forms described above is supported in varying degrees through the architecture of the system. The notion that technical choices are always already tied to social choices and values plays out at an explicit level here (Taylor 2003, 2004). At the individual-player level, there are both mechanisms to facilitate making new connections with other players as well as sustaining them. For example, the game now has introduced a tool which allows people to tag themselves as looking for a group (LFG). In the past players had to call out in zone channels or ask around to try and find partners. With the new LFG tool they are now able to submit themselves to an in-game searchable database of players who want to join together. Of course, the introduction of such a tool ends up supplanting some of the more personal touches in the process (where players, for example, try and create exciting calls to draw in other players) but also introduces the ability for players to search across the whole of the game world (and not just their specific location) for partners. At the individual level there are also commands such as /friend that allow people to keep lists of other players they deem more than simple acquaintances.[21] When issuing a special command they can then see if anyone in their list is logged on, and if so where in the game space.

Communication in the game is also a central feature of how social life is supported and in addition to public communication methods (speaking outloud so those around you can hear, or speaking on a zone-based chat channel), players are also able to send private messages ("tells") to one another across zones. In the beginning the game had a fairly rudimentary communication system. Aside from several zone-based chat channels ("shout," "auction," and "ooc"—out of character, a holdover term from role-playing) multiplayer communication was limited to those in formal groups or their guild channel. In 2002 players were given the ability to set up their own self-defined chat channels (which can work across servers), thus allowing groups of friends or family to create a private back channel for themselves. Friends who are playing at the same time but in different areas of the world can now join shared channels to talk to each other. In many instances, these systems are not primarily used to actually play together. The value can, in fact, lie in having people to talk to while off doing solo adventures, helping each other out with anything from information to equipment, and knowing that there are players for support if trouble arises. In this way characters do not have to be near each other in the game but can sustain communication across distances.

Beyond the more individual social mechanisms however, the game is particularly notable for the ways it supports collectives. Groups, for example, are formal collections in which people, once joined together, can monitor each other, use a private chat channel, and all gain experience points based on teamwork. The formal group in *EQ* also has a leader who can invite and disband members. At the guild level people are now able to bring up a tool that allows them to see all the members of their association and where they are in the world. All guild members share a "tag" on their name identifying their guild affiliation. Guilds also have automatic private-chat channels and can set "messages of the day"—broadcast messages that all guild members see when logging in.

The development of the guild tool is notable for representing a recent decision by the game's designers to more formally support the associations that long have existed in the game space. While guilds are formally recognized by the system and given some rudimentary special abilities, the more recent development of management systems represents an important facilitation of social networks. For many years guilds have relied on third-party Web sites and tools to manage their groups. While there is still a heavy reliance on Web sites for communication (guilds make extensive use of them to chat and distribute information), more functionality is now in the game itself.[22]

This is apparent even more dramatically with the introduction in the *Planes of Power* expansion of the raid tool and extending functionality for groups. Large, typically well-coordinated, events have been a mainstay in *EQ* for many years now. As previously mentioned, many of the most difficult monsters in the game can be handled only with far more people than the 6-person group allows. In the past there was no formal mechanism for more than the 6-person group to hunt together, leaving raids of 50+ in particularly tough situations. Communication had to be done in public zone-wide channels, and there was no way for the system to share experience points among the larger group. Designation of a leader for the event could not be formally signaled, and the coordination of these raids was an amazing feat of on-the-ground creativity and informal communication. Some explanation is given for this absence in design in Robert B. Marks's interesting book on *EverQuest*, where Brad McQuaid suggested raiding was never a centrally designed feature of the game. Marks writes, "To this day, McQuaid denies that raids were planned for specifically. 'Certainly there is raid content, but most players don't raid, even at higher levels, and the intent was to offer content at the higher end for all sorts of player types and their varying schedules and abilities to commit time to the game, especially in one contiguous chunk'" (Marks 2003, 83). Given the paucity of raid tools in the original game, this account makes sense. But the fact that raiding is in many ways now a central component of the game (indeed, some might contend the *only* real option left for longtime players) also highlights the ways *EverQuest* is not one singular game but an artifact developed over time by many actors. This can include, for example, design or live teams that followed after the original development members left the company. As the game undergoes serious revision in the face of strong competition, some early fundamental design choices that informed and reflected a kind of "essence" or "spirit of the game" are being reworked and often radically altered. We can similarly see how the notion of who the *EQ* player is has evolved over time and in relation to a variety of factors including market competition, the maturity of the genre, and the experience and tastes of players. The shift to a demographic of players increasingly occupying the high-end of the game has influenced how the game is altered and extended.

With the introduction of the raid tool, large groups now are able to have not only designated raid leaders but to distribute XP more fairly among participants. They share a formal communication channel and are able to monitor each other's progress better. Taking it one step further, the game developers now have added an advancement feature for a character such that the player can distribute some of her XP to acquiring leadership abilities if she desires. Interestingly, formal leadership skills as codified in the game give direct benefits to the members of the group (in particular, the function that shows all players the health of the group's target) and thus players who have spent some of their experience points on this enhancement bring a useful tool to the situation and often will be asked to serve as group leader. Improving one's abilities in this way, while not providing a bonus in terms of experience points, certainly is tied to both the pragmatic and reputational advantages such skills bestow.

Groups and Guilds

In previous work Mikael Jakobsson and I examined the layers of associations players engage in, which makes their time in the game more enjoyable as well as facilitates their play (Jakobsson and Taylor 2003). We additionally sought to uncover qualities of association—reputation, trust, responsibility—by using the analogy of mafia life. Many of the qualities we identified as mafia-like are indeed part and parcel of participation in social and community life. And as with offline life, people have a variety of social interactions—some more formal than others, some sustained and some transitory, some connected to familial relationships and some connected to friendship networks. This pattern is repeated within *EverQuest,* so the social life of the game can take a variety of forms.

For the new player who does not yet know anyone else in *EQ,* induction into the social life of the game comes first from the small, temporary connections made with other new players. As I mentioned earlier, players routinely group up with each other to progress through the game more rapidly and successfully. Groups act as a microlevel, short-term social network. By creating a group out of characters specializing in different but complementary skills, members collectively can take on and defeat opponents who are equal to or stronger than the individual characters in the group. When players join a group they also have access to a group-based chat channel for communication. Players use the channel not only to coordinate their fighting, but for small talk, joking, and general conversation. While the group functionality in the game is most narrowly intended for facilitating collaborative hunting or questing, it also becomes one of the primary methods through which players come to make new friends, learn about the world, form and learn strategies for play, and in general participate in the social life of the game.[23]

While a large portion of the game is of course focused on killing monsters, completing quests, and leveling-up your character, the mechanisms through which this occurs and the values embedded there are particularly interesting. In the example I gave earlier about trains I suggested that the player community quite often evaluates the behavior that goes on within it. People are constantly making judgments about who to trust, whether or not someone is cheating, if they want to commit themselves to a group of other players, and all kinds of other social considerations. This is not to say that players are constantly angsting over such issues, sitting at their computers consciously weighing all kinds of factors (though of course that does sometimes occur). Much like the ways we do this kind of work all the time, unconsciously, in our offline daily lives, MMOGs similarly tap into the work, evaluations, and pleasures of relationships and social networks. This kind of engagement can be seen most clearly by looking at guilds, the primary formal organization in the game.

While some players may go their whole career without having joined a guild, this is not typical given the benefits of collaboration, which become especially important in the higher end of the game. Guilds are officially sanctioned organizations of players with a hierarchical leadership structure. Membership in a guild offers players admission into a broader social network. In general two types of guilds exist: family guilds (sometimes called "social guilds") that emphasize personal connections and playful engagement with the game, and raiding guilds (sometimes called "uber guilds") marked by a very well-articulated commitment to pursuing the high-end game.[24] While social guilds involve complex social systems, raiding guilds are also heavily reliant on social mechanisms. Despite their own proclamations sometimes to the contrary—such as the guild that says, "Don't confuse ROV with a social club guild, we are a 90 MPH ultra competitive TEAM guild"—high-end guilds rely on many of the same basic social mechanisms pervasive at other levels of the game (Ring of Valor 2003). While for many hardcore players terms like "social" often evoke images of chatting, hanging out, and general undirected play, even the most ambitious, dedicated guilds rely on deeply social mechanisms to succeed. As I also discuss in the next chapter on power gamers, even high-end guilds are very adept at blending instrumental action with social work. The main mechanisms at work in all guilds, to varying degrees, are reputation, trust, and responsibility.

Reputation

Reputation plays a significant role in a gamer's success because at a basic level reputation determines both being able to secure groups over the long term, as well as being admitted into a guild. Potential members generally undergo a process in which they petition to join the guild and, in the case of raiding guilds, often list their equipment, skills, and any additional qualifications or selling points. While in family guilds the entry paths are often much less formalized, sponsorship scenarios are common and applicants are often only considered for guild membership after being vouched for by a current member. It is not unusual to find special clauses that allow "family members, RL [real-life] friends and alts [alternate characters] of current and former members in good standing" to bypass typical application requirements, thereby pointing to the power of preexisting social networks (Legion of Valor 2003).

Applicants are regularly required to spend some time grouping with members of the guild as a process of evaluation. In smaller family guilds vetting is often done through back-channel conversations and interpersonal persuasion between members. Many of the more formally organized guilds have Web-based message boards and there are typically members-only recruit discussions in which people confidentially weigh in with their opinions or vote on applicants. Through evaluating a person's skill at playing their class, their demeanor, and even their broader values (Do they put the needs of the group above their own? Are they fun to play with?) their reputation is considered. Attention is given in assessing whether they are a good fit with any codes of conduct a guild might have.

Beyond systems of reputation to get into a guild, members also work to build and maintain their status once accepted. People become known for their skills as raid leaders, accomplished class players, group organizers, and general knowledge of the game and world. In smaller guilds a high value often is placed on being an amiable play partner or flexible member of the group. There is a pleasure in the kind of validation the esteem of the group bestows in addition to the practical benefits that accrue from reputation. At the high-end game many of the most significant accomplishments simply cannot be done alone. Getting an epic weapon (a penultimate class-specific piece of equipment), defeating a particularly tough mob, or visiting a forbidding or locked zone are achieved only with mass cooperation. Being seen as a team-player, generous in helping others, or simply a powerful force whose alliance is useful can significantly affect the ability to mobilize resources when needed. While a character might be quite powerful in terms of experience level, they also need social capital to draw on to progress in the true high-end game.

A final thread of reputation is the way guild membership signals something to the broader server community. For example, players often have very strong feelings about the powerful guilds on their server. To admirers these top characters are seen as playing the very essence of the game—taking on the toughest mobs and conquering the exclusive zones. In these instances they can even symbolically act as proxies, standing in representationally for all the other players on the server. For example, when fighting the Sleeper—a particularly tough mob that would only appear once in the game—was first successfully undertaken on a server, other players cheered the guild who accomplished it. Indeed, in one case a player argued that by taking on difficult new mobs, high-level guilds help out the entire server:

They should be given a medal and a monument for being DIFFERENT! . . . Probably one of the only top flight guilds server wide going a different road and doing something original. That alone is a great accomplishment. Lots of other guilds certainly owe RoV for beta testing the loot for that entire encounter though. . . . (Dragonmist 2002)

The idea that these guilds contribute to the broader collective knowledge of the game is fascinating. There is certainly a basic way this happens in that guilds that accomplish difficult challenges on a server, such as killing a new monster, often will post details about the encounter and any loot they get, thereby helping future players prepare for their own attempts. But it is also that these guilds can hold a kind of symbolic power among their fellow players, representing a play experience that many may aspire to but in fact never quite achieve. As the quote above shows, such sentiments reflect not only the kind of esteem some raiding guilds can hold among nonguild players, but that these organizations take on a larger role within a given server culture. Guilds themselves come to act as unique agents—entities encompassing more than the sum of their members—in the broader game community. That guilds themselves might become valuable actors in the community shows the ways not only individual players, but more formal organizations, make up an integral part of the game space.

The value of high-end guilds is not always uncontested, however. Many players see the most dedicated ones as operating *contrary* to the spirit of the game. They are sometimes seen as too instrumental in their playing style— taking the fun out of the game by being too focused on achievement, which is often seen as acting in opposition to community. In these instances they are framed as valuing objects or accomplishments over people.[25] In all cases ultimately the guildtag comes to signal a reputation above and beyond any individual player's identity. It acts as a social signifier and locates the character in a larger system of reputations, affiliations, favors, and even grievances.

Guilds themselves recognize this and often require members to always keep their affiliation visible (going into "anonymous" mode hides the guildtag along with all data about the character's level). People often do good deeds in the name of their guild as a way of boosting its reputation. All things being equal, a prominent guildtag gives a player an edge. Generally this is a beneficial factor though it is fascinating when guilds develop reputations that are more contentious. Sometimes guilds get reputations for being "too aggressive" or not quite playing by the rules. In these cases the reputation a guildtag gives could conceivably hurt game opportunities. In the case of strong guild rivalries, such identifications serve as powerful boundary markers.

Underlying this issue of reputation is an implicit construction of social hierarchy. Within the guild system this is formally recognized, both socially and in the very system itself, through the designations of guild leader and guild officer. In each of these cases these members are afforded special privileges, often formulating the direction a guild will take and being given special weight, socially, in their opinions. At a structural level guild leaders and officers are granted the power to invite new members into the guild through the use of a special command, /guildinvite. The more serious command /guildremove can only be issued by the member wanting to quit the guild or by a guild officer. Quite often offenses against the guild and its codes result in banishment, sometimes temporary, sometimes permanent. Given that this removal marks a public and formal break with a member, it is not surprising that the power to issue the command is controlled.

Outside of the guild system the question of how social hierarchies are managed via these reputations is much murkier. On servers there is often debate and ambivalence about raiding guilds and so ranking in the social strata is extremely contextual. Indeed, the argument that some high-level guild members do not recognize this fact is a long-standing bone of contention such that complaints of "strutting around" zones or acting like "they own this camp" abound. Within the dynamic culture of a server, reputation and hierarchy are not stable categories but often the subject of debate and contestation, with some guilds rising in public stature while others fall. Ultimately, this very fact itself points to the distinctly social context of not only the categories, but how meaning is constructed around them.

Trust
With reputation comes obligation, and one of the first areas that shows this dramatically is the area of trust. Guild members are constantly risking their characters' lives for each other and, in turn, trusting each other that hunting and raids will be well planned, loot distributed fairly, and that if problems arise the group will band together to solve them. Trusting groupmates is a common theme throughout the game and it becomes even more pronounced at the high-end where venturing into dangerous zones brings heightened risk of death and potential loss of corpse (and all the hard-earned items carried on it). Advanced play involves immense coordination and cooperation, and participants trust each other to not only play their characters well but to see through group events till everyone leaves safely.

Beyond the trust that occurs in fights, there are other instances in which players rely on the honor of others. Many guilds operate banks serving as warehouses for the collective. Players are allowed to borrow equipment from the bank, which has been stocked by fellow members via donations.

Typically players are trusted to only use the borrowed equipment on authorized guilded characters and to return it if they no longer need the item or leave the guild. Spells, which cannot be given back, are given out on an as-needed basis. In all these instances members are entrusted with the collective property of the guild and in turn expected to respect its status and donate back when possible.

While these types of sharing behaviors are all sanctioned, if not supported, by the game, one form of trust is explicitly prohibited. *EQ*, in its End User License Agreement, states that:

You may not transfer or share your Account with anyone, except that if you are a parent or guardian, you may permit one child to use the Account instead of you (in which case you may not use that Account). (Sony Online Entertainment 2005)

However, it is not unusual to see players sharing accounts. Among friends and family members, it certainly is often the case that the prohibition seems to have no direct correlation to actual practice. Indeed, the ways players use and circulate accounts is quite often in clear opposition to the ways Sony wants them handled. For many players sharing accounts can seem a fundamental necessity to successfully play the game and as such constitutes a practice quite counter to the specified terms of play. This can be viewed as a practice in which "sensible use [is] developed in context" (Hine 2000, 10; see also Woolgar 1991a). In any given guild a handful of people have particularly high-level characters that are especially beneficial (Clerics being the most notable), and it is common for several guild members to have access to these prime accounts, despite the formal prohibitions.

Generally account access is rooted in friendship first and foremost but, given the way social networks operate, it is also the case that shared access simultaneously benefits a guild. For example, imagine a scenario in which a guild goes on a particularly difficult raid and the entire group is wiped out. An additional cleric is needed to resurrect all of the guildmembers, so one of the people present logs on another member's character to assist. On more than one occasion such an action has salvaged an otherwise disastrous play session. Though formally prohibited, account sharing represents one of the ultimate forms of trust in the game, one that is not taken lightly and is quite valued.

Responsibility

As is probably becoming apparent, very closely underlying each of these categories is a sense of responsibility binding guild members. While in family guilds this is typically unarticulated but deeply felt, in many high-level guilds there is sometimes a quite explicitly stated rule that when the guild is participating in an important raid or if your services are needed, you will "drop everything [and] get your butt to the raid." Some guilds require a certain amount of consistent weekly (or daily) raid participation and at the very least people are generally expected to, within reason, help out the guild and its members whenever possible. While many guilds account for people having "offline lives," one states its requirements quite dramatically:

You must play more *EQ* than you spend time sleeping. We need people who are dedicated and like to play a LOT. Our raid time is generally 4–12 PST in the evening. If you can't make it for that, Fu isn't the right place for you. (Club FU 2003)

In high-end guilds there is an interesting relationship, and sometimes tension, between the individual and the group. On the one hand players often join these guilds for ambitious personal reasons. They want to achieve more with their character and the high-end guild is the way to do it. It is not uncommon to see people leave their smaller family guilds to join a raiding one once they are able (though often leaving an alternate character back with their smaller guild, sort of as a way of keeping ties with their roots). On the other hand, their goals can be achieved only through massive collective action. Ultimately, even individual pursuits can be framed in terms of, indeed subsumed to, guild responsibility such that, "Our efforts will be geared toward the TEAM not any one individual" (Ring of Valor 2003). Keeping up with leveling, advancing toward an epic weapon, getting dungeon keys or flags for locked zones, working on trade skills, and more generally improving gaming ability are seen not only as personal goals to be achieved but ones that contribute to the overall good of the guild. Some guilds even push people to play their main characters so that a critical mass of higher-level players is achieved to assist the guild in taking on tougher zones and mobs.

In this regard smaller family guilds are both more idiosyncratic and, in some ways, more individualistic. While it is certainly the case that they exert informal pressures to support the group, there is also much more room for heading off to pursue individual quirky play goals, especially those that may seem to have no clear value. Responsibility is measured, if at all, in primarily relational terms. One helps guildmates and looks out for them not because of a larger collective goal, but because of who they are as people. In family guilds, collective actions arise not from an instrumental orientation (as it primarily does in raiding guilds), but from mutual value of one another.

Socialization and Its Discontents

Guild membership is not always a sure path to success, especially when characters are not quite attuned to each other. One player I interviewed addressed this when he talked about how he joined a guild for the social support only to find his character was essentially locked out of advancing: "[After offline friends left *EQ*] I was kind of alone in the game. Not having anybody to rely on, I joined a guild. That was kind of fun for awhile [but] the better people get the better items . . . so you can get better items. And I wasn't getting any of the good stuff. And that's sort of discouraging I guess." Being unequally matched with potential play partners can set up a very frustrating continual game of catch-up. Because *EverQuest* puts some restrictions on the level differences players can hold when participating in groups together for experience points, people often find themselves torn between pushing hard to keep up and sliding away from friends and guildmates if they do not play regularly. So, for example, a player who is away from the game for a couple of weeks may find that his level-25 character can no longer group with his friends' characters, which have now advanced to level 40.

With a quantified marker of game progression it should also be no surprise that modes of status and hierarchy are at work in the game. Whether it be having a prestigious guildtag or a highly valued piece of equipment, social life of *EQ* is rife with markers of success, both skill-based and "material." For many this results in a kind of pleasant competition where trying to improve a character to gain access to accomplished guilds or obtain rare spells or armor propels the player forward in the game. But over time it can leave some with the feeling that they simply cannot keep up, cannot compete, can never be satisfied. It is not unusual to hear some players express a sense of disillusionment with the acquisitive nature of the game and the amount of time and toil it takes to participate.

The burden of the social can also enact itself in ways other than the play mechanics of the game. The deep reliance on others can make the constant challenge of piecing together matched groups a bit tiring for some. Yeone, who plays the game in large part with family and friends, feels that this part of the high-level game is particularly acute. She wrote, "I'm getting tired of needing x class and z class to kill something. Verant is so fixed on that. Because of that, [we] can't do what we'd like to do, even if it's not uber. I like the challenge the game is at but when we wanna go do something for exp or whatever [we] usually have to get a cleric and enchanter. That can be a pain sometimes. I don't have any high level cleric friends too, the only one I know is a friend of Danny's [an offline friend of hers] in RL and if he comes out, he usually brings 2 or 3 of his RL friends as well. So many friends but not enough room." This balancing act between trying to find challenges and activities of interest but always within a matrix of who you know and don't, who's actually logged on and potential play partners, and built-in collaboration requirements can be quite tricky for players. This is certainly a major factor in why people often create several different characters that they then deploy contingent on whatever specific conditions—social and event-based—they encounter during any given play session. This context-dependent play strategy highlights the ways players approach *EverQuest* not with one preset orientation but often shape their play styles and activities against a variety of factors. In this regard, the "cycling through of identities" (à la Turkle) seen in other Internet spaces is as much an instrumental and relational decision about how to facilitate play within any given context.

Experienced players also can feel that they sometimes spend more time helping out guildmates or working to keep guilds together than they do actually playing. Jackie, a longtime player noted that "The majority of effort you put into guilds is not that minute or two of fighting a monster, it's everything that you are doing in between trying to keep people motivated, organized, and working as a group." This can sometimes result in people creating new anonymous characters, either on the same server or a different one, to allow them to play without the burdens their social networks may bring. On the one hand the benefits, both in terms of play and in terms of support, players receive from each other is enormous, but at times the weariness from dealing with personality conflicts, life crises, or the less exciting but quite necessary work of keeping a group of people together and coordinated can be overwhelming.

And what about the often-discussed issue of "griefing" in games? In the world of first-person shooters, for example, the issue of people cheating, causing havoc with the game, and ruining (or at least trying to ruin) the experience of players is a central concern. This issue has driven software innovations from the player community itself—anticheating program *Punk Buster* is the most notable. While there are always players who attempt to disrupt games, in the case of PvE *EverQuest,* my sense is that this is a much less pressing issue than in some other genres. The deep reliance on social networks and time investment, combined with the power of social sanctions as implemented by the player community radically shifts how this issue looks. Combined with the fact that on most servers PvP engagement (and by extension, the trouble that can arise from "player killing") is not allowed by default, the shape of griefing in a game like *EQ* is quite different from that in something like the first-person shooter game *Counter-Strike.*

Game designers and theorists debate about whether there is simply a type of player who engages, persistently, in grief behavior (Foo and Koivisto 2004; Kuecklich 2004; Smith 2004). While I am sure this is the case to some degree, more interesting are the ways even good players sometimes find themselves committing acts of grief or exploiting the system. Raph Koster suggests, for example, that "many players are willing to cheat" and indeed that cheating may actually be "a sign that the player is in fact grokking [deeply understanding] the game" (2005, 112). Though not condoning cheating per se, he argues that players will always be looking for optimal paths and that "when a player cheats in a game, they are choosing a battlefield that is broader in context than the game itself" (ibid.). While his analysis is rooted in a model of behavior linked to a story of human evolution, I would suggest instead a sociologically informed approach, but one that also problematizes the notion of cheaters (or griefers) as a rare and unique personality type. As I tried to highlight in the example of training, designations of "grief" are extremely contextual and player response runs from "letting it slide" to formally petitioning the game administrators. I have witnessed high-level, well-regarded players "kill steal" another player (basically jump in and take a monster mid-fight), for example, as an act of retribution. I also have seen very nice, thoughtful players teach younger players they thought rude or not fully socialized a "lesson" by training a monster on them. It is also the case that many actions deemed "griefing" or "exploiting" exist on the boundary lines of the game—often in spaces in which the rule set is not clearly defined or the system itself is ambiguous.

While a fair amount of rhetoric circulates among MMOG development communities about the always potentially disruptive nature of players, the power of norms in these spaces should not be underestimated. Despite the actions described above, even when players engage in behavior deemed questionable by those who run these game worlds, it is often still within specific regimes of control and socialized behavior. Ultimately my point here is that these categories—griefing and cheating—are both socially produced and only made meaningful via contextualization. Linda Hughes (1999) notes that this kind of situated understanding is found much more broadly in both children's play and within professional sports. Indeed, the meaning within the game is based in something other than formal rule structures, which often leave significant spaces of ambiguity.

Offline Connections

Over the years I have heard repeatedly of people coming to *EQ* because of a family member, friend, or coworker.[26] Kim, for example, met her husband in the game (something she does not tell too many people, given the stigma often attached) and now their family plays together. As she put it, "Four people, four computers, one server." Another woman, Katinka, who became a regular part of my game life and was in several guilds with me over the course of the years, began the game because her husband (who had himself been playing for a while with his friends) sat down one night and made her a character based on one of her tried-and-true *D&D* characters.[27] In the course of my research it was not at all uncommon to find that people were connected to other players through a variety of preexisting offline ties.[28] Indeed in the case of women and power gamers (which I discuss later) this is particularly notable. Besides providing an explanation for how people first are exposed to the game, however, offline ties between players also serve as an important component in the enjoyment of the game. In the following example, I am having a conversation with a young guildmember, Dargon, that turns to the subject of family.

Dargon: I only wanted to have an alt for awhile he is a STD

TL: A what darg?

Dargon: A STD super twinked dwarf

TL: Heh, ah.

Dargon: My uncle said i was that and i got laughed at by him so i stop[p]ed his moeny [sic] source for awhile

TL: Lol

TL: How many in your family play darg?

Dargon: I think 7 or 8

TL: Wow, nice

TL: Did you guys get them into it or them you?

Dargon: Both uncles on dads side sister brother and me dad and then 2 cousins

Dargon: We got my 1 of my uncles but the other got it for his B day by his wife (who now regrets it)

TL: Aw, heh. do you guys group together a lot?

Dargon: And the cousins we got them into it

TL smiles.

Dargon: Well the one we got in to it he is lvl 9 chanter so my 10 dwarf can and the my other uncle has about a million characters on in the guild even i group with him a lot and my cousins i group with alot but the group is different i PL [power level][29] them

TL: Ah, gotcha. still pretty cool. didn't realize you had all kinds of family in [the guild]. heh, neat :)

Dargon: We have are only little chat thing set up to wear we get on and join the chat

TL: Oh, handy :)

Here we see the way an extended family negotiates the game space. It is not unlike the stories you hear from many other players in which a kind of domino effect occurs whereby yet one more family member finds themselves picking up the game and starting her own character. One interesting aspect of this particular example is the elevated position Dargon has inside the game. When his uncle teases him about his character, he retaliates by freezing in-game monetary support. Dargon has a kind of duality to his status within the family. On the one hand because he is young he often is not in the same position of power as his parents, aunts and uncles, or cousins. But in-game this dynamic is flipped and he has opportunities to occupy the more powerful or higher status position.[30] James Gorman, in his piece in the *New York Times* entitled "The Family That Slays Demons Together," recounts a similar experience in which he found himself relying on the help—both knowledge and financial—of his son in the game *Diablo II*. He writes of one of their in-game shopping excursions:

"This one I'll buy for you," he [his son] said, pointing out the Plated Belt of Thorns (which I now wear), "but if you go for the more expensive one, you'll have to pay yourself." I could hear my own voice, in the aisles of Toys "R" Us, urging moderation in the purchase of Beast War transformers.

These situations also point to the ways families and friends bring social capital into the game space through preexisting relationships. While it is sometimes called twinking, it is not at all unusual to find players helping newbies they know offline by giving them some money, items, or, just as important, crucial game advice and tips. Beyond game objects and knowledge, out-of-game relationships give players an instant social network in the game. Cousins can introduce a new player around, coworkers can put together groups to help the new player, and in general the existing in-game networks can be marshaled to help the new player. These offline connections also provide unique situations in which people sometimes play together in the same shared physical space, where the benefits of instant easy communication or handing off keyboards, if needed, are also apparent.

While I have so far suggested that offline connections are primarily ones that predate the players' entry into the game, it is important to note that game relationships quite often move offline and that players regularly form out-of-game relationships with each other.[31] This is something we see in other Internet spaces, as well, so it should come as no real surprise that people who form regular meaningful relationships in the game space might want to pursue them offline. This can occur in a range of different ways.

Katinka—I previously mentioned that her husband created the original character for her—was only one member of a very close extended family-and-friends group that I spent much time with over the years. In fact, I first met her through her husband, Jack, who played in the game. Both being Gnomes, we found a kind of instant playful bond that many Gnomes seem to have in the game. As I spent more time with the couple, I came to see that they negotiated a very interesting set of relationships. Quite often they were in separate guilds (though regularly with secondary characters in a common one) and had an extended friendship network that piggy-backed on many other offline relationships. Katinka's cousin, for example, was a player I also ran into with some regularity, and Katinka played with a group made up primarily of husbands, wives, cousins, and close in-game friends. Figure 2.6 is a simple map of that small group.

One of the most interesting things I saw in my time with this group was the ways partners often negotiated semi-role-played extramarital game relationships and friendship bonds. Once a character reaches level 20 in *EQ,* the player is allowed to give it a last name. Several times I spent evenings with sets of couples who shared character last names but were, I would find out in back-channel, actually married offline to other players. Katinka, for example, shared a last name with Vin, one of the other members of our guild who was not her husband. She and Vin had developed a fairly close friendship over the years and while the last name signified an in-game marriage (of several years), it was as much a marker of a deep friendship commitment. After several years they decided to meet and Vin flew from his home in Hawaii to visit

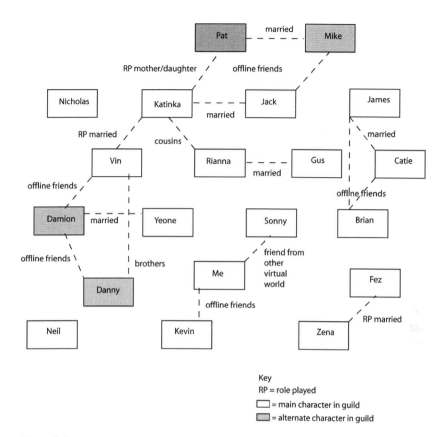

Figure 2.6
Map of a family guild

Katinka and her husband (who he also knew from in the game) at their home in Texas.

TL: How was that, meeting him for the first time?

Katinka: Oh, God, I was a nervous wreck. I'm gonna meet my best OOC friend in real life. I hadn't slept in 24 hours. Do you remember Rianna?

TL: Yeah, I do.

Katinka: Well she's my cousin.[32] She was staying with me that night. She was going to go to the airport with me, because I can't find my way out of a wet paper sack without a map, a flashlight, and a Sherpa to guide me. It's like 7 in the morning, we haven't slept, because I'm rushing around the house trying to make sure everything's just right. We get to the airport, we're sitting there, and we're completely loony by this time, so we're sitting there waiting for his plane to come in. I don't have the slightest idea what he looks like really, I've seen one picture of him. He told me what he was going to be wearing, so we gotta look for this guy wearing this. And all of a sudden all these little A- cause he's Asian, all of a sudden all these Asians get off the plane and I'm like "Oh, my God," and I'm looking for him and there he is, so I'm like "okay." So we get him and we give him a hug and we could have knocked each other over because neither one of us had slept. So, it was great, ya know, being able to meet him.

TL: Was he different than you expected him to be?

Katinka: if he had been any quieter he would have been dead. He's not a very loud person. And being from Texas, ya know, we are just loud—you don't take us out in public if you can avoid it. He's a lot like how he is in the game, just quieter. And after the first day or two we were able to relax and act completely silly.

TL: And was that your first time meeting somebody that you had only met online?

Katinka: Yeah.

TL: Interesting. Would you do it again, do you think?

Katinka: Yeah, I think so.

TL: And did it end up changing how you guys were able to interact with each other online?

Katinka: not really, because we got to be really great friends before we met, and we're still really good friends now. It wasn't very different.

This ability to have relationships that might not otherwise occur without the game strikes me as one of the fundamental ways spaces like MMOGs are reorganizing social life. As children and teens occupy positions of power, as intergenerational friendships develop, as partners find new friendship networks not solely reliant on a nuclear family, as people develop deep connections with those who live far from them or whom they never meet in person, these game spaces offer interesting possibilities to undo some of the constraint produced by traditional families and localized friendship pools.

Beyond what happens in these smaller individual offline meetings, one of the most common, and most formalized, venues for players to see each other offline is the guild meet. Guild meets are much like the Fan Faire I describe in chapter 1, though they generally are much smaller and not organized through SOE but by the members themselves. Guild members physically meet up, typically for a weekend, in some geographic location often decided based on how easy it will be for most members to attend. Guild meets are generally informal and usually revolve around eating, socializing over drinks, and reminiscing and talking about the game, which often act as jumping-off points for romantic or sexual encounters. It is fairly common for people to post follow-ups in guild forums for members who could not attend, recount antics, and often post pictures.

Extending the Network

My own experience of the game, and what I have seen with many others over the course of the years, is a progression from new, unaffiliated player to embeddedness in this variety of friendship and organizational webs. But it is important to note that it is not just the first-hand, real-time interpersonal relationships and groups that constitute the social world of the game, but also the collection of message boards, databases, comics, fan art and stories, and even game modifications that contribute to players feeling a bond and connection to the *EQ* world and their fellow gamers. Any discussion of game life must include a model of the distributed social sphere via groups, practices, and knowledge that exist outside of the formal bounds of the game.

The resources and communities available to players through various third-party services and Web sites is impressive. Sites such as EQAtlas[33] have provided detailed maps of the game world to the player community (long before they were integrated into the game interface), and Allakhazam[34] offers extensive searchable databases on everything from game monsters to clothing. Notably, the knowledge available at sites like Allakhazam or Graffe's Wizard Compilation[35] are built from player input and represent a kind of collective experience repository where players can benefit from the play (and work) of others. Information-gathering sites can also act as anchors for player communities. For example, one of the primary ways I learned how to be not just an *EQ* player, but a Necromancer, was through a message board/database site for the class. The site, EQNecro,[36] provided a space for people playing the Necromancer class to talk about game strategies, note new things in the world, complain about particular aspects of the game, and joke around. It offered a common meeting point with other players. As has been noted in many other Internet studies, participants often find such spaces invaluable and meaningful communities of affiliation, and this is certainly the case with *EQ* (Baym 1999; Danet 2001; Wellman and Gulia 1999). Whether it is a message board based on playing a Druid or focused on the social life of a particular server, discussion lists and Web sites expand the definition of the game world.

Another category of Web sites worth mentioning are the comic, humor, or art sites. A large number of daily comics, fan-produced humor pages, and movies have emerged around the game. These productions are particularly interesting in that while they do not have any community-communication component (no one is talking to each other and no data is being shared) they can form a powerful connection to the game for players. Relating shared experiences through art (be it comic or not) is a common way players circulate feelings about the game to others and reflect on their own experience. For example, when new fan-produced movies turn up—on all kinds of subjects including sitting at tiresome camps or, in a more poignant one I recently saw, a long-time player touring the world as a way of saying goodbye and leaving the game—links to them often circulate rapidly. While sharing information about the game or passing along a link to a favorite comic can be a way of connecting with an existing social network, it also becomes a powerful mechanism for participating in a larger game public.

From Gift to Commodity: How Design Influences Social Life

Because of the organic nature of the culture in games, it is quite malleable and can change over time, often in relationship to the underlying structures of the game. Two examples of this are buffing and porting. Buffing is a basic action in *EQ* in which players cast spells—either onto themselves or another—that assist them in the gameplay. Buffs can increase the number of hit points (HP) a player has (the numerical measure of health such that more HP means you can take more damage in a fight), make them stronger, hit harder, regenerate mana (a kind of reservoir of energy required to cast spells) at a quicker rate, help them be resistant to opponents' spells, and various other advantageous qualities. When a buff spell is given, the caster loses some mana, which can generally only be regained through time and, on occasion, requires an expendable component like a gem.

Buffing is an integral part of play, but how has the player community negotiated this aspect of the game? In the early years of *EQ* it was very common for people to ask for buffs with a fair amount of frequency. It was typically only done in particular environments—common areas where people gathered—and not when someone was in the middle of a battle. Generally social norms required people be polite and, in fact, this was one of the few spaces in which a role-play "voice" would often occur. So, for example, a player might approach a Druid and say "Kind sir, can I ask you please for a SoW," the Spirit of Wolf spell, which increases running speed. It was very unusual for such a request to be turned down as it was typically seen as costing the caster very little and was in some ways interpreted as part of the work associated with being a class that could bestow such spells. Casting particular spells could be seen as a public-service duty, a way of contributing to the larger player base. Sometimes the player who received the buff would try and give the caster a bit of money in return, though just as often it was refused. Players who did not stick to some basic conventions were often thought of as rude, newbies, or young and socially inexperienced. In fact, the generosity of buff-giving was such that it was also not uncommon to see higher-level characters wander through lower-level zones buffing people randomly as they went. For a lower-level character, a "drive by" buff or regeneration heal could be an enormous advantage for their hunting session and in such cases public acknowledgement of the good deed was typical via shouts of "thanx" on the zone-wide communication channel.

As the game has progressed, however, this dynamic has changed somewhat. While there are still random acts of generosity in regards to doling out spells and within formal groups it is still the norm that people do not pay for buffs, it is now more common to see buffs advertised (or requested) in zone-wide channels via calls: "Donating 100 plat for a virtue for me and my partner." This is certainly in part because the cost to the caster has risen over the years. Whereas in the past spells were typically purchased from game vendors or "dropped" off killed monsters with a fair degree of frequency, the scenario for acquiring new spells at the higher levels has changed. Spells themselves have been altered such that they do a lot more relative to what they used to but are also now much rarer to find. This has produced an expensive market, where players pay upwards of 80,000 platinum for some of the most powerful spells. As the personal costs have become higher the social norm toward nonfriend gift-giving has decreased. Players now see charging for buffs as a way of recouping their costs. Requests to be buffed for free are met with replies about the high price of obtaining the spell. We can see in the shift from a gift to market economy around buffs how the design choices—combining very powerful, highly sought-after spells with scarcity—has produced a companion effect in social behaviors.

It is also just as likely, however, that the age of the player base in relation to the game (i.e., there are more longtime *EQ* players than new ones) has contributed. In the beginning most characters simply could not afford this kind of monetized buff system. Over time the player base has become more experienced in the game, has acquired more wealth, and in turn can sustain not only a commodity orientation, but a fairly inflated pricing structure. The social norms of politeness and gift-giving have in part morphed into a kind of capitalistic exchange in response to a combination of design and character demographics.

However, it is certainly not the case that gift-giving and acts of generosity no longer occur in the game. They certainly do. But they now operate in a much narrower sphere—tighter associations form a more central part of the game and, in turn, gift economies more closely map onto friendship and formal affiliation networks like guilds. This is in part a result of a change in mobility within the world and the advanced experience of the player base. The issue of mobility brings up the example of porting.

In the beginning *EQ* was a game in which the work, and potential peril, it took to cross the vast geographical distances was not insignificant. Aside from the risks of encountering higher-level monsters, there was at a very basic level the need to run great distances to get around. Crossing continents required running through zones to get to a dock to wait for a ship that, when you got on it, actually simulated sailing by forcing the player to wait while the character crossed a virtual sea. For members of an evil race or class that was not allowed in good-aligned cities, journeys were even more dangerous and involved hiding, sneaking, taking underground passageways, and all kinds of additional time-consuming activities. For lower-level characters, travel often necessitated companionship to avoid being caught alone having to fend off a tough monster.

Into this structure the designers gave a helper—the classes of characters known as Druids and Wizards. Both are able to instantaneously transport (known in the game as "port") other players to locations all over the game world. Each are constrained a bit in this ability in that they are granted the spells to do so only as they progress through levels in the game and can only port to specific areas. Given how valuable a resource porting is, both classes quickly realized they could make some additional in-game money through the service. In the early days of the game it was common to hear shouts such as "Porting to WC, SR, NK, Nek, BB, Toxx + SoW, just send me a tell" or "Taxi to NRo, WC, NK meet at spire." Players would then contact the porter, meet up, and receive their transport. Quite often Druids would include an additional buff like Spirit of Wolf, making receiving a port from them often preferable. What was always striking was the way this service emerged from the player community and how it regulated prices associated with it. There is certainly no outline in the game manual for how the procedure should work, nor any specification of whether it should be free or cost. The stability, of both the price (there was very little competitive pricing around porting, and on my server the price never wavered from 10 platinum coins, for example) and the practice once again testifies to the ability of player communities to self-organize and regulate.

Landscape and mobility in *EQ* now have a different configuration. Since newbies no longer are so tightly bound to their home and adjacent zones, only a handful of people still try to make a living by porting. People are, aside from zones requiring specific porters to get in, no longer reliant on each other for mobility.[37] Indeed, even the boat that previously provided all travel from the continent of Antonica no longer runs. While the world has quantitatively grown (from 65 zones when I started to 222 now), in many ways it feels smaller. This radical change in culture occurred in large part because of two key design decisions—the introduction of a centralized transport zone with NPC porters and the inclusion of automated self-service porting. The first of these was the creation of a zone named Nexus and nonplayer-character porters as part of the *Shadows of Luclin* expansion to the game. Players were now able to visit Wizard spires (the previous sites used by actual Wizard player porters) and meet NPCs who, when asked, give a free token for travel. Every seven minutes the spire automatically transports anyone holding the token and standing in the vicinity to the Nexus zone. The Nexus zone, a centralized transportation area located on the new moon, simply provided access points not only to new Luclin locations, but to Wizard spires in other parts of the world. It instantly became a way to port all around the game without the help of another player. Of course, one could still only port to preexisting wizard spires, but this limitation was soon eroded as well.

The ability of the general population to self-port was enhanced further in 2002, as part of the *Planes of Power* expansion to the game. While the previous change had kept intact the notion of needing someone to assist in porting (even if it was an NPC), in the *Planes* expansion this work was taken over by an object, a book on a stone pillar located in various zones in the game. When a player clicked on this book they were instantly transported to another new hub—the Plane of Knowledge (PoK)—where another appropriate stone could provide transport to any other zone needed. Almost overnight the economy around porting crashed. Players who had formerly made a decent living as a kind of in-game taxi service found themselves practically out of work. Just as significantly, however, was the way this simultaneously changed the nature of the locales throughout the world that were once transportation zones. In the past people often gathered around popular porting spots. They were not only the places for picking up rides but for finding buffs, safely resting surrounded by other players likely to help out if something attacked, or simply a convenient meeting spot. With the automatization of porting and the introduction of centralized transportation zones like PoK and the Nexus, the regional gathering places died, as did the social life around them.

The Shift from Provincialism to Cosmopolitanism

The change in porting and mobility in the world is an example of a much larger transformation in the game from a kind of provincialism to cosmopolitanism. People are now able to encounter a wider variety of players much earlier in their game life, can easily travel far more of the world, and rely much more on a mass player base than the small, idiosyncratic local ones of the past. The original world of *EQ* relied on a distributed system of towns (for example, Freeport on the continent of Antonica or Kaladim on the continent of Faydwer) and vendor villages, and whether or not a player could visit them was very much dependent on their character and skill. "Evil" characters, such as Dark Elves, would be "killed on sight" (KOS) in good-aligned towns like Eurdin. Conversely, if good characters wanted to visit an evil city such as Neriak, the home of the Dark Elves, they either needed to be quite skilled in sneaking or making themselves invisible, or get the assistance of another player (for example, having an Enchanter cast a spell to hide the actual identity). But these localized towns and player-driven hubs, though still present in the game, have become nearly obsolete with the implementation of the Plane of Knowledge zone. PoK exists as a kind of metropolis that hosts not only a game-wide transportation system, but banks, libraries, and vendors that can be used by all characters of the game. Marks quotes one of the expansion designers, Shawn Lord on the intent, saying, "We wanted to build this place that was out of the ether. It was completely detached from everything that you understand and it's dedicated to all three approaches to acquiring knowledge. So we ended up having a neutral, good, and evil district" (Marks 2003, 96). This shift from regional activity to a centralized hub is also clearly seen in the move from local zone-based markets to the megastore that is the Bazaar.

One of the most fundamental and indeed most powerful design choices made for the game was the creation of money, objects, and the ability to trade. It may seem a bit odd to call this a choice given how ubiquitous these things are in MMOGs, but it is certainly the case that you could build a game that includes none of them (Farmer 2004). Like many MMOGs, *EQ* has included all of these, and as a result of these basic design decisions it has an economy and culture of not only gift-giving but of buying and selling.[38] Not insignificantly, *EQ* has for many years now had a permanent zone-based auction chat channel for players to use in advertising and looking for goods. The formal inclusion of this communication channel lends legitimacy to the action of buying and selling game items, something I return to in more detail in chapter 5. As a young player I was of course used to people buying and selling goods, but I remember finally seeing this side of the game in sharper view when I found myself in a zone called East Commonlands (EC). Given its location between several busy areas as well as the fact that a number of NPC vendors were housed there, EC was—at least on my server—one of the central hubs in the game not only for picking up buffs and joining player-run games of gambling (games of chance using the /random command) but for buying and selling goods. People would hang out in a tunnel, a safe area with no wandering monsters, and advertise their wares via the auction channel. While purchasing also happened in other zones via the auction channel, EC was a player-distributed store offering a constant supply of vendors with things to sell.

This market configuration required a number of things—people had to be "physically" present in the zone to hear about items and see goods, and the seller had to be present to continually call out auction information and make the transactions. With the advent of the Bazaar zone, processes changed radically. The Bazaar, located on the new moon in the game, was built for the sole purpose of buying and selling. Players now can purchase special "trader satchels" and, if they stand in a designated area, can initiate a command putting them into vendor mode. Vendor mode allows players to set fixed prices on their goods and automates the process of selling. If a player approaches and offers the designated amount, the trade is processed automatically. This allows the player to turn on vendor mode and leave her computer, turning the character into an automated merchandise machine. While the player must remain logged in, the character no longer needs to call out auctions, haggle prices, or manually initiate trades.

On the buyers' side, they can enter into the Bazaar and do fairly complex searches on items for sale, looking for things by name, by statistics, by price, by vendor, and by many other subcategories. Buyers can comparison shop instantly among all sellers present (and it is now fairly rare to find anyone selling things outside of the Bazaar). They no longer haggle. Indeed, 99% of the vendors a player encounters in the Bazaar are simply placeholders, avatars who will automatically carry out the formal wishes of their now-absent players. In the beginning the Bazaar was an extremely "laggy" zone to be in. There were simply too many people (equating a graphics overload) engaged in too much processing-heavy activity. Anyone with a less-than-lightening-fast computer often had to walk, avatar eyes on the floor so as not to see any complex graphics (read: other people), and try to find the particular vendor he had chosen. In another interesting change, the Bazaar has now be redesigned such that all other trader graphics can be turned off when entering the space. Instead of showing all the vendors selling their goods, the screen shows only the character's avatar in a large hall, maybe with a few other shoppers, and the one vendor chosen to purchase from.

This scenario certainly recalls situations like the rise of WalMart or the mall versus Main Street. But many players feel that life is much easier now and that running around buying and selling, paying outrageous prices because there was no competition, and all the time "wasted" having to sit and sell things has been fixed.[39] It is hard to not look at the empty wizard spires and druid circles and hear echoes of the death of local culture and public space, but many players claim that waiting for ports, sitting on ships that crossed virtual oceans, and paying for help were not any meaningful part of the game.[40]

Of course, people do form social networks even though these old meeting areas are gone, and emergent culture has not simply given way to centralized systems. While there is no vibrant East Commonlands tunnel culture on my old server anymore, people still hang out and chat in places like the Plane of Knowledge. Indeed, many players simply shake their heads in the face of the nostalgic old-timers who bemoan the way the game has developed. I do think there are some losses that come, however, with the conveniences of the Bazaar or teleportation devices. One of the tricky aspects about a game like *EQ* is that many of the things that are seen as nuisances or difficulties are exactly the mechanisms that propel the creation of emergent cultures and social networks. The lack of easy transportation options forced people to deal with and rely on each other, to set up practices that foster and facilitate that engagement, simultaneously creating value around a set of skills. Having to deal with an actual buyer for your goods can lead to negotiations of value, moments of generosity, and even trust. Just as in offline life, the move from provincialism to cosmopolitanism, from localism to globalism, may bring with it many quality-of-life improvements, but we would be remiss to not at least be clear-eyed about the costs associated with it as well. The design and structural choices by game developers are always deeply connected to the forms not only of play, but of sociality, that participants enact. As Michel Callon notes, "Indeed engineers transform themselves into sociologists, moralists or political scientists at precisely those moments when they are most caught up in technical questions" (1991, 136). In a game like *EverQuest* where the social aspects of the game drive its success and some of the pleasures derived from playing it, the relationship between design and culture, and the importance of understanding the ways those intersections feed into the game, cannot be overstated.

3   Beyond Fun: Instrumental Play and Power Gamers

I was in Los Angeles for work and decided to try to meet up with one of the people I had become friends with in the game. I met Mitch, a mechanic living in one of the sprawling suburbs outside L.A., fairly early on through my connections with Katinka and people in our small family guild. When we first met, I was a midlevel character trying to make my way through *EQ*'s first game expansion, *Ruins of Kunark*. Mitch befriended me and we grouped up, providing a much-needed change from my recent soloing grind. We spent quite a few days camped on a hillside in the Overthere region killing the local monsters, and I gained a number of levels during that period. In retrospect, that small window of time was about the extent of our playing together. On later occasions he would start up a new character and we would have a chance to group again, or he would find a way to meet up in the game to pass along some items he could no longer use. But what quickly became apparent is that Mitch consistently passed me by in advancing in the game. If I were gone for a day or two, I would come back only to find him several levels ahead and off in another part of the world. Most of our game friendship, while in many ways rooted in those early sessions on that hill, was held together through in-game chatting.

As my small family guild fell apart and regrouped in various forms (with different names and slightly different membership rosters), Mitch found himself a place within one of the top raiding guilds on our server, and he remains there today. I figured my trip to L.A. would give me a good chance to meet face-to-face this long-time, but somewhat sporadic, in-game friend. We decided to meet at his house along with Josh, another in-game acquaintance I had played with a few times. Mitch gave me the tour of the house, ending in his game room. There he had several desks piled high with CDs, papers, magazines, and assorted stuff. On his desks were my first introduction to a very different world of *EverQuest* gaming—two computers side by side running the game simultaneously. Later Mitch increased this to three machines, but even with two it was clear why I—a researcher dedicating quite a bit of time to the game—still could not keep up with this guy who, despite holding down a full-time job, seemed to advance exponentially faster than me.

The conversation pretty quickly shifted from our idle chat about my trip and movies to *EverQuest*. Almost immediately Mitch opened up a Web browser and talk began flying about the previous night's raid (he and Josh were at this point both in the same high-level guild) and the loot that had dropped. Recounting fights is a common topic of conversation among players, but with Josh and Mitch the talk had a slightly different quality. They seemed to know an incredible amount about the items' statistics and often carefully looked over all their properties (additional HP or intelligence points, for example), closely examining what had been won when the monster was killed. They quickly rattled off comparisons with items their characters currently wore and debated which were really valuable in terms of gameplay statistics and which were novelty items. They knew what they wanted, what they needed to improve their character, and thought about their goals in very quantitative terms.

They pulled up another page at their guild Web site that already chronicled the same fight, describing in both text and pictures, what had occurred. The page became a kind of artifact propelling the conversation—they talked around it, recounting the strategies and tactics used, remarking on who did what, what worked, what failed, and also what was the next challenge. Previously I had felt that whenever I mentioned the game to nonplayers I seemed completely off the map, that I was speaking a language they did not understand and talking about a world they could not fathom. This was the first time, however, I felt out of my element in an *EverQuest* conversation. Despite some paltry attempts at joining in, I was essentially unable to relate to their experience of the game. It was unfamiliar. What they focused on and highlighted generally were not the things I paid careful attention to. While I was not an unknowledgeable player—I certainly knew which was my best weapon and set of spells, knew where to hunt, even had my eye on a new outfit to upgrade my abilities—their intent and focus had a different quality. Like those nonplayers I had tried to talk to in the past, this time I was the one just listening, somewhat confused, somewhat bemused, and mostly feeling like I was peeking at an unfamiliar world. Mitch and Josh played a different *EverQuest* than I did.

The growing body of literature on massively multiplayer online games, and indeed in game studies in general, typically has focused on a generic player—a sort of ideal type, the imagined player. Given the newness of computer game studies, this kind of homogeneity is understandable—the terrain is still undergoing a basic mapping, so fine-grained distinctions have not yet emerged. Earlier work by people like MUD creator and game designer Richard Bartle, however, provide some indication that not all players are the same nor enjoy the same aspects of a game. He proposes that there are a variety of types of activities people prefer in multiplayer games and that we can characterize such players through a basic taxonomy. His now oft-repeated categories—achievers, socializers, explorers, killers—form a continual basis for discussions of player types and are frequently referred to by game designers as a way of understanding how they might shape their product to appeal to different audiences.[1] Though he has refined the categories in his recent book and provides a fascinating discussion on the variables that intersect any such modeling of behavior, the basic framework Bartle suggests in the 1996 article based on his experience with MUD players is that people generally enjoy four things.

Achievement within the game context. Players give themselves game-related goals, and vigorously set out to achieve them. This usually means accumulating and disposing of large quantities of high-value treasure, or cutting a swathe through hordes of mobiles (i.e., monsters built into the virtual world).

Exploration of the game. Players try to find out as much as they can about the virtual world. Although initially this means mapping its topology (i.e., exploring the MUD's breadth), later it advances to experimentation with its physics (i.e., exploring the MUD's depth).

Socialising with others. Players use the game's communicative facilities, and apply the role-playing that these engender, as a context in which to converse (and otherwise interact) with their fellow players.

Imposition upon others. Players use the tools provided by the game to cause distress to (or, in rare circumstances, to help) other players. Where permitted, this usually involves acquiring some weapon and applying it enthusiastically to the persona of another player in the game world.

In Bartle's model, players fall on an X and Y axis based on their general orientation and game interest. The horizontal gradient runs from "players" to "world" and the vertical line runs from "acting" to "interacting," so that those who are more oriented to other players and interacting fall in the "socialisers" quadrant and those more oriented toward the world and acting fall within "achievers." While such distinctions often are overstated as complete archetypes, it is worth exploring different styles of play to understand better the more complex nature of engagement in multiuser game worlds. Abstract notions of a "game player" may offer some initial paths into understanding games, but we also can learn quite a bit more about the varieties of ways people think about rules, play, and game worlds by looking at the multiplicity within the game community. The notion that people play differently, and that the subjective experience of play varies, is central to an argument that would suggest there is no single definitive way of enjoying a game or of talking about what constitutes "fun." We need expansive definitions of play to account for the variety of participants' pleasurable labor and activity. Those definitions must encompass both casual and more hard-core gamers. Suggesting that games are always simply about "fun" (and then endlessly trying to design that fun) is likely to gloss over more analytically productive psychological, social, and structural components of games.

One of the most interesting distinctions I have found in my research on MMOGs is the difference between casual and power gamers. Both terms are likely to evoke a stereotyped figure. The casual gamer is often seen as someone "with a life" who invests only moderate amounts of time in a game, while the power gamer appears as an isolated and socially inept player with little "real life" to ground him. Such distinctions echo what is often said about virtual worlds more generally, that those who find online spaces compelling simply do not have much happening offline. For the most part, dialogue about the difference between types rests on unproductive rhetoric and tells little about real styles of play, everyday experience, and what brings people back to a game over and over again. It dichotomizes and oversimplifies the much more complicated social experience of players in each category.

The question about styles of play and gamer types is an old one debated in both designer and player communities. There are often normative aspects to the divisions. For example, players sometimes refer to others as "roll players," "power gamers," or "munchkins." Having roots in tabletop role-playing, these designations are given to players seen as perverting a pure game-space by distorting some aspect of play (too much hack-and-slash, loot greediness, and underdeveloped characters) or by taking advantage of the game design itself (through loopholes and actions not intended in the system but nonetheless not prohibited). In an article by Anablepophobia (2003) at the GameGrene Web site entitled "Just Say No to Power Gamers," the author suggests that such players ruin role-playing games (RPGs) by their insistence on being as powerful as possible and "see[ing] no other purpose in the game besides winning."

While some put the blame on the system, the designers, or the GM (suggesting that the structure of a particular game may produce this kind of behavior), others claim it is an unethical choice on the part of the gamer—that they are simply not playing fair or "right." Some suggest power gamers are inclined to cheat more readily. Bob, a college student who played quite a bit of the game, did not label himself a power gamer because he saw it as an identity that came with a questionable value set. He summed up a fairly common notion about power gamers and their guilds: "They were not interested in playing by what was basically the rules. They realized the disadvantage they were at by playing by the rules so they just bent them." On his previous server, Bob had grown very unhappy with the way power gamers seemed to always skirt the borders—and indeed, sometimes even push at them—between questionable and fair play. The notion that power gamers are out to spoil everyone else's fun or that they are inclined to cheat more frequently looms as a stereotype in the player community. But untangling the specter of renegade players set on cheating from the more general group of regular players allows us to consider this style as a serious play strategy in which typical notions of fun and pleasure are upended.

Straight, clear-cut cheating is not something I found to be a defining feature in the power gamers' style of play. Instead, it is just that somehow power gamers, while sharing the same world as their fellow players, seem to be at times *too* focused, *too* intent, *too* goal-oriented. To outsiders it can look as if they are not playing for "fun" at all. Bob is an interesting case in this regard because at some level he is certainly a dedicated player and devotes much time and energy to the game. Yet he felt a kind of resentment based on his constant inability to keep up with the power gamers:

They did things I would consider just ridiculous like getting three or four accounts or having an entire group that was just them [i.e., a single person playing multiple characters at once, enough to support a formal group] and level themselves up and get items for themselves. I have lots of hate for the power gamers. I think like, for me I felt I played the game a lot, I would play probably 4–6 hours a day, almost the equivalent of a fulltime job and I couldn't even keep pace with them cause they were on probably 10 hours a day.

Clearly for Bob, and others, power gamers push too much at the bounds of legitimate play. Whether they seem to have too much time, employ strategies that look like cheating or seem against the spirit of the game, or make their involvement look more like work than play, the controversy about power gamers highlights the diverse orientations people can bring to the exact same game.

After reflecting on my visit with Mitch and Josh and talking to more power gamers, I wondered how our understanding of the nature of play might be extended if we take the power gamer as a legitimate participant in game space.

Rather than dismissing them as simply odd or dysfunctional players, power gamers play in ways we typically do not associate with notions of fun and leisure. They, therefore, tell us something about the ways we construct those categories. In worlds like *EQ,* power gamers often are juxtaposed with role players. As one player remarked, "There are people that play for the role play aspect who say 'thus' and 'forsooth' a lot . . . and then there are people who have their statistics and what's best for advancing their character." In querying players for their definition of power gaming, the comparison with role players and casual gamers often emerged. Role players in *EQ* (though fairly infrequently found outside the dedicated role-play server) are seen as people dedicated to the back-story and narrative structure of the world. They game through developing characters, alliances, and plots—though there is no formal mechanism in the game for rewarding this activity and it therefore has little part in leveling. More casual gamers, on the other hand, typically do not develop elaborate back-stories for their character or follow plot. They may change characters frequently, level more slowly than some, and focus on quests or skill development. They can be involved in guilds, but most often of the "family" sort (as described in the previous chapter). Casual gamers may never attend a high-level raid, those fights in which advanced players take on and kill particularly challenging monsters, and likely never have the opportunity to visit some of the areas in the game. Despite playing with varying degrees of regularity, they nonetheless find the game engaging. For many casual gamers then, making sense of the intensity power gamers bring to the game can be perplexing. And for those like Bob who think they are already running pretty fast to keep up, a power gamer can almost feel like a nemesis.

This sense that somehow these players are just too dedicated, indeed almost bordering on the psychologically pathological, is a popular theme. What I found in conversations with power gamers, however, is that they consider their own play style quite reasonable, rational, and pleasurable. There are several qualities to their approach that emerged: a focus on efficiency and instrumental orientation (particularly rational or goal-oriented), dynamic goal setting, a commitment to understanding the underlying game systems/ structures, and technical and skill proficiency. One of the reasons power gaming occupies an "othered" space in games is that it appears to operate directly

counter to a popular understanding of fun and leisure. The activities and orientations power gamers bring to games often look more to the outside world
as work which leads to a much broader ambivalence about what constitutes
legitimate play.

One of the issues that sometimes arises with an examination of this style of
play is whether or not women can, and do, occupy the position of power
gamer. Is there anything inherently gender-biased about the approach? My
answer is no, but with two caveats. I have certainly talked to several women
who fit the bill of a power gamer and heard from others about women in
their own guilds they would identify as such. The caveats arise not around
internal psychological orientations to the play style (i.e., "women are not
competitive enough"), but structural considerations. There is debate, for
example, about how much time is required to be a power gamer. Some feel
that power gaming has more to do with how time is used than the amount
of time devoted to the game. Others, however, suggest that many women,
because of domestic or work pressures, simply do not have the required
amount of leisure time needed to fully embody the play style. My sense is
that time definitely plays some role, especially at the high-end game where
participation in raiding guilds, a natural home for the power gamer, comes
with significant responsibility.[2] The fact that many women still perform an
enormous juggling act with domestic labor, social-familial responsibilities,
work outside the home, and their leisure time certainly plays a part in their
ability to inhabit the power-gamer play style. The other factor, which I discuss a bit in the next chapter, is that (just as offline) dedicated ambitious
women often are seen as abnormal, not fitting within traditional feminine
roles. This can carry a certain amount of stigma that has to be cautiously negotiated. Rather than saying that women do not enjoy this style of play, I am
more inclined to note that the social barriers to becoming a power gamer are
worth taking into account.

Efficiency and Instrumental Action

One of the most notable characteristics of the power gamers I observed and
spoke with is their fundamental adherence to a cause-and-effect model of
game involvement. Such gamers in *EQ* are particularly attuned to making the
most of their time in the game and so undertake actions to produce efficient
reward paths. John, a small-business owner who was introduced to the game

by his brother, early on in our conversation self-identified as a power gamer: "I look at *EverQuest* as the numbers. If you do this you'll get this, this is a better combination, you'll have a better chance to kill. That's all it is for me—to see the new stuff and do the new stuff and find the new stuff."

This kind of efficient, almost quantitative orientation is something I saw again and again. Chris, an undergraduate in computer science, came to typify for me the play style. While he had started the game with his college friends, he found himself quickly surpassing them and eventually shifted his networks from offline to online connections, turning solely to better matched in-game players for groups. He described how knowing the best, most efficient way to play was central to success, especially at the high-end game. For players like Chris the game is seen as a problem to be broken apart and solved. Working out solutions and strategies with focused intent then becomes central for players with Chris's mindset: "Efficiency is probably they most important word [for a power gamer]. Leveling is all about efficiency." While a player certainly can advance without this kind of orientation, power gamers structure and evaluate actions in terms of productive or wasteful strategies. In comparing how a casual gamer approaches the issue of in-game items that provide the wearer with beneficial properties and statistics (figure 3.1), Chris said, "If you want to be the best you've got to get everything to mesh. You can't have 'Oh, this is the best item from this guy, this is the best from this guy.' You have to say 'I have 47 points to get to my current cap [point limit]. How do I get that based on what drops what?'"

This intentionality extends to all aspects of play, even failed encounters and mistakes. One player suggested that average players do not confront failure as a learning opportunity in the same way that power gamers do: "When we die we say 'What went wrong?' and try to understand what happened." While it is certainly not unusual to hear even casual gamers talk about trying something a few times to "get it right," the level of attention power gamers give to understanding mistakes is notable. What are often viewed as the best player-guides—written tips and walk-throughs, usually put on Web sites—tap into this impulse, with their rich accounts of how to handle a monster or zone that specify down to the very pacing of the encounter how to proceed (though often the nuts and bolts are left to private, password-protected member areas). Just as frequent are pictures and documentation for successful encounters. This willingness to critically examine others, let their own tactics be reviewed, and repeat encounters until they succeed distinguishes the

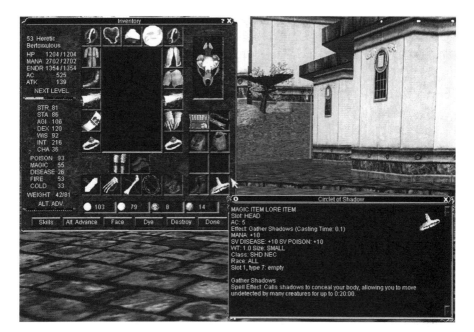

Figure 3.1
Inventory screen and breakdown of statistics for specific items

power gamer from the more casual one who may move onto a different location after several unsuccessful attempts.

Dynamic Goal Setting

As is probably clear, the focus on efficiency is typically driven by the desire
to be the best. In a game like *EverQuest* that goal is particularly tricky given
the ongoing expansions which increase level caps (when the game began, the
maximum level was 50, now it is 70), the diverse race/class character structure
that produces varying skill sets, and the variety of arcania to be mastered. In
the face of this complexity, what distinguishes the power gamers is their constant engagement in dynamic goal setting and the focused attention to
achieving those goals, which can range from gaining levels to securing particular weapons and armor, killing certain monsters, gaining admission to a
specific guild, getting special skills, and exploring difficult zones. As many *EQ*
players comment, the game never ends, so players must be self-directed in
how they progress. People continue to play well after reaching the highest

level in the game, which is a testament to the multilayered and locally defined nature of the win condition.

What is striking to me with power gamers is their willingness to go through
very hard work to achieve their goals. It is not the activity itself that becomes
the measure of fun, but the possibility for success that pushes them forward.
Chris, for example, told me about a fourteen-hour session to reach level 50 (at
the time the highest level in the game). By the last few hours of his session, he
found himself going "snowblind" and yet pressed on. When I asked if he had
enjoyed that evening, he replied, "I'd still rather be doing that than other
things. This is my goal, it's going to be fun when I get there. It's the grind
sometimes but then you get there." In *EQ* players of all levels often talk about
"the grind," which is the experience of going through painfully boring or
rote gameplay with slow advancement. Everyone knows and accepts this is
a (flawed) part of the game, but the threshold for tolerating it varies widely.
Power gamers seem willing to endure much more than many other players
and are particularly adept at breaking down the game—dividing the challenges into discrete parts and then working on each area like a puzzle—to
meet their personal goals, which they are constantly revising and developing
as they progress. As Chris put it, "These individual goals you set determine
what kind of player you are. I want to be 50. I want to be 50 first. I want to be
50 in three weeks. How am I gonna do that?"

This was echoed by Jackie, a computer programmer and one of the women
who, while not self-identifying as a power gamer, expressed many of the qualities I have come to see in them. She described her time in the game:

I enjoy progressing in the game, having a sense that there is this path that I'm going on
and I've made some progress toward it. I used to enjoy xp'ing [gaining experience] and
leveling a lot, in and of itself as a kind of progression. I have enjoyed in the past kind of
competitive xp'ing, like on my previous server I was the first enchanter to get to level
50 on the server. And that was a competitive thing, I definitely put in a lot of effort . . .
I'm also competitive in other goals too. Like, I wanted to be the first platinum jeweler
on the server and then it became focused on doing other server firsts like trying to kill
this dragon before anyone else, that sort of thing. I've enjoyed that sort of thing. I'm
very goal oriented I think so I like setting goals and going for it.

Game Knowledge: History and Experience

It is important to keep in mind that all participants in a game come to it
with some history of play. Bob, for example, was a longtime game player who

started out in the first grade with the *King's Quest* series on his PC. Jackie had started playing offline RPGs when she was about ten years old then continued into the online world of MUDs in college, finally making her way to *Ultima Online*. Players of all types come with a diversity of game experience, be it drawn from board games played around the family dinner table, a first-person shooter (FPS) game on a home PC, or maybe even a live-action role-playing (LARP) experience. They may have never played on a team and only against the computer. People bring with them a play history that in varying degrees informs their interaction with any particular game. This historical and contextual specificity of play should not be overlooked in an analysis of gamers. In the case of power gamers I found that they often drew from a broad base of game knowledge as a way of advancing their play in *EQ* and were good at figuring out what skills they could lean on from past experience. In the most basic instance, specific game commands may be transferable. *Star Wars Galaxies,* for example, has added an interesting feature by allowing players to select an *EQ* keymap, which minimizes the time it takes to learn how to execute basic actions and gestures. Some *EQ* players were likewise familiar with the game's structure based on their previous experience with MUDs.

Beyond these interface considerations, however, are the ways specific games in effect teach players to be gamers in a general sense. Chris saw his time in *EQ* as a part of his larger biography as a gamer, saying, "*EverQuest* was training for *Dark Age* [*of Camelot* (*DAoC*), another MMOG]" and, similarly, his previous experience with games like *Quake, Unreal Tournament,* and *Halo* also provided useful information for "how people move" in *DAoC*.[3] Power gamers seem particularly adept at creating knowledge that is transferable between games (and, conversely, realizing the limits of such an endeavor based on how unique the games are). Jackie, for example, had spent time in tabletop *D&D* both as a DM and as a player. Like many others, she brought her tabletop knowledge of that game and previous characters (in terms of race and class combinations) with her. But she noted that in *EverQuest* "class balance is very different" and that, while she had played Clerics in other games, in *EQ* she found them much too passive for her taste, so she instead picked other classes based on her goals at the time. This willingness to adapt to the specific affordances and limitations of the game is something less pronounced in the players who find themselves, no matter what the game, drawn to a particular character type.

This general game knowledge, of course, becomes grounded in figuring out the particularities of each system and the specific mechanics at work. Power gamers often push systems to their limit by trying to "break" them or find points at which the game architecture is internally contradictory or malleable. In many ways it is these kinds of behaviors that are seen by the broader game community (and quite often the administrators) as looking quite similar to cheating. But power gamers generally see these kinds of explorations into the dynamics of the game as smart—that only by understanding the constraints of the system can they play most effectively. How do mobs path (walk or move) through a zone, and what is the most efficient route to take when fighting them? What are the rates of respawn on a particularly rare monster, and what triggers that process? How do different spell combinations work in breaking up a tough group of monsters? What happens when I do this? Or this? As power gamers work and rework such questions, their knowledge of the game can at times appear "too good." They seem to understand how things work at a level the average player does not quite grasp. Given the gap in understanding how power gamers actually play, this kind of knowledge sometimes is labeled negatively as cheating or trying to exploit the system.[4]

This boundary-pushing is one of the first instances in which my account of power gamers differs from Bartle's consideration of the "achiever." In many ways the achiever fits the mold of the power gamer with the attention to goals. Bartle, however, suggests that for achievers, "Exploration is necessary only to find new sources of treasure, or improved ways of wringing points from it" (Bartle 1996, 3). By contrast, he posits, "Explorers delight in having the game expose its internal machinations to them. They try progressively esoteric actions in wild, out-of-the-way places, looking for interesting features (i.e., bugs) and figuring out how things work" (ibid.).

In my discussions with power gamers I have found that this line is not so clear. Certainly there is a goal behind the system exploration that power gamers engage in, but it does not seem to have quite the peripheral "only if I have to" quality Bartle hints at. Indeed, there seems to be a kind of pleasure attached to mapping out such mechanics and responding to them in creative ways. While detailed explanations of effective strategies (the outcome of "explorer" labor) on the one hand serve a functional purpose in sharing knowledge so others can replicate a tactic, such rich recountings of strategies through informal chatting, stories, and written-down guides also seem to mark a pride and pleasure for the power gamer. In this regard there is a distinct social pleasure that arises from the power-gamer orientation that is not fully captured within the rubric of "achiever." Be it the status that comes from accomplishments or the ability to help others with one's knowledge, power gamers seem to be deeply embedded in the social processes of the game world. Power gamers also may refine strategies of others, seeking increasingly esoteric (but more efficient) methods of play. Indeed, in a game like *EQ*, power gamers cannot simply be achievers but seem to require a fairly complex set of social and exploratory skills . . . and even enjoy them.

Technical and Skill Proficiency

The final category worth mentioning is the role technical proficiency plays in the life of a power gamer. While *EQ* is a fairly straightforward game that requires little technical know-how (which is often seen as contributing to its popularity with a fairly diverse audience) players can deploy higher degrees of technical engagement. The use of macros or remapping keys is one way power gamers often streamline their sessions for maximum efficiency. While the average player either may not know about or take the time to learn how they might "script" an encounter, power gamers often spend time distilling down essential strategies or customizing the game in a way that makes their play more tuned to a unique style. They do not just accept the interface but alter it to suit their own methods.

Another common activity among power gamers in *EQ* is what I saw at Mitch's house, the practice of "2-boxing": playing multiple characters simultaneously on two machines. There are players who extend this even further, with 3-boxing being not uncommon (though generally the additional characters are not quite as active as the primary one). Before *EQ* was allowed to run in a windowed mode, this might additionally require using a hack program such as *EQWindows* to allow for several instances of the game on one machine.

Beyond actually playing multiple accounts, there are also tools like *ShowEQ*, a program that runs on Linux and gives a detailed accounting of any zone including what mobs are present and what they holding, a listing of exits, and a listing of other players. *ShowEQ* is certainly one of the more debated "helpers" for the game and is often seen as a cheat. While it is by no means the case that all power gamers use it (or even see it as ethical to), players relying on such a program are more likely to be power gamers. The program runs only on Linux and, in that regard, was explicitly created with a big built-in barrier for use. Only those with some specialized technical knowledge, not to mention a computer running Linux, can use it. But for those who do get it running, it can be very useful in providing a kind of god's-eye view of the game world. Yet it is certainly a contested "helper," something right on the border of legitimacy for all players. John, for example, speculated a bit more about his self-identification as a power gamer when he reflected on the use of things like *ShowEQ*, saying, "I guess I'm not that much of a power gamer, I still go by the rules."[5] In general, though, this kind of active engagement with, and sometimes pushing back on, the technical constraints of the system seems to be another notable feature of the play style of power gamers. Programs like *ShowEQ* and the more general ways players build up competencies within a game also highlight the important ways players bring to any given game a history, replete with skill sets and technical knowledge. These take on a direct role in the game experience and should not be considered external to the enterprise but central to game play. Focusing on the larger context a player operates in can move us beyond abstract (sometimes idealized) notions of "player" to grounded experience that can highlight not only creative play strategies, but difficulties between player (as user) and game (as system).

The Myth of the Isolated Gamer

With this description of power gaming, it easily could be imagined that the type of player engaged in this style of play is quite isolated, grinding away with a hyper-focused efficiency out of sight from other players. While there has been some interesting work done on FPSs that taps into their sociological aspects (Morris 2003; Stald 2001; Wright, Boria, and Breidenbach 2002), MMOGs as a genre and *EverQuest* in particular actively facilitate the production of a very specific power-gamer identity that problematizes notions of individualized play. *EQ* power gamers are distinctly social players, although at times such sociality may not look like what we see in casual or role-players. Nonetheless they are typically linked to both informal and formal social mechanisms which facilitate their play.

As we have seen *EQ* is a game in which success (especially at the high-end) can only be gained through a reliance on social networks. Players not only socialize in the simplest sense (through chatting and hanging out in the virtual world) but form complicated systems of trust, reliance, and reputation. Play in *EQ* is grounded in the production and maintenance of social relationships and larger organizations such as guilds. These kinds of connections are no different for power gamers, and in *EQ* they certainly are not the "lone ranger" figures one might expect. Indeed, in many cases the deeply social quality of the high-end game and guilds, where power gamers inevitably end up, is even more pronounced than for lower levels. The reliance on, and involvement with, social networks and resources—Web information and bulletin boards, guilds, and off- and online friendship networks—indeed reveals power gamers to be some of the most socialized players in MMOGs.

Community Knowledge

Power gamers are constantly evaluating, planning, and organizing their game sessions. With the wide variety of locations and monsters, the reliance on statistics, path progressions (needing to make sure you have "keys" or "flags" before proceeding onto the next challenge), large amounts of armor and weapons (all with their own statistics that modify the player), and spell/combat strategies, there are numerous factors of gameplay that players, and power gamers in particular, need to juggle. As a response to this complexity, a broad knowledge base grounded in the community has developed in conjunction with the game. In the previous discussion of the social life of the game I suggest that we consider the ways Web sites, message boards, and the like operate as extended social networks. We similarly can think about how these sites form the locus for a kind of "collective intelligence," an idea Henry Jenkins (2002) picks up from Pierre Levy's (1997) work on the reconfigurations occurring in contemporary society around technology and knowledge. Jenkins (2002, 1), following on Levy's argument, suggests that:

The new knowledge communities will be voluntary, temporary, and tactical affiliations, defined through common intellectual enterprises and emotional investments. Members may shift from one community to another as their interests and needs change and they may belong to more than one community at the same time. Yet they are held together through the mutual production and reciprocal exchange of knowledge.

The screenshots taken from the popular Web site Allakhazam (figures 3.2 and 3.3) show the ways players contribute an immense amount of information to the broader community. Figure 3.2 shows the front page at the Web site that provides links to maps, detailed character information, play guides, region information, and equipment data along with long lists of "new" and "updated" items being cataloged. These are objects in the game that have been

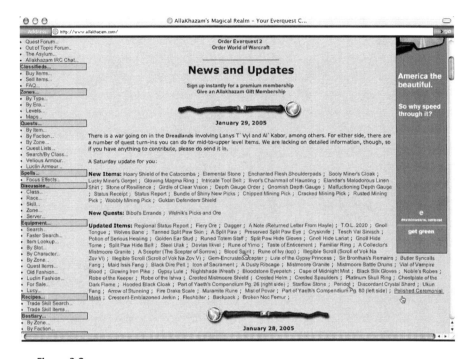

Figure 3.2
Image from Allakhazam Web page

submitted to the Web site's database by players, for players. Users can click on any of these items to bring up detailed information about the object. As shown in figure 3.3, players collectively submit information about an item, adding bits and pieces to flesh out its record. This item, the Faithbringer's Boots of Conviction, has been submitted to the database by a player named Rithina of the guild named Paradise of the server Nameless (as noted in the tag that has been added to the image of the item). The information includes a variety of statistics, where the item is found, and how it is obtained. Note that both the "where" (Wall of Slaughter) and "how" (part of the Trelak's Plate Armor quest) are themselves links to further information in the database, also provided by players. Matt Hills (2002) points out the ways fan-produced culture intersects with status claims, which is quite visible here. He notes that paying attention to this aspect of engagement "allows us to consider any given fan culture not simply as a community but also as a social hierarchy where fans share a common interest while also competing over fan knowl-

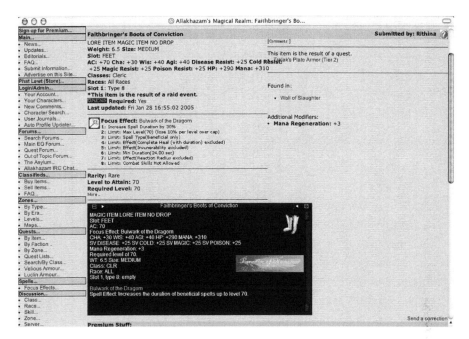

Figure 3.3
Item information from Allakhazam user-built database

edge, access to the object of fandom, and status" (Hills 2002, 46). Knowledge about the game simultaneously circulates through gift, status, and reputation economies (Kollock 1999; Sun, Lin, Ho 2003). Within the world of *EQ* players seek and acquire status not only through the items they own, but more generally via their knowledge of the game, its artifacts, and how to acquire them. Below the item details is a message board (not show in the screenshot) that allows players to comment on the object, extending the range of participants that can contribute to the database. This communicative space allows players an opportunity not only to add to the information given, but to rebut and challenge each other's contributions. Such critical collaborative practices around which *EQ* artifacts are embedded points to the ways they are constructed as meaningful objects only within complex networks that include not only the original designers, but Web-site managers and the various players that interact with them both within and outside of the game world.

It is also common practice for Web sites to link to each other, thereby extending the network even more. For example, clicking on maps at Allakhazam launches another site, EQAtlas, in a new browser window. While much of the game is confined to very specific server-based experience, sites such as this form a meta-community for the game. Information found on one server is just as applicable for another, and in this regard such sites also act as a central umbrella organization for the larger *EQ* community. Information found at sites like Allakhazam are invaluable for *EverQuest* players, particularly those operating at the high end of the game.

Jakobsson notes that the boundaries of the game can be seen as extended through such spaces, suggesting, "It is very hard to imagine a game like *EQ* without all the resources on the web helping players with maps, information about spells, equipment, etc. From the players' point of view these websites are an integral part of the game itself."[6] Play strategies, maps, and databases of monsters and items, not to mention information and tips for playing particular kinds of characters, are available online. Combined with the detailed records of tactics, items, and raid encounters guilds regularly track, information outside of the game is crucial for the power gamer.

Indeed, these players are active visitors and contributors to such sites, especially via their own guild pages. They often will make daily rounds, visiting key Web sites to get information and strategies. As John put it, "We have these goals, and we go onto those websites and see what people got on other servers and what we want." This kind of labor is a massive collaboration in the production of valuable game knowledge and presents a fascinating example of player sociality. While the casual gamer may visit a map site on occasion or sometimes peruse a message board, power gamers regularly consult, dispute, refine, and build knowledge through the more formalized mechanisms of Web sites and bulletin boards. By participating in guild sites, gaining status through contributions, and entering discussions with others, players bond to the collective and enact social modes of play.

Friendship Networks

While one type of coordination occurs through Web sites like those mentioned in the previous section, at a more basic level knowledge about the game and tactics are distributed through peer and friendship channels. And these information networks regularly cross off- and online boundaries. One player I interviewed talked about how his playing was intricately woven into his offline relationships with people in his dorm. His ability to be a power gamer was supported by a kind of supplemental processing with his "real-world" friends:

We'd play for a couple of hours and go to the dining hall and be talking about it and go to class and be talking about it. It's a pretty consuming game. A lot of the game was items so we were talking about items we wanted to get and stuff like that. And some of it was stuff that happened. The adventures. Since we're on a PvP server it was a little different. We'd talk about the encounters we had with other people.

He went on to describe how he had access to several of these friends' accounts at various times, which aided him moving his character around, doing item transfers, and other game tasks.

Of course offline friends sometimes get left behind and new ones in the game are made. As Chris put it, those new in-game connections often are not built around common (outside) interests but on "mutual respect" for each other's abilities in the game. The social networks of power gamers are incredibly important at a couple of different levels. The first is a basic need for interaction. In talking to players I noticed how often they referred to strategies they employed for making it through the "grind" parts of the game. As one player put it, "Killing the same monster for four hours and not do[ing] something else is very boring. So if you don't have someone to talk to or something else to do you'll go crazy. You needed to chat if you wanted to get level 50." While some will watch television or read during these periods, it is just as typical to hear them talk about using in-game communication to entertain themselves during these boring play periods. The amount of downtime and dull moments should not be underestimated, and it is something even the designers acknowledge (albeit implicitly). Players noted with amusement the introduction within *EQ* of a *Tetris*-like game called *Gems* (figure 3.4). The game allows people to play a very simple puzzle within *EQ* (overlaid onto the standard interface). As one reviewer wrote:

Somewhere, a merciful programmer noticed that certain aspects of the game were SO GODDAM DULL and downtime was SO EXTENSIVE that people were doing things like laundry and watching television while they waited to hunt, level, cast spells, travel to meet friends . . . in short, to play *EQ*. Out of the goodness of his heart, he leapt into action (on his own time) to solve the problem. The result? *Gems*. (Thomas n.d.)

Beyond chatting with people in the game to get through lulls or simply to socialize, as detailed in the previous chapter there is a deep reliance on each other to be able to progress. The reliance on not just groups but good groups

Figure 3.4
Gems, a *Tetris*-like game within *EverQuest*

(productive ones in which a player gets a decent rate of experience with minimal deaths and downtime) become central to high-end game play, which is
where power gamers in *EQ* cluster. "Knowing people you trust to play the class
well" becomes crucial. A simple example is of group members being able to
trust that the group's Cleric, a healer character, will follow the fight attentively
and cast healing spells on members in a timely manner so they do not die.

Being a good team player is key, and power gamers are particularly good at
not simply knowing the strengths and limitations of their own class, but that
of the others in the game as well. Chris suggests that the key is to ask "how am
I going to work in conjunction with people based on class, skill, and equipment" in any given group? Rather than being asocial, power gamers seem
extremely *relational* in their orientation—paying attention to how the competencies of people relate to each other and how they can be coordinated. On
the more sophisticated end, then, it is not simply that the Cleric, for example,

knows which heal spells are most effective, but that the main melee (weapon-wielding) character also knows what kinds of assistance the Cleric can provide, including the precise timing at work, a sense of how much healing can be given before a monster starts attacking the Cleric, and what specific buffs to ask for. Power gamers also can bring much more flexibility to bear than average players in how characters are played. They are more likely to innovate an encounter, asking how, given a current group configuration (and any constraints it brings), tasks can be divided up best.

Power gamers rely on building strong social networks so they are able to call on help as needed, form well-balanced groups for particular tasks, and propagate raids. They are also quite clear on their need to be seen as good players, ones who can be counted on to valuably contribute to a group. The better a player's reputation is, the more likely her opportunities to advance. Ultimately the benefits of swapping strategies and sharing knowledge (not to mention accounts) cannot be underestimated for this play style. Because of the kinds of investments power gamers can put into the group, it is worth noting that they can often travel in packs, sometimes even from game to game, porting their collective knowledge with them. It is not uncommon for people to start and leave games with each other so that entire groups move for example, from *EverQuest* to *Star Wars Galaxies* to *World of Warcraft*. Power gamers know the value of a good working team and can go to some lengths to preserve it.

Guilds

As shown in the previous discussion, reputation systems play a significant role in the construction of the high-end game, thus not only linking power gamers to a broader community but at times making them quite beholden to it. The development of high-end raiding guilds provides social support and legitimacy to the power gamer. These guilds are often central to player success as they provide a consistent and reliable source of not only game knowledge, but labor (in the form of help from guildmates). As Jackie suggests:

The evolution of the game environment was becoming more and more guild focused and less and less individual focused. I saw that guilds gave players a large advantage in terms of organizing and the game has become more focused on defeating large powerful mobs that require a lot of organization and coordination . . . it's impossible to do it [reach the high-end game] without a guild.

Within a guild, power gamers not only have a very local mechanism for sharing knowledge and tactics, they also are called upon to support the other members and advance the cause of the guild. Most raiding guilds in *EQ* are very dedicated to tackling ever-increasingly difficult or unexplored zones. New challenges always are being sought after and created. Doing so becomes in part a status marker, but it also serves as an important mechanism for continuing to enjoy the game. I would argue that the participation of power gamers in guilds points to a sociability we do not normally associate with this kind of focused play style. Not only is there a broader community the players are involved in, they quite often are called upon to put aside their own individual needs for the good of the group. As Chris put it, "Somebody calls a raid, you get there. You drop everything. '[But] I'm half a bub [bubble, a visual marker of progression through a level] to level!' No, you get there."

This commitment to a larger group moves the idea of socializing beyond simply chatting, or informal friendship networks, to a recognition that there is a fundamental necessity to rely on others in a game like *EverQuest.* The power gamers are not exempt from this. Their intense focus, commitment to instrumental action, and love of efficiency does not in the context of *EQ* produce an isolated and individualistic player but a highly networked one.

The Pleasures of Instrumentality

In the examination of power gamers, we begin to confront a model of play that at times looks and sounds quite unlike how we usually speak of gaming. The simple idea of "fun" is turned on its head by examples of engagement that rest on efficiency, (often painful) learning, rote and boring tasks, heavy doses of responsibility, and intensity of focus. Indeed, many power gamers do not use the term "fun" to describe why they play but instead talk about the more complicated notions of enjoyment and reward. At times it almost appears as if they are speaking of work. One of the problems with the term "fun" is that it cedes the discussion of the pleasures of play to an overly dichotomized model in which leisure rests on one side and labor on the other. The question about where the boundary between work and play lies is something Roger Caillois has taken up, writing that play is "an activity that is free, separate, uncertain, unproductive, regulated, and fictive" (2001/1958, 43). He speaks of the "contamination" of play when it is encroached upon by reality, obligation, or professionalism. He writes that in these instances, "What used to be a pleasure becomes an obsession. What was an escape becomes an obligation, and what was a pastime is now a passion, compulsion, and source of anxiety. The principle of play has become corrupted. It is now necessary to take precautions against cheats and professional players, a unique product of the contagion of reality" (ibid., 45). This feeling, that once outside factors begin to leak into the world of play it loses its specialness, its sanctity even, still circulates with some frequency. But might we imagine a space in which our games at times are not always "fun" and, conversely, our labor can be quite pleasurable? Does the framework in which work is about suffering and play is about its relief get us very far in understanding the multiple ways people not only game but experience the activity? Certainly when we look at power gamers we see a production of pleasure that may seem unfamiliar at first glance. On the other hand, even the most casual of gamers probably has experienced those instances in which their play slides into boredom or repetition or where they feel compelled to finish just one more round of their game. And what do we make of professional players in this model? Ultimately it strikes me as a fairly narrow formulation not only of what constitutes a game, but just as significantly what constitutes pleasure in the broader sense.

Julian Dibbell, an astute long-time observer of virtual worlds, has, for example, pushed this question of the boundaries between fun and work even further with his attempt to earn a living solely by buying and selling in-game goods from *Ultima Online* for real-world cash (Dibbell 2006). Through his year-long experiment to earn a living (well, $11,000 in 9 months) just by selling items from *Ultima Online,* he explores the ways our play time is increasingly intersecting with work and productive activities. Whether it is the gamer who decides to sell off a character on eBay once he has grown bored with the game, the companies that arise and marshal cheap labor to send into game worlds for the purposes of creating massive storehouses of virtual goods, or, just as powerfully, the webs of connections and practices that weave between the game and "nongame" space, the idea that there is an autonomous circle of play set off from the "real world" seems increasingly tenuous. Researchers like Brian Sutton-Smith (1997), whose fascinating work on children's play historicizes this divide by pointing to the ways play has always been tied up with weighty notions of identity, community, and the very process of civilization. Similarly Johan Huizinga (1955), whose work is undergoing a kind of renaissance through its use by designers and theorists like Jesper Juul (2006) and Katie Salen and Eric Zimmerman (2004), while circumscribing the sphere of play through its "spatial separation from ordinary life," simultaneously notes how it is often entangled with the serious—indeed the civilizing—in complicated ways.

As Dibbell suggests, "It is precisely because of the proliferation of play in the digital age—and of the peculiar compatibility of digital logics with the logic of games—that modernity's longstanding balance between the productive and the ludic now stands threatened with undoing, the realm of work verging now on overwhelming that of play" (Dibbell 2004). While some see this development and worry, he notes a provocative call from the Situationist movement of the 1960s, which sought for "the central distinction that must be transcended" between play and ordinary life (ibid.). While quickly noting that this development, as it so deeply intersects capital and commercial culture, may not exactly be what they had in mind, he raises a crucial question about the status of play and the pleasures found in it.

The rhetorical linking of cheats with professional players strikes me as not unlike the kinds of arguments people make when they equate power gaming with cheating—both are seen as styles of play to be mistrusted.[7] They are seen as corrupting some kind of "authentic" game-space. In this model there is a notion of what pure play looks like, and it is inherently incompatible with instrumentality, extreme dedication (such that it appears sometimes to look like "work"), and even occasional boredom. The model of legitimate play that underpins much of this rhetoric is one that continues to bound off play and work, pleasure and pain or suffering (or boredom!). This kind of dualism does not appear to match the varying experiences players report about their engagements with a game like *EverQuest*. Unpacking the complex pleasures of play—even when they do not match common notions of fun— is the only way we will be able to understand the power gamer like Chris who said, "It's learning a skill and getting better at a skill. Even if they are pixels, it's rewarding."

Sentiments such as Chris's prompt us to think more about what engagement in games brings for players. Some find Mihaly Csikszentmihalyi's (2002) notion of "flow" particularly useful for understanding the attraction mastery in games can have for people. He proposes that optimal experiences arise when

one's skills are adequate to cope with the challenges at hand, in a goal-directed, rule-bound action system that provides clear clues as to how well one is performing. Concentration is so intense that there is no attention left over to think about anything irrelevant, or to worry about problems. Self-consciousness disappears, and the sense of time becomes distorted. An activity that produces such experiences is so gratifying that people are willing to do it for its own sake, with little concern for what they will get out of it, even when it is difficult, or dangerous. (Csikszentmihalyi 2002, 71)

While there is certainly something about this model that expresses some of the "zones" power gamers find themselves in, it is also one in which the "flow channel" is fairly narrow and unforgiving to boredom or more socially-embedded forms, something we see a lot of in *EverQuest*. I find Torill Mortensen's examination of "alternate pleasures," drawn from her extensive research on a role-playing MUD useful in broadening the discussion. In Mortensen's 2004 article, she highlights how the kinds of nuanced social play found in role-playing spaces might be better understood in terms of seduction and "mutual interplay." While she is basing her work on a particular genre of game, it highlights the ways the production of, and engagement with, the social can form a pleasurable and motivating experience. In a related spirit, Espen Aarseth's (1997) work on the (potentially illusory) "pleasure of influence" evokes something more than flow. In his formulation, there is a kind of relational quality between player and game, one that is founded on taking risks and asking "What happens when I do this?" (1997, 4). As he notes, it is the potential to "explore, get lost, and discover secret paths" that animates this engagement (ibid.). While power gamers certainly inhabit the functional and instrumental orientations to the game, they simultaneously—through their affiliations, networks, and engagements—point to these more relational pleasures, be it with others or the game artifact itself.

So what can power gamers teach us about "fun," about work, about the social life of gaming? The recognition that online participants are not isolated individuals but more often than not "regular" people having meaningful everyday connected experiences with each other is something being discussed in relation to general Internet use more and more. Rather than simply framing the power gamer with a throwback isolation rhetoric, they can typify the kind of sociability we see not only in games, but online in general. Their reliance on social networks and their contribution to broader collective knowledge locate them as decidedly networked players. And the way they refigure popular notions about the distinction between work and fun is striking. The simultaneous weaving of both instrumental and social orientations is notable and something we typically hear little about.

Recognizing power gamers as a unique type also pushes us to refine categories we often gloss over. In much the same way that Internet studies has moved from speaking about generic Net users to focusing on particular activities and specific communicative environments and acts (newsgroup readers, bloggers, MUDders, file-traders, etc.), we are coming to a stage in game studies where we would be well served to tease out specificities around not only different game genres but styles of play, forms of interaction/communication, and the various pleasures of gaming. The variety of subject positions and forms of engagement available to players can help us understand the lived meaning of play in diverse sets of communities.

4   Where the Women Are

Think for a moment about "gamers." Who do you imagine? If you create an image in your mind, what do they look like? Who are they? What is their life like? So far this book has proposed some counters to the common stereotypes. I hope that the notion of gamer as social isolate has been eroded somewhat. But what about the gender of the imagined player? Typically the picture of gamers remains that of boys and men. Powerfully, this is often even the case for the women who themselves play games and who, when asked, still hesitate to call themselves gamers.[1] Women and girls who play computer games are, if not invisible, typically seen as oddballs and anomalies. But is it time to alter that internal model we often have? What can games like *EverQuest* tell us about the present, and future, of women and computer games?

A 2001 study by the market-research firm PC Data Online received a fair amount of press as it, for the first time ever, placed women as surpassing men in the population of online gamers (Guernsey 2001). While the margin was quite slim (50.4%), similar studies since then suggest a more diverse community of game players than previously thought. Aleks Krotoski, in a 2005 white paper commissioned by the Entertainment and Leisure Software Publishers Association (ELSPA), has found that women make up 39% of all active gamers in the United States, while in Korea they go well beyond 50% of the market. She additionally suggests that they make up a sizable portion of the market for online browser-based gaming. While statistically gauging where female players fit in still requires more work, the image long held that women are not interested in or are not actually playing computer games (a potentially powerful distinction) must be reevaluated. This is not a trivial methodological point. As Simeon J. Yates and Karen Littleton suggest, "By focusing on their absence from gaming culture such research ignores the voices of those women and girls who do engage with computer games" (1999, 567).

While many of the women playing online are involved with more traditional sorts of games such as *Hearts* or *Bingo* (often played through major portals like Yahoo! Games),[2] a growing number play MMOGs. Though the number of women do not outpace men, officials at three major MMOGs (*Asheron's Call, Ultima Online,* and *EverQuest*) counted women as 20–30% of their subscriber base (Laber 2001). For more "casual" MMOGs, like *Yohoho! Puzzle Pirates* by Three Rings, women make up 40% of their player base.[3] Indeed, *EverQuest*'s Gordon Wrinn has suggested that "the gateway for getting women into gaming is going to be through these role-playing games" (Laber 2001, 2).

This genre, then, offers a chance to revisit the question of women and gaming. While much of the literature so far has focused on the look of *Tomb Raider*'s Lara Croft or the need for more "girl games," MMOGs push us to think about the pleasures those 20–30% of players are experiencing. Often the women and girls playing what are typically defined as masculine games are considered simply exceptions, data points that are outliers to be written off. But taking this demographic as a central focus of research is key to understanding the complexities around gender and computer games. Why is it women enjoy this kind of game, despite the fact that it has not been explicitly designed with them in mind, and in fact at times actively disenfranchises them?

Social and Identity Play

Women's general use of technology and the Internet often is framed around how they enjoy communicating with others and how engaged they are with experimenting with identity. Similarly, this is the major focus when women and gaming are discussed. As Patricia Pizer, a lead designer at Turbine (makers of the MMOG *Asheron's Call*) notes, "what women are finding so interesting about these games is that they provide a sense of community and social structure you don't see in other games" (Laber 2001, 1). Chatting, connecting with other people, forming relationships and maintaining them are all aspects of the interpersonal pleasure MMOGs afford, and multiuser games have benefited by drawing in this component of online life. It is certainly the case that the women I spoke with over the years enjoy this aspect of the game.

However, it is important to recognize the multilayered nature of social life in such spaces. The most basic understanding of online socialization frames the activity in terms of "chat"—that you simply talk to people in the digital environment. However, much as offline, there are variations to social life and community that are quite rich, so we should be cautious about using short-hand explanations of the depth of work that goes into the social life of a space. Approaches that frame women as "wanting to talk" underplay the ways in which they are social actors whose interactions and identities are diverse and context specific. People move through a variety of spaces, all having their own set of norms and goals that have to be negotiated. We have seen, for example, the ways MMOGs put the user in many settings: within a guild, among intimates, among acquaintances, among strangers, with enemies and opposing guilds, with teams, within message boards, and within particular servers. Each of these settings bring with it an attendant group of specificities that must be accounted for when trying to understand not only how people game, but why they game in particular ways at particular times. Talking about how women simply like the "social" component of games, or how they like to "chat" can flatten a fairly rich play landscape and trivialize the work involved in sustaining social life within a game.

"Identity exploration" is also typically seen as a primary play goal for women and girls. Both because of the nature of the game (in which a character is created) and the engagement with avatars, users can construct identities that may or may not correlate to their offline persona. Much as with work on MUDs, we find examples in *EQ* of people experimenting with creating selves. Sherry Turkle, noted MIT researcher specializing on identity in a digital age, has argued: "When we step through the screen into virtual communities, we reconstruct our identities on the other side of the looking glass" (Turkle 1995, 178). Users are not formally bound to play only characters that correspond to their offline gender or to create identities that simply mirror their "real world" temperaments. Indeed, there is a long tradition within RPG culture to try and inhabit characters that are quite opposite of how a player might normally think and act outside of the game.

While we must consider critically how much freedom people have in reconstructing themselves online, virtual environments without a doubt remain a space in which users are constantly creating and performing a variety of identities.[4] Given that *EverQuest* allows people to create up to eight distinct characters per server, there is at least formally a potential to explore a range of personae. It is not uncommon to find longtime players with several active or semiactive characters per account, though generally confined to one server.

When users do branch out onto other servers, it is often to play within particular rule sets, such as those that support strict role playing or PvP activity.[5] One notable phenomenon is the way information about characters is shared with friends and guildmates, thereby plugging into preexisting community structures. Rather than keeping identities secret from one another, it is not uncommon for players to know who their friends' alternate characters are. There are exceptions to this of course (sometimes people only share such information with a select group) but overall the terrain of identity play in *EQ* is something more akin to parallel or linked character threads than firm persona boundaries.

The power of the avatar, however, does not have to come strictly through role playing, but also in the ways it serves as the key artifact through which users not only know others and the world around them, but themselves. Avatars are objects that not only represent people in the virtual world, but influence and propel the formation of identity and relationships. Jackie described the connection that developed:

[I] spent so much time expressing myself as her and interacting with people as her. And that's one of those things of course, as you develop your relationships with people as your online avatar you understand that they generally relate to you as your online avatar and not as you the person. I mean they know you aren't really an Elf and they probably, like, don't socially regard you as an Elf or anything like that but nonetheless they refer to you by your avatar's name, they base their experience and perception of you entirely on events that have occurred in the game involving your avatar. . . . There are all these people I know who exist for me only in terms of my interactions with their avatar. I don't know really how old they are, what they do. It's all based on the avatar thing.

From the initial moment of character creation through the life of the player in the game, they fashion for themselves unique identities in the world. As they progress they are able to further customize themselves by choosing a surname and obtaining different objects. In a world in which you might very well run into two Barbarian Warriors with the exact same face, distinguishing oneself through naming and outfitting becomes key. While there is a significant focus on choosing particular clothing and weapons for very utilitarian reasons (better statistics being predominant), many women I have spoken to discuss enjoying how they have been able to customize their character in particular ways.

In nongame virtual worlds users often find the lines between their offline and online self fairly blurry (Taylor 2002; Turkle 1995). My sense is that while this happens much less in *EQ,* in large part because of its "gameness" always foregrounding its own intentionality—it is never *just* about identity play—avatars continue to present themselves as evocative vehicles for identity and MMOGs offer some unique possibilities. The issue of how virtual-world experiences "filter back" is particularly striking, though, when women report that playing the game helped them become more confident or assertive. One female player recounted encouraging the younger women she encountered in the game to use conflicts as an opportunity to practice more assertive behavior. Speaking about a guildmate in particular, she said: "So I've been telling her, build a little backbone, don't be afraid to tell people what you think. It might hurt their feelings, it might make you an enemy, but what can they do?" Given the kind of identification with characters some users experience, this can be a powerful component of the game. As Katinka put it: "There's a little bit of yourself in your character, for my characters anyway. With my druid [I'm a] raw nature, nature-loving, tree-hugging girl. [And] I love animals, I love nature, so part of me is in her." While gender swapping is also certainly something that occurs in *EQ,* one of the more interesting aspects to consider is the way the game may allow access to gender identities that often are socially prohibited or delegitimized offline—a simultaneously sexy and powerful or masculine and beautiful persona. Women in *EverQuest* are constantly engaged in playing with traditional notions of femininity and reformulating gender identities through aspects of the space that are tied directly to its nature as a game. Identity is formulated in relation to formal play elements within the world such that active engagement, embodied agency, and full participation are guiding values for men and women alike. This is a potentially radical framework and one that can challenge stereotypical forms of femininity.

Exploration

The role of this active engagement in the game extends to the way one can interact with its "worldness." One of the notable things MMOG environments (and many computer games in general) offer is the way their construction of worlds lets users actually wander a landscape and explore. Most women I have spoken with express a real enjoyment of engaging with the game as a world and environment. Given the geographic organization of a space like *EverQuest,* users are able to move through an entire world and explore different lands and inhabitants. Gareth R. Schott and Kristy R. Horrell similarly found that girls who game were engaged with exploration, suggesting that "respondents were focused around the freedom that RPG's gave to exploration of its virtual environment for the accumulation of symbols that possess general life enhancing qualities" (2000, 43). One woman I spoke with recounted her experiences trekking her own Necromancer around the world ("from one end of Norrath to the other") and the peril and excitement such a journey brought. Jackie noted she specifically created a Druid because they "were the ultimate explorers and at that stage of the game I just really wanted to explore." Mary Fuller and Henry Jenkins (1995) have noted the special kind of "landscape" games provide, and MMOGs present some of the clearest examples of movement through elaborate virtual spaces (though with a much richer sense of character and embodiment than early videogames offered).

While men and women alike can enjoy traversing these spaces, women are afforded an experience they are likely not to have had offline. While both the landscape and its creatures might threaten the explorer, in the game space this threat is not based upon gender. Unlike the offline world in which gender often plays a significant role in not only the perception of safety but its actuality, in *EQ* women may travel knowing they are no more threatened by the creatures of the world than their male counterparts are. While this may seem an odd reassurance, it is far from minor. Risk of travel in-game is tied to more general categories of faction (does a particular town or zone's inhabitants hate your class or race?), power (do the area's creatures know you are more powerful than they or are they confident in their ability to kill you first?), or skill (can you effectively hide, sneak, or pass through undetected?). Because of this gender-neutral approach to threat and safety, there is a kind of freedom of movement that women often do not experience otherwise. It is also the case that as one levels and obtains greater mastery of the game space, zones of free exploration are broadened. An area that was previously quite dangerous to a character was not dangerous because of gender, and eventually it might become accessible with game competency. This is an important pleasure of the game, and many women enjoy extended travel and exploration of the virtual world.

Beyond Pink Games

Typical accounts of women and games tend to focus exclusively on identity, exploration, and socialization. The mid-1990s saw a fair amount of scholarly work, not to mention commercial investment, around the issue of girls and gaming. Justine Cassell and Henry Jenkins's edited collection *From Barbie to Mortal Kombat* (1998), one of the best and most widely cited collections on the subject, offers an excellent snapshot of that period. While some work in the 1990s was notable for its nuanced approach in understanding the relationship between gender and games, much of it presented stereotypical formulations of girls' relationship to technology. In addition, little was done to disentangle the experience of play across age and the life cycle. Research on girls thus often was extrapolated to apply to women. While animated by a deep concern for enfranchising girls into not only computer gaming but technology more generally, such approaches typically suggested that we needed games geared to traditionally feminine interests and sensibilities. This kind of approach is typified, for example, by the perspective that sees women enjoying the socializing or ethical quandaries of games and men the raw power they are able to exert in them (Brunner, Bennett, and Honey 1998). The model is also one in which girls do not particularly enjoy violence or direct competition in games but instead prefer to funnel their energy toward interpersonal issues, indirect competition, environments, puzzles, or character-based genres (Graner Ray 2004; Kafai 1996; Koster 2005; Subrahmanyam and Greenfield 1998).

To this end there were a number of products launched that sought to bring games to a market traditionally underserved by game companies. While titles like Mattel's *Barbie Fashion Designer* stand at one extreme, Girl Games's *Let's Talk about Me* focused on topical life issues. The work of Brenda Laurel and her company Purple Moon probably best exemplifies the developments to come out of this movement. Known for its *Rockett* series of games, Laurel's company sought to design games around interactive narratives as a way of, very basically, engaging girls with computers. Rather than trying to make a gender-inclusive game, the Purple Moon approach was to design for girls "because we wanted to protect the experience as being something girls could own, something that could be theirs, so that they could say, 'This is mine, this is for me, I own this and you don't get to make fun of it'" (Cassell and Jenkins 1998, 119). The company's *Rockett* games focused on relationships, secrets, identity negotiation, and interpersonal skills. As Laurel writes in *Utopian Entrepreneur*:

I took a lot of heat from some people who call themselves feminists for portraying girl characters who cared about such things as appearance, popularity, belonging, betrayal, and all the other sturm and drang of preadolescent friendship. Some people thought I shouldn't do that because girls shouldn't behave in this way. But they do, you see. And who they become depends a great deal on how they manage their transit through the narrows of girlhood. (Laurel 2001, 3)

Not simply meant for fun or entertainment, the intents of products like those from Purple Moon were laden with social and political ambitions.

The approach of the pink-games movement has close ties to work on gender that suggests that women are more inclined to focus on, and prefer to invest in, activities such as caregiving, interpersonal orientations, cooperation, and internal discovery (Chodorow 1978; Gilligan 1982). Of course, all of these are highly valuable activities, but do they accurately reflect a total vision of femininity? As critical work on the subject points out, femininity and the very notion of "woman" is not an identity category that exists separate from considerations of age, race, class, ethnicity, nationality, sexual orientation, or indeed the matrix of practices that constitute the performance of gender (Butler 1990; Collins 2000; Dugger 1991; Halberstam 1998; hooks 1981; Kerber et al. 1986; Lorber 1991; Romero 1992). Does the 12-year-old, middle-class girl negotiate and perform her gender within the same vertices that the 48-year-old, working-class woman does? Are the stakes the same? Or, maybe better put, does the negotiation of those stakes look the same? Does the same girl enact her gender in the same way across her lifespan? Do the practices, the social maps, the various contexts to understanding particular permutations of gender, transfer across all women? While I certainly do not want to suggest we cannot identify some common stereotypes that circulate in the dominant culture about what women and men do, how much those ideas correspond to actual lived practice and experience is another matter. Far too often I have heard students, for example, talk about how women dislike first-person shooters, only to have them quickly follow up by noting that they themselves do enjoy FPS's but "those other women" do not. I have also encountered men who want to suggest that women dislike competition, but those men are stumped when asked to explain that assumption given the women in their lives who play sports or tabletop games. The current models through which we understand women's engagement with games, including one in which women are seen as "intruders" rather than inhabitants of gamer culture, are linked to a much older rhetoric touching on not only issues of women and technology, but their engagement with sports (Bolin and Granskog 2003; Hargreaves 1994; Kay 2003; Scraton and Flintoff 2002; Wajcman 1991). By keeping in mind the historical context, we can begin to draw on past battles (and victories) over the role of women in technology and science, "masculine activities," and claims for active subject positions.

By focusing on the historical pattern of these arguments, and the variability of gender as it intersects with other factors, we can begin to unpack the apparent invisibility of women gamers. For far too long researchers have overlooked the broader structural and social influences on how the category of "gamer" (something women do not always feel authorized to occupy) has been shaped. The overreliance on fairly narrow psychological understandings of femininity has tended to foster diminished examination of the role of marketing, social networks, technical proficiency, and the actual configuration of game devices as artifacts. Echoes of old and familiar "men are hunters, women are gatherers" and "different brains" stories are also on the rise, and we are seeing tenuous sociobiological theories emerge as powerful rhetoric to explain what games women play, or why they do not.[6] Fortunately for both the field and for women gamers, there is an emerging wave of research tackling these more structural and contextual relationships between gender, technology, culture, and games. Work by researchers including Jo Bryce and Jason Rutter (2003), Diane Carr (2005), Aphra Kerr (2003), Gareth Schott and Kirsty Horrell (2000), Helen Kennedy (2002), and Simeon Yates and Karen Littleton (1999) examine everything from the physical design of game consoles like Microsoft's *XBox* to how the circulation of games within social networks highlights paths of entry (and legitimation) into gamer culture.

There is another layer of critique with the pink-game approach, though. It is the notion that good game design originates by asking people what they want. While companies certainly want to avoid alienating a potential audience (something I discuss a bit more regarding avatars), discovering what appeals to a person when it directly intersects with issues like gender is profoundly tricky. The investments in retaining a cohesive performance of one's gender, at least publicly, makes it quite difficult methodologically to tap into the nuances of desire and potential pleasures. Suzanne de Castell and Mary Bryson argue that we cannot untangle the production of "girl games" from the production of gender itself:

The question we urge is simply: Whose interests will be served in making use of these purportedly "essential" differences as a basis for creating "girl-friendly" computer-mediated environments? Most importantly, are we producing tools for girls, or are we producing girls themselves by, as Althusser (1984) would put it, "interpellating" the desire to become the girl? By playing with girlish toys, does the girl learn to become the kind of woman she was always already destined to become? (1998, 251–252)

People may not know what they *could* enjoy. Trying to design from gauging existing tastes or play preferences is one of the most conservative approaches and rarely results in innovation. As Jesper Juul has suggested, if ten years ago designers had asked people if they might like to spend time in a game washing dishes or cooking, replies probably would have focused on how boring or uninteresting that would be. And yet *The Sims,* a game that often centers on mundane activities, has proven one of the best-selling titles ever. Juul astutely points out, "What this tells us is that game development and innovation is often about finding that something previously considered dull can actually be interesting, and that in a sense, innovative games are a discussion about what games are" (Juul 2003). The dangers of a design approach that relies on only asking people what they want (which is actually more like a marketing strategy) is even more dramatic when it comes to gender as it often puts all players (men and women, boys and girls) in the position of trying to imagine the pleasures of activities that may very well be prohibited, indeed sanctioned, in their nongaming lives.

Mastery and Status

If we look at some of the examples that we could easily frame as identity performance, we can begin to see aspects often simply rendered as "feminine" (identity play) may have more complex underpinnings signaling a breech in the all too easy feminine/masculine dichotomy. The linking of power and sexuality we find in women's *EQ* identities, for example, highlights a broader pleasure derived from advancement in the game. Marsha Kinder has pointed out how many video games rely on placing women as the "object of the male quest—various sleeping beauties who wait to be rescued by male winners" (1991, 106), and while some of that is a part of *EQ*'s backstory, the ways the game allows women to occupy active roles is quite notable. As we see in the example of power gamers, players like Jackie are incredibly focused on mastering the game. This competitive game orientation (either against others or via one's own set goals) is often overlooked as a powerful motivation for women. Even for players who are less intently focused on achieving specific leveling goals within clear time periods, the excitement over reaching a new level or getting out of a particularly bad one (a "hell level") is not lost on any players, including the women. Within the gaming space itself mastery and status can be performed and signaled in a variety of ways. Users are able to see the level of others (as long as the person is not in role-play or anonymous mode), and, as previously discussed, guild membership carries special meaning. Sometimes particular skill sets are required for crafting special armor or items, and competency can be demonstrated through mastering the ability to create highly valued game objects.

As players advance through the game they also can gain autonomy as they perfect their skills. Katinka notes that her choice of playing a Druid was connected to wanting options and control over the terms of her play. She said, "With the druid, I have the option to solo or group if I want. Some days I might feel like grouping and then others I don't feel like dealing with people so I can solo. Just being able to put RL behind me for a little while and get into this fantasy world where I can control animals and mess with the weather and things like that." Practices often simply noted under the category "identity production" may in fact be tied up with more complicated issues of game competency and social status. Sharon Sherman (1997) has noted the development of "social power" that men obtain through time spent perfecting gaming skills, and it is worth considering the access women have to this experience in the game. Obtaining epic weapons or more generally owning impressive equipment (weapons, armor, robes, rare items—especially when won from a fight and not bought) all become artifacts of mastery and signal to both the user and the server community their skill at the game. In these cases while objects do play a role in creating the identity of the user, it is not simply a neutral performance but one tied up with signifying power and status—qualities rarely attributed to women. Katinka described her relationship to the gear her character wears saying, "I'm proud of myself. I have no problem with people inspecting me [clicking on an avatar to get a detailed look at their items] because you know, I've worked hard for what I have."

In addition to the in-game performance of status and power, female players actively transfer their accomplishments to out-game venues. Given the widespread use of message boards within the game, we also can examine how women tie their game experience to this venue. Authorizing and signaling oneself as a person to be taken seriously is reflected in signatures (".sig" files) appended to posted messages. These .sigs (whether in textual or picture form), while serving to keep the community informed about "who is who" and acting as a way of customizing a posting, provide some clear markers of mastery and status. This information also can lend legitimacy to the author's comments because experience is seen as a valuable asset in the game. Knowledge, and by extension the speakers themselves, can be authorized through these kinds of public signals of status.

The text-based .sig has a long history going back to the early days of e-mail and Usenet postings. Within the *EQ* message boards, a fairly common form is for people to list their characters and levels, as well as any server, guild, and role-playing information. For example:

Asherea Lonewolf 47 Druidess—Prexus

Naharet Darkhealer 31 Cleric—Prexus

Shadowclaw

The author of this .sig has more than one character (Asherea and Naharet) of particular levels (47th and 31st) and classes (Druid and Cleric) in the guild Shadowclaw on the server Prexus. Each of these elements communicates to the reader the poster's game status, level of mastery, and authority to speak. Such signatures thus act in several functional ways. They become a method for users to draw continuity between virtual spaces (game and "off-site" communication forums) and lend legitimacy, authenticity, and authority to their words. The importance of these should not be understated. As Jeff Moyer, founder of Allakhazam notes, "The forums are really a community in themselves. Frequent posters gain reputations through the quality or type of posts they make, and friendships and rivalries develop based solely upon the posts people make" (Marks 2003, 114). While on the surface such devices might be tagged as identity markers, we would be remiss to not understand that they also serve as examples of the ways women communicate their game status and mastery to others.

Also common on message boards, .sig pictures are images used by authors similarly to convey meaning or commentary. For example, figure 4.1 is a representation of a character in a vulnerable, even sexual, pose. The kittens seem to have gotten the best of her and give the picture a playful quality. What places this image in the category of mastery and status, however, is the sword. Players of the game will recognize this as an epic weapon, an object that requires not only a high level to achieve, but typically involves several long quests and the coordination of much game talent and support. As a marker of player identity this image represents a rich example of both a nuanced rendering of power and femininity, as well as a very subtle deployment

Figure 4.1
Druid epic fan-created art

Figure 4.2
Bard and dragon fan-created art

of symbolism quite meaningful to a targeted community of readers (knowl-edgeable *EQ* players).

The second image (figure 4.2) also combines several elements to signal in-game power. The image itself is a pastiche, with components drawn from both the game and other artwork. The character is positioned in a fairly ag-gressive stance over the slain body of a dragon. Based on the avatar itself, the gender of the character is somewhat ambiguous. The name, and the context in which it is used (a fan site for women who play the game), signal a performance of "woman" but with a show of power not typically accorded them.

Dragons in this world are among the hardest creatures to kill. They generally are not defeated by a single person, yet this image represents a lone victor, alluding more to abstract power than any single instance of combat. The digitally altered backscene, of a nearby lightning storm, plays on a familiar trope of power and dominance. To push home the point, the author has inserted the tagline "Never underestimate the power of a bard"—referring to the character's class. There is something quite amusing about the whole scene being framed at the top by the name "Mysticpurr," especially given the somewhat ambiguous gender of the avatar. The juxtaposition of the seemingly playful, even feminine, name against the representation of power is common and is one of the ways women often mediate the intersection of traditional gendered identity and more provocative representations of accomplishment and status.

Team Sport and Combat

Being in a group (a team) brings with it a range of traditional issues associated with sport. Groups have leaders (either informal or formal) and participants engage in various roles and tasks for successful play. Within the context of a group there also will be instances of praise and critique, as well as the ongoing negotiations that take place with informal pickup groups. Women's sports have only recently come to be valued in any serious way in the United States, most notably after the introduction of Title IX of the Education Amendments of 1972, which "prohibits sex discrimination in federally assisted education programs" (U.S. Dept. of Education 1997). Access to group sports in any lifelong way has been something denied to most women, and Title IX marked a crucial turning point in changing structural values around play though the requirement of equal funding to girls' and women's athletics programs. In addition, team sports have thus far been gender divided, with men and women occupying different teams and leagues. Grouping in worlds such as *EverQuest* provide an interesting opportunity for women not only to participate in group play, but to work closely with men and even lead them. Women do at times occupy this position in the game with some difficulty. Claire, for example, felt that women have to work harder and manage relationships carefully if they are going to be guild leaders. This is not dissimilar from offline gender politics when it comes to leadership, but the possibilities within *EQ* for widespread active roles for women is notable. Grouping involves proving worth and skill, as well as the benefits afforded well-regarded and valued players. The enjoyment of this kind of new team sport is something women have direct access to in these games.

In fact, it often is around grouping issues that women articulate why they prefer active, powerful characters. While within the *EQ* community there are heated debates about the value different classes bring to a combat situation, generally most people articulate group usefulness as a key component in valuing a character. Women frequently speak about wanting to have powerful or valuable characters for team situations. One woman, for example, discussed why she chose the different characters she did. In her tabletop gaming experience she often had picked Clerics but found that in *EQ* they did not suit her. She found them "very passive. They pretty much rely on everybody else doing whatever needs to be done and the cleric just sits there and keeps everyone else alive." After experimenting with several different classes she finally picked an Enchanter for its specific nature in *EQ*. She said, "In that environment an Enchanter is just very powerful. In a group situation they could make or break the group. They required skill, a lot of skill. I found them challenging and interesting and the ability to control the flow of combat was I thought really, really interesting."

While attention to group processes is something typically coded as "feminine," I want to reframe these actions to simultaneously highlight the way they speak to women's desires not to be simply participants but powerful active agents within the game. Quite often similar behaviors in men and women are called different things, and the naming is formulated along fairly stereotypical lines. So, for example, men who manage guilds are called "leaders" and seen as wanting to be powerful players, while women who do so are called "facilitators" and praised for their commitment to the group. How does our understanding of women's engagement in computer games change when we unpack the black box of the "social" or "cooperative" and begin to explore underlying motivations and the ways participants themselves think about their own actions.[7] The value a skilled person can bring to the game, and the pleasure of being such a player, was a common issue in my observations and interviews with women.

The activities players engage in (both in groups and solo) to fight monsters gets to the heart of the pleasure of combat. The traditional girl-games line of reasoning has not left us with a complex understanding of the ways women might approach the issue of violence in a game. The standard line—that women do not like violence or that they prefer using more subtle (sometimes coded as "manipulative") tactics over force—leaves us unable to adequately explain the draw combat and violence in computer games can have for women. Helen Cunningham, for example, recounts how girls she interviewed explicitly avoided genres like *Barbie Fashion Designer*, saying "I'd rather play violent games any day" (2000, 222). She further suggests that "In most areas of society this violent and aggressive side of a girl/woman's nature has to be repressed in conformity to socially expected norms of what is acceptable 'feminine' behavior. Playing violent games gives female players the chance to express this aggression in a safe context" (ibid., 223).

In general the intersections of mastery and power previously discussed are quite complex for female gamers and they cannot be unlinked from the violence of these games. Women often remark on enjoying jumping into the fray of fights, taking on difficult monsters, and, as one put it, "kicking ass and taking names." This is not unlike some of the reports about "grrl gamers" and women who play FPS's (H. Jenkins 1998b). Women's relationship with game violence is complicated. Women gamers I have interviewed speak about the pleasure of hunting and jumping into fights, saying things like "Yeah, I enjoy going out and beating down evil mobs" or "If I'm in a bad mood, ya know, I'm in a bad mood so it's time to go kill something, take my aggressions out." Often they playfully contest gender stereotypes around women and fighting, like one whose Halfling Cleric (a very short character of a "support" class) engages in head-to-head combat as she shouts, "Ah, get in my belly!" (mimicking the character Fat Bastard from the Austin Powers movies). She says:

I think what turns me onto the gaming is the feeling of empowerment. In real life I'd never be able to go up to a giant and beat it down or whatever. But when you're in the game, you can become whatever you want. If you want to be this really, really tough character one day or you can just be whatever . . . In the game if you don't like something you can kill it. I don't know, I just feel more "rawr"! I am druid, hear me roar.

Combat in the game is quite extreme (you kill monsters and potentially other users) but also muted (there is graphically no blood or gore), and my sense is that the enjoyment of violence takes place at an abstract level for most participants. The pleasure is closely tied to the skills involved to take down a mob, the precise timings and movements required, the skill of playing the class well in a battle situation, the adrenaline rush involved with a fight, and the general ability to even engage in this type of activity. Of course, more work needs to be done on understanding the embodied experience of fighting in computer games. When we play we negotiate a duality of presence (between the offline and the game world), and as we gain embodied competency over our avatars, we come to experience a satisfaction reminiscent of what is felt when we master a sport or embodied activities in corporeal space. The pleasure of embodying technique, skills, and control in our corporeal bodies might have interesting correlate points in computer games. The joy of game combat is then a product of the more elaborate and valuable activity of competently embodying a character. In this way the actual fight is as much an opportunity to demonstrate the qualities of game mastery as anything.

Design Limits

While there is much to praise in what MMOGs afford women and the multiple pleasures we can find there, it is important to consider the ways they represent partial systems and ones in which we see limits on how gender is being figured into game space and the demographics associated with it. Designers often have bold, even progressive, visions of what their virtual world might be, but it is worth exploring the subsequent gaps between those imaginations and their implementation (Taylor 2003). Brad McQuaid recounted his approach to this issue: "I guess my philosophy when it comes to gender is somewhat akin to how I feel about race—I prefer the 'color blind' approach. Just as when I encounter someone who is of a different color I don't really ascribe much relevance, so also did we approach *EverQuest.*"[8] While this stance is well intentioned (and something I have heard from virtual-world designers of all sorts), unfortunately there are many mechanisms—be they marketing strategies, community practices, or preexisting sociocultural frameworks and value systems—along the way that intervene.

The idea that color-blindness (or in this case gender-blindness) can be achieved simply through discounting the power of these categories—in the organization and practice of everyday life—is risky. Indeed, the ability to even suggest such a position often can be taken only by those who are not subjected to its force and weight (the priveledged group seen as without color, white, or gender, male). The rhetorical effect is that issues pertaining to gender and race are taken off the table as areas to be articulated, debated, and confronted. For example, Patricia Williams writes about the ways "scripted denial" can lead "visual images to remain in the realm of the unspoken, the unsaid filled by stereotypes and self-identifying illusion, the hierarchies of race and gender circulating unchallenged" (1997, 18). While the impulse behind adopting a color-blind approach often is well intentioned, and may in fact work well for some aspects of design, in the absence of explicit critical thinking and practice it can feed back into stereotypes. For many computer games the biggest problem lies around avatars and the way gender is represented. In a multiplayer game like *EverQuest,* this is a deeply important area.

Avatars are central to both immersion and the construction of community in virtual spaces. They are mediators between personal identity and social life. As a respondent in one of my previous studies put it, they are the "material to work with" when you are in a virtual world (Taylor 2002). Debates over the ways women are represented in games, as in discussions of Lara Croft and other prominent game heroines, touch on this, and when dealing with multiuser spaces the question of representation becomes central to the experience of the user (Edmonds 1998; Funk 2001; Goodwin 2001). Katinka considered the ways her avatar's appearance influences how she acts, suggesting that, "When I play a Wood Elf with the happy expression on her face I kinda try to be more cheery. I do notice a difference of how others treat my characters." As with offline life, bodies come to serve as mediation points between the individual and the world (both social and material). What they are and, more important, what social meanings they are given matters.

Unfortunately, what I continually have found is that women in *EQ* often struggle with the conflicting meanings around their avatars, feeling they have to "bracket" or ignore how they look. As I discussed in my own considerations of avatars when faced with the character-creation screen, it can feel as if one is choosing the best of the worst. While there is a fair amount of diversity among female players about which avatars are preferable, there seems to be a consistent message that they want a choice in how they look online. This is not about women not wanting to look attractive or even sexy. Women hold complicated relationships to even stereotypically gendered characters. As Lisa Edmonds has argued of *Tomb Raider*'s female hero, "After seeing so many games in which women are little more than background props, or in which the protagonist's only objective is to blow up everything in sight before he is blown up, Lara Croft is a joy to become during a brief escape from reality" (1998, 2). Helen Kennedy (2002) similarly points out the limitations narrow textual analysis of the character can produce, noting that Lara Croft can occupy multiple meanings based on broader cultural readings of action heroines or even serve, more provocatively, as a potentially transgressive mediator based on the complicated rendering of the subject/object relation in computer games. One woman I spoke with, Kim, points to the nuanced relationship women can have with their avatars. She says of her selection:

I went with the really cute female Wood Elf, with dark hair, and I really believe I identified with her strongly. I wanted to be her. She had a 3-inch waist and didn't have any problems swinging a sword around. I, at the time, if I carried a couple bags of groceries in the house I was pooped. Obviously her boobs didn't sag, she didn't have to wear a bra, she didn't want one. I have two children, I have to help mother nature. So I really wanted to be her.

It does, however, often turn on the issue of choice and the desire women players have to decide for themselves how they will look in the game and, by extension, what the nature of their experience will be. As Kordama, an *EQ* player who wrote a review of gender representation in *EverQuest* puts it:

So what do women want from role playing games? I cannot speak for all women but I can for myself, that the answer lies in simple choice. I certainly want the ability to play a woman, and I want to be able to decide what she looks like as much as possible. I want my characters to be beautiful, but not necessarily brazen. I certainly don't want to be forced to display even virtual buttocks to the world to the howls of laughter from my fellow players. (2001, 1)

While the discussion around her article generated some fascinating dialogue, not the least of which highlighted the diverse ways female players think about "sexiness," the theme of choice recurred. This point is not seen as unique to women, however, and game designers are aware of the desire of many of their users to have more agency in deciding how they are represented in the world. Brad McQuaid notes that, "Players want to be able to configure their character's appearance" and certainly many MMOGs have developed this aspect of the game by providing more customization choices to the player (Walker 2002). But does it go far enough? As another player writes,

I would like the choice of character coverings, and I would like the chars to not look like they all have some bizarre scoliosis. I don't have a problem with a "sexy" character; I just don't want to play one where body parts are hanging out to the world (half elves, dark elves). This did influence my choice of race, because the dwarven women are allowed to stand straight and keep themselves clothed in something that makes sense. Guess I have a gripe with representations of fantasy women; who would go into battle wearing a chain bikini? Really? OUCH! Anyway, it is annoying, but I keep reminding myself that Verant probably did not consider women a viable market share of the game when they designed it. (Tryne 2001)

What is striking about this post is not only the way the player frames her critique, but how she tries to imagine her place in the designers mind and whether or not she is seen as having a legitimate seat at the gaming table. This idea of the imagined user is key in shaping design and, by extension, the possibilities actual players encounter (Akrich 1995; Oudshoorn, Rommes, and Stienstra 2004; Woolgar 1991b). As Jerry McDonough notes in his research on virtual-world designers, while they have some understanding that their "users are a diverse and heterogeneous group, they nevertheless tend to form a singular vision of their users—an ideal type (Weber, 1958)—which provides them with a reference point for a 'typical' user when designing the virtual environment" (1999, 862). He goes on to say that this inscription is not just in relation to the content of the world, but "a normative statement of who their users should be, and how they should behave" (ibid; see also Taylor 2003 and 2004b).[9]

When the subject comes up (not infrequently) on message boards, it often is noted that the original avatars were designed by a woman, thus suggesting the entire subject is more complex than might first appear. Brad McQuaid gives some background on this matter:

Rosie Cosgrove, our Art Director, felt strongly that the male and female playable characters should be "exaggerated" or, more precisely, "glamorized" . . . sort of like "Barbie and Ken," I suppose. The result was the somewhat controversial appearance of many of the female characters, they being rather voluptuous and often scantily clad (although, really, not worse than what you can see at the beach). We received all sorts of feedback, ranging from praise to outright outrage at the "sexism" allegedly employed. And while I don't want to speak for Rosie directly, I do recall her reacting as follows: 1. many of the female characters were how she'd personally want to appear in a "fantasy" game and 2. because our core demographic (not by design, but rather simply by fact) were approximately 18–30 year old males, their appearances made sense. In retrospect, I think heroic, exaggerated player characters can be depicted with less controversy and probably a bit more conservatively . . . but that's just my opinion.[10]

The writer of the post about fighting in chain-mail bikinis was, indeed, not entirely off the mark in her analysis of the place of women in the game. They are seen as valuable additions to the player base but not part of the "core" demographic. There is a dual system often at work in representational design. On the one hand the "fact" of the existing market is constructed and maintained through images that support a (very particular) imagined heterosexual male user.[11] On the other hand, the color-blind language often makes it quite difficult to talk about the ways representations (or advertising, gaming costs, etc.) may in fact contribute to the nature of the market because it sets up a rhetorical ideal not actually supported either organizationally or in practice. But because we are always working around, through, and with notions of race and gender, only by acknowledging how they circulate and the meanings they hold can critical practice be achieved.

I appreciate McQuaid's sentiment that, upon reflection, there is probably a more sophisticated method to handle gender and avatars. Only by moving to a framework that openly acknowledges the thorny terrain and critically considers these issues through the design process might the progress he suggests be possible. The additional complication here is that when the issue of gender finally is put on the table, more often than not it is in service of reifying imagined difference rather than trying to unpack more complex formulations of femininity and masculinity. The question often becomes: "Well, we all know women don't really want direct competition or fighting games, so what can we make for them? What does a women's game look like?" It is as if suddenly the entire experiences of women *who right now do play,* of women who *have played for years,* are hidden off in a corner lest they overly complicate our notions about what "real" women and men take pleasure in. And, rather than trying to understand how those women may tell us something about paths into gaming or how we might learn something for future design, they are seen as the oddballs, the nonmainstream, the exceptions. There is a devastating cycle of invisibility at work here, one in which game designers, companies, and sometimes even players render an entire demographic as tangential. This move, to marginalize women and to not imagine them as a *core* demographic, in turn helps enact design decisions and structural barriers that create the conditions for disenfranchisement.

Similarly, the issue of race, as traditionally understood in the social sciences, is particularly complicated in relation to *EverQuest* and intersects this question of avatar representation.[12] Each avatar's skin color is set by a game artist. All humanoid characters (Elves, Barbarians, Dwarves, Halflings, Humans, Gnomes) are by default white/tan skinned except for two, the Dark

Elf (blue) and the Erudites (dark brown). As briefly mentioned before, Dark Elves are an "evil-aligned" species, and while they are particularly well suited (because of their base statistics) to become characters like Necromancers, they also are able to occupy more "neutral" professions like Enchanter. Their home city is located fairly centrally in the world and they are one of the most popular avatars played. Erudites, noted in the original manual as "high men," are a fascinating counterexample. Though they are the only representationally "black" avatars in the game, their base statistical configuration gives them some additional intelligence points making them, at least statistically speaking, an enticing choice for those wanting to play a magic-caster class (Wizards, Enchanters, etc.). Erudites' backstory suggests a kind of noble heritage with a focus on learning and knowledge arts. So how can we think about the design of the races in the game? While how they appear and the properties they have is heavily informed by a longer tradition in the role-playing genre, there are also more *EQ*-specific considerations at work.

Marks quotes McQuaid on the design of the races saying, "We wanted to make each race attractive, and to make those races we feared might be less attractive more appealing by giving them special abilities. Which classes a race could be came from both the desire to make that race compelling to play and also what we thought made sense from a role playing standpoint—for example, a Troll Paladin obviously doesn't make sense" (2003, 90). While in this statement McQuaid is not trying to address the more general issue of "race" as understood outside gaming contexts, it is worth thinking about how it nonetheless enacts broader considerations of racial identities in the game. If we take McQuaid's design imperative to heart, we can see how adding additional base intelligence to the one black avatar, in effect boosting their skills to make them an appealing class to play, in some sense points to a compensatory model at work. Eric Hayot and Edward Wesp argue that within *EQ* there is a kind of dual logic in how racialization operates via the Erudite avatar. Within the frame of the game world "recognizable, real-world 'racial' features" are both a "defining visual characteristic" for the avatar but the game simultaneously "relates those cosmetic elements to a fantasized history that explains the Erudites' genetic predispositions [high intelligence and some diminished strength] solely in terms of the *EverQuest* game world" (2004, 415). While the game itself seeks to frame (and contain) how we might understand the Erudites, the seeming intentionality of the designers to work against type by "inverting a number of pernicious racist stereotypes" should not be overlooked and reflects the way in-game choices (be they design or play ones) always are in dialogue with out-game considerations, whether consciously or not.

On the one hand this design intervention is certainly a welcome refusal to go down the familiar path in which black game characters are positioned, as designer Ernest Adams (2003) notes, either as rappers or athletes (see Dines and Humez 1995; Entman and Rojecki 2001; Gray 2004; Hall 1997; hooks 1996, on the deployment of racial stereotypes in traditional media). But alternatively this kind of move can slip easily into the formulation in which the "other" is the exceptional, the model (minority), or the noble. Homi Bhabha suggests that "the chain of stereotypical signification is curiously mixed and split, polymorphous and perverse, an articulation of multiple belief" which can simultaneously traffic in, for example, the image of the savage and the dignified, the primitive and the accomplished manipulator (1999, 377).

Of course, as Hayot and Wesp note a player may choose to play an Erudite against type as proscribed by the game and not particularly benefit from the inherent intelligence bonus. They argue there is some loosening in *EQ* between racial characteristics and strategy, suggesting that it presents a more open structure to racial encodings than that of, for example, something like *Age of Kings* where strategy can seem almost "genetically" encoded within the structure of the game. This tension, between how much the game structures any individual play and the possibilities for moving beyond any formal guides is always present, but the move toward reverse stereotyping adds another complication in which the representation of average (in some cases read as "normal") seems to remain at least formally encoded beyond the reach of the nonwhite character. Of course, most races in *EQ* certainly are not average. This is a fantasy world. But because Erudite avatars also are tied to particular racial representations that have links to the offline world, they circulate in a much broader economy of images (and ideologies) beyond the formal bounds of the game. It is also important to keep in mind that this should not simply be a formulation in which "brown avatar" equals "race" but that they are located in a much larger context whereby whiteness simultaneously is always being constructed through the other avatar choices available.

Despite the gameplay advantage this race brings for those wanting to play magic casters, Erudites appear to be a relatively rare avatar choice in the world. While statistical data on preferences are hard to come by, the *EverQuest* Web site posted percentages for the avatars that had been selected by players. Erudites accounted for 6.6%, with Human ranking highest at 17.3% and Troll lowest at 3.5% (Sony 2001). The language here should be noted, given that "Human" is the actual name for a race of white avatars in the game. The rhetorical history of such formulations (with white equaling human and nonwhite being indeterminate, nonhuman, or "other") is important and, while appearing at this top level, is simultaneously a bit complicated by the fact that the Human character model figures predominately in how all humanoid characters are handled by the system's graphics. Nonetheless, the language structures the races, and by extension the representation, in ways we should not simply dismiss. Erudites, as a race, cluster down at the end of the scale with the nonhumanoid figures such as Dwarf, Gnome, Halfling, Ogre, and Troll.[13] While there is some apparent selection by players, on only a handful of occasions have I seen Erudites in the world. In this regard it is probably worth noting how another design feature may play a role in their scarcity. All Erudites begin on a small continent named Odus. Unlike other races their cities are not centrally integrated into the major zones of the game, and the Allakhazam Web site remarks that their starting area for characters is "probably the worst newbie zone in the game." As I discuss in chapter 2, travel restriction is (or was) one of the primary constraints on new players. Being on a peripheral continent, cut off from the rest of the world, may not be the most appealing starting path. While on the one hand Erudites were made more attractive by the intelligence booster, they were simultaneously disadvantaged geographically. This, combined with possible reticence among the player community more generally to engage in "race-swapping" has ultimately led to the one black avatar choice going relatively unplayed.[14]

The issue of race and representation in games is a large problem in the industry and in many ways mirrors what we see in traditional media. Games, however, provide particular challenges in trying to understand how to "read" representations because their structure encodes not only aesthetics but strategies, rules, and play choices.[15] In the case of *EverQuest* the picture is made even more complex by the fact that avatars always circulate as social objects (and, indeed, players constitute them through culture even prior to their encounter with another player). While I do not want to engage in an oversimplified textual reading of the Erudite race, when we draw in analysis on how they function within the game, both in terms of formal design and practice, we can see that they stand as somewhat troubled figures.

Embodiment Online

The lack of meaningful attention to avatars is rooted in an impoverished view of the nature of the body, both off- and online, and its relationship to identity and the social world. Poor models, architectures, and underlying structures that rely on easy stereotypes overlook the power of these spaces as embodied, with all the possibilities that entails. A serious recognition of a sociology of the body might drive more interesting design. Bodies are not simply neutral objects that have no bearing on our experience but act as central artifacts through which our identities and social connections are shaped. Bodies carry particular social meanings and are often profound sites of contestation (Bourdieu 1984; Featherstone, Hepworth, and Turner 1991; Foucault 1979; Goffman 1959; Grosz 1994; Mauss 1950; Shilling 1993; Turner 1996; Williams and Bendelow 1998). As Anthony Synnott has put it, "The body is not a 'given,' but a social category with different meanings imposed and developed by every age, and by different sectors of the population. As such it is therefore sponge-like in its ability to absorb meanings, but also highly political" (1993, 1). Some bodies are ascribed legitimacy and some are not. They not only become places in which we express our identities but, because they are socially constructed, they offer or deny particular formulations. Bodies act not only as the conduit through which we participate in society but as a mechanism through which communities themselves are performed. They facilitate not only the production of identities (shaping persona through the look and actions of an avatar) but social relationships and communication. They are not neutral, and indeed their power lies in the very fact that they cannot be. People move their avatars through virtual spaces, using them to interact with each other and with the world. Avatars are crucial in producing a sense of presence, of "worldness." Just as corporeal bodies are integral to our personal and social lives, avatars are central to our experience in digital environments.

The virtual-world inhabitant who told me she sees her avatar as "material to work with" hits on the complicated ways bodies (and their corresponding digital incarnations as avatars) act as both social and personal artifacts. While rhetoric of the fluidity of identity performance and meaning online has been dominant, Allyson Polsky (2001) importantly notes that avatars themselves are never unencumbered, suggesting that, "even in virtual reality they are subject to organizational practices which, because they are a product of the social, never fully escape the social" (para. 10). Avatars do not appear in the game world simply as blank objects that allow users to construct independent meaning systems on them. They present themselves as complex symbolic referents that then circulate in a broader social economy.[16] Several researchers have explored the ways status systems and hierarchies express themselves in virtual worlds, undermining the myth of online life as inherently trouble free (Donath 1999; DuVal Smith 1999; Jakobsson 2002; Kolko and Reid 1998; Reid 1999). As each user encounters an avatar (their own or another's) he makes sense of it through a variety of social and personal "stories." Those stories help form the structure through which avatars act as agents for users. This experience can be expansive or constraining and can foster further immersion, identification, and affiliation or limit it. The chain-mail bikini and the "fantasy-size" breasts are not neutral markers but decidedly shape both identity and social interaction. The kind of bracketing women are forced to perform when playing these games is thus unfortunate, from both critical and design perspectives.

Attention to not only the power of embodied virtual spaces, but to the meaning of the body more generally is something many designers continue to overlook. Kathryn Wright of WomenGamers.com reports on a fascinating roundtable she conducted at the annual Game Developers Conference (2001b). She discusses how dismayed some of the male designers are when the topic even is raised and their claims that the subject of representation is not an issue of poor female body design but merely one aspect of all avatars being exaggerations. This is akin to viewing the design of *EQ* avatars as simply "glamorized." Certainly many of the male figures we see cropping up in games suffer from a hyperarticulated stereotype of masculinity with overly developed chests and biceps. However, Wright notes that such replies, "Seem to miss the significance of the fact that female characters are not simply portrayed in a physically unrealistic manner, but are overly sexualized as well" (ibid., 1). Sheri Graner Ray, a senior game designer at Sony Online Entertainment and author of *Gender Inclusive Game Design* (2004), points out that male avatars are not hypersexualized in the way that female ones are: they do not walk around with erections and signal constant sexual receptivity, for example.

Although an argument might be made for the ways chests and biceps on male characters act as symbolic sexual characteristics, they are simultaneously able to represent more general, nonsexual, power. This can be contrasted with the way women's large breasts typically act only as sexual markers in the game, their meaning remaining fairly one dimensional. Katinka described the frustration this can produce, saying, "You're sitting there minding your own business and somebody says 'Hey, nice boobs.' That's not what my character is. There's more to my character than her chest—much more than her rack."

Several women I interviewed expressed concern for the way a younger generation of girl gamers would have to make sense of these types of representations and the behaviors that often follow them. While *EQ* tries to provide some hurdles to minors playing the game, it is not unusual to find teenage boys and girls in the space. Claire reflected on the issue, "I just try and ignore it but I guess the one thing that bothers me is the young girls that play. Like one of the little Druids in our guild, she's 11 in RL. Her mom sits with her while she plays. I see how guys react toward my character and some of the rude things they've said to me I would not want them to say to an 11 year old child." It is unfortunate if some of the positive experiences women can find in games like *EQ* continue to be countered by such familiar offline practices.

Shaping Markets and Contextual Models

Within the game industry there are two major prongs driving regressive gendered divisions: design and advertising. Avatars are one of the central fronts on which real change can be made easily. Graner Ray acknowledges that while better design choices might cost a bit more up front it also "becomes a matter of weighing the entire potential of the market versus the initial cost of development" (2004, 106). But what happens when the product leaves the hands of the designer? Advertising for computer games is one of the core ways of generating interest and cultivating markets. It is also in the realm of advertising that potential players come to understand a game as a gendered product.

Far too often games or game equipment that have no gender-coded play mechanics or design features get inscribed by marketing departments as such. They become "for men." The most notorious example of this is Nintendo's Game Boy line of handheld consoles.[17] Gareth Schott (2004) conducted a small but instructive study with women, asking them to play with a Game Boy Advance SP then following up by showing them ads for it. Though their initial response to the handheld game was quite positive and the participants perceived it as largely gender neutral, when confronted with the marketing for the device responses ranged from aggravation with the marketing campaign ("Why can't we have it?") to even retracting their previous, more positive perspective on playing with the device. The power of advertising to frame the use and context for games can have a double edge. Marketing campaigns can both be off-putting to potential players, disenfranchising them from the product, and simultaneously put women gamers into the awkward position of reevaluating their own previous use and pleasures in gaming.

Marketing remains an issue for *EverQuest* and MMOGs more generally. Despite their success in bringing in female players the preponderance of advertising and box art (figure 4.3) that is displayed on the shelves at stores remains unimaginative in its approach to constructing a diverse audience for its products. When we do see women in ads for games they are usually there not for the benefit of engaging potential women gamers but instead to evoke sexual-

Figure 4.3
EverQuest box art

ity or a fantasy context. For example, an ad for *EverQuest* in *Maxim*'s 2001 "best of" issue shows two women in a nightclub setting, dressed up and holding drinks. One is leaning over to the other and saying, "He's opened up a whole new world for me!" Such formulations of women's relationship with the game, or more accurately, the location of *real* women as peripheral participants, also is reproduced in products like the "Babes of Norrath" calendar (which presents female NPC characters from the larger mythological world of Norrath) or the "Quest for Antonia" model competition, hosted in cooperation with *Stuff* magazine, that searched for the "real life" woman who "most closely resembles Antonia," a character who rules a region in *EQ2*. Probably unsurprisingly, both the images used in the calendar and the Antonia character on the Web site looked like models with large breast implants, posed in ways that evoke nothing of the power, the activity, or the challenge of *actual* female characters as played in the game. While they sometimes hold weapons, I would argue they are not intended to trigger an imagination of actual use but are simply props and strongly mediated by the way the rest of the image sexualizes the woman.

My sense is that some (though certainly not enough) game designers themselves find this disconnect between their product and how it is marketed at times distressing. While a designer may develop an innovative form of play or representation in a game, we cannot overlook that these artifacts (and their creators) exist in larger organizational and cultural structures that shape and distribute products in particular ways. Despite my critique of *EverQuest* on the issue of avatars, I think it has done remarkably well in not encoding gender into play mechanics, and this certainly should be factored in when considering the numbers of women who subscribe to the game. But sales, marketing and promotional departments must realize that large numbers of women and girls are playing their games *despite* campaigns that alienate them or position them as outsiders to gamer culture. As Graner Ray (2004, xv) highlights, a very basic commercial issue must be considered: "developers need to think about the future growth of this industry and what the market *could* be" (emphasis hers). Why do game companies continue to, often willfully, overlook potential markets for their products instead of cultivating new and diverse communities of players? How long can the 15–25-year-old-male demographic not just sustain, but grow, an entertainment industry in interesting and innovative ways? This is also an ethical and political matter. Being able to engage in particular leisure activities is not neutral, and affording diverse audiences equal access is socially important (Wearing 1998). If we think women should be able to play sports—and not just special "women's sports"—why should we give them any less when it comes to computer games? Given the ways computer games afford challenges, exploration, risk taking, learning, competition, teamwork, and the pleasures of agency, full and equal access is important for girls and women.

A Call for Visibility and Inclusiveness

As the MMOG genre emerges we are beginning to see the ways that the traditional approach of "pink games" lacks a rich picture of girls' and women's play. Jeanne B. Funk points out that games focusing on friendship and sociality may overlook the fact that "girls are looking for games which also push them to take risks and where there is a chance to be absolutely and unequivocally dominant" and further suggests that there "may be unintended consequences to gender-specific software: girls may be less likely to benefit from developments in the gaming mainstream if they believe that only 'girl games' are appropriate for them" (2001, 3). Helen Kennedy writes that ultimately "We also need to offer a critique of the entire discourse around gaming which serves to create the illusion that it is a masculine preserve" (2002, 6). Citing the success of changes in the movie industry, she notes, "It is similarly vital that in the construction of a critical discourse about games we encourage and stimulate innovative and alternative images of men and women that do not simply reinstate doggedly rigid gender stereotypes" (ibid.).

Brad McQuaid proposes that one of the strengths of games like *EverQuest* is precisely that it was built with these broader design goals. As he puts it, "It's also worth noting that, due to what makes MUDs and MMOGs compelling (character development, immersive worlds, strong community building tools and functionality), we always knew [it] could be fairly gender-neutral."[18] It is clear that designers and their companies need to rethink not only who their users are but what is at stake in the artifacts they provide. Brenda Laurel suggests a link between the lack of gender diversity within game companies and the products they create, arguing that the game industry has been "horribly stunted" because it has "been unwilling to look beyond itself to its audience" (2001, 36). Akrich (1995) notes the variety of techniques designers employ to try and represent the users to themselves (for example, via consumer testing or looking to experts) and suggests that reliance on a kind of "I methodology" remains one of the most widely used techniques. For example, in Nelly Oudshoorn, Els Rommes, and Marcelle Stienstra's (2004) research on the creation of the *Digital City of Amsterdam* platform, they note that the designers "generally took their own preferences and skills as major guides" (an approach simultaneously tied up with producing a notion of "everybody" as user), which led to a system that privileged experimentation and "innovation" over user-friendliness (53). The reliance on this approach is particularly short-sighted given the heterogeneity not only across users, but within *any particular user's* context.

Revisiting the numbers of women playing the major MMOGs shows that the figures are quite remarkable given they are not the demographic being targeted. In many ways, women play in spite of barriers to entry. Women gamers are finding fascinating and complicated pleasures in online games, and while most of what we have seen in the literature so far points to the social aspects that draw women in, it is clear that this does not tell the full story. Games like *EverQuest* appear to be offering venues for the interesting exploration of activities typically bounded off from each other—sociability and power, mastery and cooperation—and women are finding dynamic ways to inhabit these virtual worlds. Helen Kennedy (forthcoming), drawing on the work of Betsy Wearing (1998), points to the ways we might see these game spaces as offering possible "heterotopias," which are counter or compensatory sites for the reformulation of gender identities. She begins to help us imagine a type of space Henry Jenkins proposes is necessary to avoid simplistic distinctions between girl and boy games.

We need to open up more space for girls to join—or play alongside—the traditional boy culture down by the river, in the old vacant lot, within the bamboo forest. Girls need to learn how to explore "unsafe" and "unfriendly" spaces, and to experience the "complete freedom of movement" promised by the boys' games, if not all the time, then at least some of the time, to help them develop the self-confidence and competitiveness demanded of professional women. They also need to learn how, in the words of a contemporary bestseller, to "run with the wolves" and not just follow the butterflies. Girls need to be able to play games where Barbie gets to kick some butt. (H. Jenkins, 1998a, 291)[19]

Cassell proposes an ambitious and valuable challenge for game design, outlining a method to "build girls' games in such a way that the game itself participates in the construction of a child's gender and other aspects of the self, without a preconceived notion of what a girl is" (1998, 299). While focusing on games for girls, her more general framework of feminist design principles intersects nicely with the ways participatory design processes might extend the range of virtual worlds. If designers would rise to the challenge presented by a sociology of the body and a more complicated understanding (and rendering) of gender, the possibilities for evocative and immersive environments might begin to truly draw in a diverse gaming population and legitimize those already playing.

5 Whose Game Is This Anyway?

In November 2004 Marvel, holders of the comics line that includes *Spider-man* and *X-Men,* initiated legal proceedings against NCSoft and Cryptic Studios, makers of the popular MMOG *City of Heroes,* for copyright and trademark infringement. *City of Heroes* (*CoH*) gives players the ability to create for themselves characters rivaling anything seen in comic books. Using the avatar-creator tool players can piece together their own superheroes (by picking fantastical costumes, bodies, and names) to fight villians in the *CoH* world, Paragon City. Though the game specifically notes in its end-user license agreement (EULA) that players are not allowed to use character names that violate any "third party's trademark right, copyright, or other proprietary right" Marvel asserts that the game allows players (indeed encourages them) to "create and utilize Heroes that are nearly identical in name, appearance, and characteristics to characters belonging to Marvel" (Marvel 2004).[1] The fact that Cryptic describes their "Creation Engine" as a "high-tech version of a box of crayons" only shows how thorny the relationship between these systems and user practice can be.

In other corners of the virtual-world scene "tax protests" by players in *Second Life* contest a change in the way objects in the world are reconciled against player accounts (Grimmelmann 2003); a researcher claims to have been booted from *The Sims Online* for reporting less-than-appealing aspects about the game world involving underage prostitution (Harmon 2004) and public demonstrations in *World of Warcraft* by players demand attention for their concerns about the Warrior character class (Castronova 2005).

While past multiplayer gaming spaces such as text-based MUDs were built around noncommercial models and freeware systems, many of today's most popular online games are owned and operated by major corporations. Though previous text-based worlds were always owned by someone (perhaps an undergraduate running the game on his dorm computer) and often hierarchical (game administrators, for example, occupied powerful positions over players), a fairly dominant ethic of shared-world creation and experience prevailed. At a basic level the source code for a wide variety of MUDs was freely available and customizable by anyone with the technology and skills to undertake game creation. But the current terrain of multiuser game-space looks quite different. Whether it is Sony's *Star Wars Galaxies,* Disney's *Toon Town,* or Electronic Arts's *The Sims Online,* the move to commercialized virtual environments is presenting some unique challenges for users negotiating between their private lives and corporate interests. Indeed, this designation of private versus corporate becomes problematized with the everyday experience players have in commercialized systems. The boundary between these categories, and ultimately between that of consumer and producer, is increasingly messy. Rather than simply waiting to see how the matter sorts itself out, we must engage in critical inquiry about what is happening in game worlds. The struggles, discussions, and debates taking place in game communities about the status of player and company ownership, as well as questions of responsibility and accountability, go to the heart of contemporary concerns not only around intellectual property, but about the nature of citizenship in commercial society and the status of culture and technology in our everyday lives. The decisions being formulated now are particularly powerful because they set precedents for the networked future in which spaces and experience come to be mediated primarily through commercialized systems of authorship and exchange.

It is, however, not simple. As we have seen, gameplay in MMOGs is a complicated mix of social and instrumental actions that are located not only in individual players but among collectives. The boundaries of the game often are not recognizable because Web sites and fan forums push at them, providing invaluable information for actually playing. The collective production of game experience and knowledge does not simply constitute a helpful "add-on" to the game, but is a fundamental factor in both its pleasure and sustainability. Most radically put, the very product of the game is not constructed simply by the designers or publisher, nor contained within the boxed product, but produced only in conjunction with the players. Beyond the role that players now regularly take in shaping game products by their (unpaid) time spent beta-testing them or providing feedback, embedded within the game world is an emergent culture created and sustained by players. What then are the challenges that arise when culture, communities, and commerce intersect? Once games such as *EQ* are seen as an embodied social world that not only incorporates elements of play as formalized through a given rule set, but extending beyond it and indeed transforming it, a range of issues emerge around the status of the culture of that world, the autonomy of its inhabitants, and their relationship with both designers and games as technological objects. Circulating around a game and, in fact, always co-constructing it, are a variety of actors with their own, often conflicting, agendas and demarcations of the game space. Designers and world-management teams typically focus on notions of fair play, authorial intent, game integrity, and mechanics. Legal counsel for game companies often are actively invested in pursuing strong intellectual-property claims for their products. Marketing departments spend much of their time shaping the public identity of the game and framing patterns of consumption. Into this mix enter the everyday players with their own specific ideas about play, their own histories and contexts (both game, media, and technological), their own situated practices in networked space, and their own understandings of the various claims and agendas held by other actors. A constant push and pull exists among all these parties around not only the question of what the game is but also whose game it is.

Culture Matters

One of the most significant issues to be considered in this discussion is the status of culture. The current climate seems to be one marked by the vigorous and widespread extension of authorship rights (via trademarks, copyrights, patent holdings, and the like). In the face of strong tendencies not only to brand cultural space, but to aggressively protect those brands, we can ask how much of our general culture individuals have creative access to any longer. As Naomi Klein suggests in her book *No Logo* (1999), the extension of multinational branded space and the commodification of culture is fomenting a moment when consumerism is colliding with citizenship. What is the status of public space and, by extension, its domain in virtual environments? Rosemary Coombe, legal scholar and anthropologist, has presented a compelling analysis of the corporate ownership of culture and the consequences of the commercialization of symbolic space. She writes that "increasingly, holders of intellectual property rights are socially and juridically endowed with monopolies over public meaning and the ability to control the cultural connotations of their corporate insignias (trademarks being the most visible signs of their presence in consumer culture)" (Coombe 1998, 26).

While the preservation of the rights of authors certainly is an important standard to be upheld, the balance has turned lately to an overextension of those rights. As Lawrence Lessig notes regarding the creation of the 1998 Digital Millennium Copyright Act (DMCA), it not only sought to extend previously granted protection mechanisms, but also to "regulate devices that were designed to circumvent copyright protection measures. It was designed to ban those devices, whether or not the use of the copyrighted material made possible by that circumvention would have been a copyright violation" (Lessig 2004, 157). The romantic notion of the single author toiling away on manuscripts or pieces of music, one whose work is preserved through intellectual-property rights and whose enthusiasm for further artistic creation is fanned through assurance that her work would be recognized as hers, is a powerful image. It is one, however, that has not quite kept pace with the range of authors we now find, most significantly corporate ones—entities who outlive any "real" human beings and whose property never slips out of their grasp and into the public domain. As James Boyle suggests, this authorial image is powerful but double-sided. Though originally speaking to an understanding of the lone individual working at his craft, it now underpins a regime with quite different agents at work such that, "A striking feature of the language of romantic authorship is the way it is used to support sweeping intellectual property rights for large corporate entities. Sony, Pfizer, and Microsoft tend to lack the appeal of Byron and Alexander Fleming" (Boyle 1996, xiii).

Though actual people are creating the literature, the music, the images that we encounter, just as often those creators do not hold the rights to their own works. Or, just as significantly, the space of public domain is increasingly diminished with the extensions given to the life of copyrights. The ability for individuals to legally reappropriate symbols for critique, or even satire, has been seriously wounded. Coombe provides a multitude of examples of our everyday symbolic lives being dominated by a sea of trademarks and copyrights. Branding has assumed such a prominent role in our cultural lives that it becomes difficult to imagine spaces not touched in some way by corporatized signs. Stories abound of people being charged with unauthorized usage of Disney characters, Barbie dolls, Benetton ad imagery and the like. More recently this symbolic turf war has extended into the digital realm, where cease-and-desist orders are doled out quite liberally (Coombe and Herman

2001).[2] Unfortunately, when an average person receives such an order the prospect of challenging it may be overwhelming and financially impossible. We are left, then, in a cultural space in which people may have little say in shaping the artifacts they find in their daily lives and are simultaneously prevented from using or reappropriating those symbols.

It is not difficult to see that the terrain of culture is now a battlefield in which corporate "authors" vigorously monitor the use of their work and are granted wide latitude in "protecting" their property. But is there some point at which artifacts, images, and symbols move from the narrow domain of single ownership into a sphere where we recognize they are meaningful only through participation in the public, the social? At what point does something shift from being solely the property of an original author to being that of those who not only use it but give it meaning? As Coombe puts it, "one could argue that if the public creates meanings for Barbie in excess of the signifier's capacity to signal Mattel's toy, they have done the sowing and thus they should do the reaping" (Coombe 1998, 67). The point becomes even more acute if, in fact, artifacts are introduced into everyday culture in a way that intends them to be persistent and pervasive. Do people then have any right not only to reinterpret those symbols, but to lay claim to them in some form?

While file-sharing networks such as Napster and BitTorrent have brought property and ownership debates to the foreground, similar negotiations also are taking place in the emerging world of computer games. In many ways game-spaces make material the deep tensions now endemic to daily offline life. For example, what is the jurisdiction of ownership when we are speaking about a person's body or identity? While we are familiar with the more weighty examples that are arising from genetic patents or information surveillance, the debates around avatars (a kind of digital body) and character autonomy fold into similar concerns. Mix artists, T-shirt bootleggers, and fans producing literatures all have signaled key debate points in the question of cultural ownership. We might inquire how the daily dynamic culture of a game-space like *EverQuest,* which is significantly constituted through the labor of the players, also intersects these issues.

Game worlds do not lie outside of our ongoing cultural battles, anxieties, or innovations but very often mirror them quite well. Looking at a game like *EQ* can lead us to ask what the status of culture is in such spaces, especially when that culture intersects with commercial interests. Are players coproducers of the game worlds they spend time in? Do users have any meaningful stake or say in what constitutes their game-space? Are players of a game world simply consumers, or can they claim any form of citizenship? Should players be afforded any rights? What kinds of responsibilities might corporations be seen as holding when they are framed as the primary world managers for thousands of people on a daily basis?

Selling Swords, Selling Bodies

In April of 2000 Sony Online Entertainment secured cooperation with the Internet auction sites eBay and Yahoo! to prevent *EverQuest* users from selling game accounts and in-game goods. Up until that time a cottage industry had sprung up in which users were turning their online labor into offline cash. Jessica Mulligan (2002) notes this is not a new phenomenon but likely dates back to the 1980s with the sale of accounts in games like *Islands of Kesmai* and *Gemstone II.* A search for *EQ* items on eBay in 2000 would have found a wide variety of available items, ranging from equipment such as armor, weapons, and spells to in-game coins being bought and sold with real-world currency. Players not only would sell odds and ends from the game but the ultimate item—their avatars and character accounts. Auction descriptions such as "Awesome Dark Elf Necro!" or "The Most Well Rounded Account of the Year" would appear, quite often with impressive screenshots of the avatar outfitted in its finest gear. At the time it was not unusual for a high-level character to fetch several thousand U.S. dollars on the auction market.

Someone who bid high enough could walk away with not only a new body (via the *EQ* account), but a new identity. Such purchases circumvent quite a few hours of developing a character and gaining levels. Many in the *EQ* community find this a loathsome practice, of course, and often derogatorily term such purchasers "eBayers." While high-level players actually do buy accounts as a way of bypassing what is seen as tedious work (a fact rarely considered in this debate), the term is typically used to mark those who have bought loaded accounts and characters but themselves have no real game skills and have not "paid any dues." While the *EQ* community has had one set of reasons to frequently scorn this practice (formulated around how good a person can or cannot play versus abstract notions of "fairness"), others bring their own sets of issues to the table. At a basic level one of the major problems with allowing users to buy and sell player accounts is it short-circuits the economic model that is the current lifeblood of many commercial virtual environments—sub-scriptions. Since *EverQuest* users must pay a monthly fee to play the game for unlimited hours, the number of months they subscribe is a crucial considera-tion for the game company. While it is hard to say what the average time is for users to level characters up, it can take months—if not years—which in the case of *EQ* translates into lucrative fees. If users can bypass the long process of leveling, though, and simply go to eBay (or at this point any of the number of other game auction sites) to purchase high-level characters or equipment that otherwise would require a fair amount of gameplay to achieve, the eco-nomic repercussions reverberate. Customer-service departments often have an entirely different argument for prohibiting auctions, but one also tied to the financial and organizational structure of the game company. Who would a customer turn to with their complaint if they were scammed by an auction? Many game administrators who handle the day-to-day aspects of running the service envision a nightmare of calls and hassles that could arise from third parties intervening in the customer-account system.

Beyond these more economic considerations, though, are deeper questions about the nature of the game and the status of the artifacts in it. It is often ar-gued (certainly by many game designers) that the integrity of the gameplay is damaged by such end runs. John Smedley, president of SOE, has said "A per-son's out-of-game status should not be able to affect their in-game status. For example, a rich person should not be able to buy their way into a great char-acter. My personal feeling, and that of the rest of the team, is that it is some-thing that could be harmful to the game. Grave harm? Probably not—but something we decided to take a stand on all the same" (Marks 2003, 75). Oth-ers have noted that the economy of the game itself might be altered by these external market forces (Castronova 2001). Possibly more significant, games that rely on reputation systems and social connections (as *EQ* does) to facili-tate cooperative gameplay indeed may be undermined by auctioning. A strong case probably also can be made for the ways having to progress on your own builds game skills and social networks central to future play and enjoyment. While concerns about subscription revenue or internal costs to support such third-party action certainly form major reasons for the prohibition of auc-tioning, there is also an underlying sense that such outside activity can fun-damentally undermine the nature of the game and the integrity of play. This argument, of course, is particularly thorny given the ways people innovate play, either through strategies or extending the games' bounds through collectively produced sites. MMOGs, at a basic level, are collaboratively authored spaces and, as such, complicate approaches that rely on any single person or group holding the final true vision of game integrity.

This issue of preserving the authorial intent of the play space is not entirely dissimilar from the ways game companies often regulate the content of the game as solely their intellectual property (IP). Both models place actual players as consumers, not authors, of the game. On the design end this can be heard in comments that frame users as "not playing right" and on the legal end as players simply "renting" the game contents for the duration of a play session. In both models the role of players as active, creative, core agents not just in the consumption of the product, but its creation, is underplayed. What is fascinating are the ways, for many designers, legitimating this kind of activity poses some serious threats to not only their game, but the status of MMOGs in general. As Brad McQuaid notes regarding auctioning, "Everybody in the massively multiplayer industry was certainly concerned about the situation. When people claim that having time invested in the game somehow gives them authority or ownership over elements of that game, you certainly have a situation that could threaten the entire genre itself" (Marks 2003, 75).

The case of banning *EQ* auctions is instructive as it highlights very clearly a narrow conception not only of IP, but of culture. In a *CNet News* article Kevin Pursglove, a spokesman for eBay addressed *EQ*'s membership in VeRO (the Verified Rights Owners program): "VeRO members list items that they own the property rights to. Should they find an auction selling items that a member believes violate their property rights, eBay will shut down the auction" (Sandoval 2001). The ban on the practice initiated a move to regulate not only the boundaries around a specific kind of virtual property but also broader claims on the activity of players. The issue is complicated, however, by the fact that the game facilitates in-game buying and trading and formally provides the ability for players to give each other items and coins via a trade window. *EQ* does not, then, prohibit wholesale the transfer of items from one player to another and even supports an economy via these mechanisms. This makes more pronounced the ambiguity of the offense. Is it that users are obtaining items outside of a definition of appropriate gameplay or that some are profiting from it? And that indeed that profit is not simply in "virtual" money (as any longtime player is likely to have acquired through normal buying and selling over the course of gameplay) but actual money? How much of a right do users have to artifacts they invest enormous amounts of time in securing? Do they have any claim on a given character or account?

While the debate both in player communities and among designers often has focused on the IP claims, we also should pay attention to the broader cultural imperatives at stake.[3] Outside of any individual player's time the account is, in fact, devoid of meaning or game status. It takes a player to create a character, and it takes the time of the player to develop that character. Through her labor she imbues it with qualities, status, accomplishments. Indeed, while the owners of a game provide the raw materials through which users can participate in a space, it is in large part *only through the labor of the players* that dynamic identities and characters are created, that culture and community come to grow, and that the game is made animate. One of the main issues the auction ban highlights is the impoverished view of the relationships between technologies, users, and culture. Players do not just consume, or act as passive audience members of, the game but instead are active cocreators in producing it as a meaningful experience and artifact. As a media product, a game, and a technology, *EverQuest* is constructed through the joint practices of designers, publisher, world managers, and players. This collective construction of the space across multiple actors is key, but often it seems to fall out of the narrow IP formulations that circulate. It is not simply that the objects themselves exist in the space, but that the time and meaning to support them is always being given. Indeed, those who argue for the legitimacy of auctions have turned to claiming that what actually is being compensated is the time any given player invests in obtaining an item, not the item itself. While that claim is seen as a kind of "easy out" by many, it does highlight a more complex framework for understanding these objects as collectively constructed.

While it is certainly the case that some users operate from a view of culture production that is just as limited (claiming they have the total right to do whatever they want with their accounts and not paying serious attention to the role of game designers and managers in the construction of their game world), when the tilt comes from corporate owners it tends to carry the full weight of their access to legal and judicial remedies. Individual users may try to assert digital property claims (and by extension particular understandings of cultural production) by auctioning accounts and artifacts, but the systemic undermining of more nuanced notions of authorship can be located squarely in the corporate realm. The battle over user autonomy would not be nearly as worrisome if people were operating on a level playing field with the corporate owners.[4] More often than not, though, they are simply ill-prepared to challenge the deeply embedded notions of authorship currently supported by legal decisions and legislation. The cost of challenging the owner of a game world, indeed the space one's digital body and identity inhabit, has been borne out by users who have been banned from the game, generally without recourse and certainly never with the benefit of third-party mediators. Such examples travel quickly through the player-community grapevine, serving as powerful reminders to other users about who has the ultimate say in setting the terms of participation.

Of course, the sticky point here is that such spaces are not only private and for profit but based on voluntary participation. Many argue that game owners have every right to set any terms of service they want. This is not unfamiliar territory, and computer games are laden with elaborate end-user license agreements. *EverQuest* in fact requires players to accept their EULA each and every time they log into the game. At a formal level, by clicking the "accept" button when they launch the game, *EQ* players agree to play by the specific rules and terms of service as outlined by the company. We might ask, however, about the legal validity of some of what is contained in EULAs and what it might mean to opt out of systems that require our begrudging assent. All too often we have seen instances of companies overextending rights or claims that may not be defensible. Rebecca Tushnet, for example, discusses a case in which the modification of game characters was allowed, noting that "one court has recognized that enabling consumers to play with and alter video-game characters has the potential to improve the market for the official product" (1997, 17). In general the growing tendency to try to police the "essence of the game" (an actual phrase in the EULA of at least one MMOG) suggests that game companies often have not quite reckoned with the actual nature of their worlds as artifacts created (and sometimes even improved upon) by multiple actors.

A number of legal scholars have turned their attention to MMOGs and sought to examine the underlying claims being made.[5] Most notable in this field is the work of F. Greg Lastowka and Dan Hunter, who wrote one of the first scholarly considerations on the subject, "The Laws of the Virtual Worlds" (2004). Based on their understanding of both legal precedent and the nature of objects and property in these worlds, they suggest that "there is no descriptive disconnection between our real-world property system and virtual assets. From both descriptive and normative positions, owners of virtual assets do, or should, possess property rights" (2004, 20). Though they qualify their statements throughout, noting that this argument is not really an indication of how those interests "should be allocated, and who owns the property," it nonetheless suggests a stronger validation of the materiality of virtual worlds than is often thought. Lastowka and Hunter additionally note that "As people increasingly come to live and work in these worlds, the domination of legal property issues by EULAs and practices of 'wizardly fiat' may appear one-sided and unjust. If corporate wizards continue to assert complete ownership rights over virtual lives, cyborg inhabitants will bring their concerns to real-world courts to prevent certain fundamental rights from being contracted away" (2004, 29).

It is sometimes suggested that if players do not like the terms of an agreement, they should simply take their money and go somewhere else. That problems raised around intellectual property and player engagement in games can be solved through the market (or through consumers' wallets) strikes me as a naive hope on several levels. The common framing of games as "simply entertainment" often obscures the ways they act as key cultural sites in which forgoing participation may have real costs. We increasingly live in a world in which opting out of technological systems is more and more difficult and yet participation within those systems pushes us to accept structures we might oppose. Try eliminating a technology (especially a communication one) from your life for a week and see how you fare. As people find their friends, family, colleagues, and the broader culture engaging in some sphere, the desire to participate can be quite strong and even can form a social imperative. We might also consider the ways participating in particular forms or places always are tied up with questions of power. Separate does not mean equal, and sometimes we can see quite clearly the benefits that come from being in *particular* spaces. I do not want to suggest that we do not have choices that we can make, but instead want to highlight that there can be meaningful benefits and costs attached to those choices.

It is also the case that game companies are very good at following precedent. In many ways it is a fundamentally conservative media outlet, taking minimal risks and building on well-established conventions. If anything I would argue that the idea of a growing diversity of offerings overlooks the narrowing and monopolizing tendencies actually found in contemporary capital. Markets are rarely free (see, for example, McChesney's [1999] excellent work on the structure of media and patterns of ownership). Usually there simply are not a wide-variety of playgrounds on offer and the strong, narrow conception of not only intellectual property but producer/player dichotomies that predominates can be worrisome. Pegging progressive IP regimes on a market model of action strikes me as woefully insufficient.

(Il)legitimate Play

The formulation that understands actors in MMOG game-spaces strictly along lines of producer and user overlooks the ways these games are co-constructed by a variety of agents. Game designers increasingly rely on productive player communities, be it to prepare a product for commercial launch or to update and refine a game once it has reached market. And as we have seen in other chapters, players are engaged actively in producing the culture, indeed the playability, of a game like *EQ*. There is, however, often an underlying rhetorical tension at work. The notion of the romantic author not only dominates legal framings but is circulated by game designers themselves. Those who have found themselves working within the multiplayer genre are, not surprisingly, a bit more nuanced than some about the status of their games. They know as well as anyone that once they put a product out there the players will do with it what they will, often playing in ways the designers never anticipated. Farmer and Morningstar note that in their own development experience:

Again and again we found that activities based on often unconscious assumptions about player behavior had completely unexpected outcomes (when they were not simply outright failures). It was clear that we were not in control. The more people we involved in something, the less in control we were. We could influence things, we could set up interesting situations, we could provide opportunities for things to happen, but we could not predict or dictate the outcome. (1991, 288)

Despite the widespread acknowledgment (at least informally) of this everyday reality, a thread of authorial control that can remain at times expresses itself with statements about players "not playing right," "causing trouble," or "ruining gameplay." My intent here is not to understate the power of the structures designers do provide, nor somehow to rob them of acknowledgment for the hard work they do. But it is worth watching how instances of "unruly play" are handled as a way of interrogating the deeper understandings about who the imagined player is and how they should behave. As Mulligan and Patrovsky try to emphasize to future designers, "It isn't your game; it's the players game. Developers spend years focused on making a game. If they're not careful, this will breed certain assumptions, such as the world they created will remain their world and the players will play the game the way the creators want it played. That will not happen. Players have their own motivations and objectives" (2003, 217).

When *EverQuest* first was launched, the game only ran in full-screen, so players were unable to use Alt-Tab to switch to other programs. The interface was nonmodular and could not be customized. The interface was, in fact, a regulating device. All players saw the exact same desktop and were expected to share an identical configuration of game-space. All players, that is, except those who had downloaded a small program called *EQWindows.* It allowed users to put the game into a window mode to open other programs—most commonly a Web browser, MP3 player, or second copy of the game. This modification offered players an opportunity to extend their game-space and use the product in ways not authorized by the company.[6] Its prohibition, primarily rooted in security concerns, made use of the application technically a violation of the EULA and was deemed a bannable offense. Some public discussions of the program said it constituted a kind of unfair advantage. By forcing people to rely only on the given game world—meaning the boxed product provided by the designer, as presented in its full-window mode—a level playing field was created where outside resources and helper sites like those described in previous chapters would not create unfair advantages for those accessing them. But as a design choice it also represented an underlying orientation of cautious and protective suspicion—some players will try to cheat, to hack client programs, to gain unfair advantage, so locking down the interface is one small step in creating a tight system. Indeed, within MMOG design circles the motto is to "never trust the client." And while the "client" specified in this phrase is the software application used to interface with the game, it belies a similar sensibility regarding the user.

In the history of the game there was another product, *EQ Macros,* that allowed players to record and play back keystrokes. According to its developers, the intended use was not to create unfair advantages but instead that *"EQ Macros* takes the grunt work out of playing *EverQuest,* and makes it more fun."[7] These same developers produced a tool called *Xylobot,* which was conceived as "a generic game tool that works with many DirectX games" and boasted a feature list that included on-screen maps, waypoints, and auto-start options. In a somewhat different model than the other modifications mentioned, these programs were not freeware, though trial versions could be downloaded.

Those who used *EQWindows* or, more often, had second computers attached to the Internet, were able to use map sites and the vast helper databases available. Players using *EQ Macros* or *Xylobot* found a range of functionality not proscribed by the game's designers. With an abstract notion of "fair play," such helpers certainly could constitute cheating in the minds of some, though I think they are better seen as pointers either to underlying design insufficiencies within the game itself or alternative play models deemed illegitimate or not fully accounted for. As games like Blizzard's *World of Warcraft* actually build into their initial design opportunities for these kinds of player creations, it is clear that there is no singular definition for what constitutes legitimate engagement. One might argue that people only turn to such resources because there is a distinct need for them, an additional pleasure in consulting the minutia of the world, or in participating in the collaborative construction of the game. Interestingly, in recent updates to *EQ* both the interface and its information extensibility have been radically altered. *EQ* now can run in either full-screen or windowed mode. A detailed mapping function, which can import player-produced maps, now exists. Additionally, players now can transmit to each other within the communication channels links that allow them to click on the name of an item and have its picture and statistical information pop up. Each of these developments is a kind of homage to the innovation done within the player community itself. Play interventions previously deemed bannable or "extracurricular" now have been integrated into the heart of the game. As such, they point to the ways emergent play forms an integral part of innovation and the development process.

While features such as a windowed mode and maps represent the ways the player and designer community negotiated divergent notions of what the game-space should be, two other programs speak to the more heavily contested status of some artifacts. As introduced in the chapter on power gamers, *ShowEQ* remains one of the more controversial add-ons to the game. To those that do not have the program, one that allows users to extract additional information about the game, it certainly can appear to be a cheat. Designers are just as invested as their most vocal players in protecting the game world from these incursions and as such, *ShowEQ* exists as an artifact that extends the bounds of the game-space but in a way that is deeply contested by both fellow players who do not use the program and *EQ*'s designers.[8] My intent here is not particularly to weigh in about whether or not it constitutes a violation of the game space; I am more interested in the way its existence prompts discussions about not only what fair play is, but what the legitimate bounds of the game are.

Similarly, a program like *EQEmu*—an emulator program that allows people to run their own instantiations of the game, free of SOE account management and subscription fees—represents one of the more debatable player-produced developments around the game. *EQEmu* undermines the dominant authorial and ownership rhetoric of the game by allowing players to engage with it on noncommercial terms and outside of the jurisdiction of the game company. Interestingly, however, *EQEmu* fundamentally relies on collaborative contribution. It only can work if participants play the "legitimate" version of the game and report back to the *EQEmu* development team the statistics and information around various items in the *EQ* world.[9] Continued information from players about monsters and other details from actual encounters within the live SOE game are necessary for the emulated world to replicate the details therein.

Fanfic and Reappropriated Orcs

While the above cases point to some game artifacts and play strategies that exist on the boundaries, we might also consider how the very identity of the game and its content is a site of negotiation. The regulation of player activity within out-of-game and third-party-owned space is similarly instructive on the question of user autonomy, corporate control, and the nature of cultural authorship in game space. The banning of the *EQ* user Mystere raises provocative issues around the way individuals and player communities are negotiating a commercialized cultural sphere.

In 2000 Mystere posted a piece of fan fiction (fanfic) to a Web site neither owned nor operated by SOE. This independent venue offered a place for players to share their written work (based around *EverQuest* characters and *EQ*-style elements) with others in a noncommercial setting. The content of the story admittedly is charged, involving the graphic rape of a character "in her 14th season" and the subsequent revenge in which the character kills her attacker. The story remained on the board for three months until it came to the attention of *EQ* representatives, who were alerted to it by a visitor to the Web site. In a move that startled many in the game community, Mystere's *EverQuest* account was closed and the piece of fanfic subsequently was deleted.

The justification for this action was defined quite broadly and spoke not simply to a concern with intellectual property but to larger reputational considerations. Gordin Wrinn, Internet-relations manager for the game, stated:

We make determinations based on information at hand regarding who is or is not having a positive effect on *EverQuest*'s community. If we determine that one person's actions make *EverQuest* a game that other people do not want to play based upon those actions, we will exercise our right to refuse service to the extent necessary to provide a reasonable and enjoyable gaming environment. (Mulligan 2000c)

John Smedley spoke with one of the major online game magazines and further clarified the company's position, saying, "In this day and age we are very concerned about the perception of online games to the mainstream public. What we don't need is people equating this story with *EverQuest* and therefore assuming this is the kind of stuff that everyone is involved in" (Parker 2000). Citing violations to their intellectual property and the production of "derivative work" Andrew Zaffron, general counsel for SOE, made clear the company's belief that "the laws governing the use of copyrighted material, derivative works, trademarks and trade dress—gives us the exclusive right to permit or disallow the outside use of our intellectual property so that we can properly manage our business and nurture the *EverQuest* brand" (Mulligan 2000c, 3).

What is striking about the incident is that it points to something beyond the standard IP concerns we encounter in the auction debate. The very identity of the game, as a commercial product with intended uses and audiences, is always being constructed by its owners. But the practices and appropriations in which it circulates through actual players and their communities simultaneously co-construct the game itself. It is not, of course, that the "community" is any coherent whole either. There were vigorous debates among players about the merits of the story and whether or not its content constituted grounds for banning. The significance of the "14th season" phrase was considered by users—did it mean 14 levels, in which case the age of the character in question is indeterminate or did it mean she was 14 years old? Mystere himself finally addressed the matter in an interview with Jon Goodwin of *Joystick101:*

The word [sic] was absolutely NOT child porn. First off, as I have always said, fantasy settings are generally viewed as being from medieval or the Renaissance period. During this period of time in real life, 14 years old was quite old enough to have been married off and have at least one child . . . Basically, in the setting given, the girl wasn't a "girl" but a young woman. Also, it is quite clearly stated that the villain in the story is doing something illegal, even in his "evil" society. (Goodwin 2000)

The author's formulation makes simple decisions on the issue even trickier as it does not take the easy out and claim it was just a fourteenth-level adult, but instead historicizes and contextualizes the story beyond the bounds of the game.

It is important to note that the story was not posted on any SOE site and involved a mix of both original characters and story elements drawn from the game. In many ways it was a classic piece of fanfic, which has a long media history. Fans have been actively appropriating television, movie, and comic book imagery for years now and creating entirely new cultural products through rewriting characters and storylines. Henry Jenkins, in his fascinating study of the practice, states that "fans assert their own right to form interpretations, to offer evaluations, and to construct cultural canons. Undaunted by traditional conceptions of literary and intellectual property, fans raid mass culture, claiming its materials for their own use, reworking them as the basis for their own cultural creations and social interactions" (Jenkins 1992, 18).

What is clear is that it is precisely *unclear* whether or not corporations and authors have the legal right to take action against fan authors of this sort, or to act on reputational concerns that may arise in the course of creative production such as this. As several articles suggest, the legal status of noncommercial fan fiction and media reappropriation in general may fall quite notably outside the claims of IP that typically are used (J. Hughes 1999; Tushnet 1997; Madow 1993; Tussey 2001). Tushnet has argued, for example, that "the interest in the integrity of the characters is not an interest in market share, but a general reputational concern, which copyright law does not formally recognize" (1997, 22). This can be contrasted to trademark law which "does recognize reputational concerns, but copyright's special solicitude for parody demonstrates that its concern for creativity requires a different kind of analysis" (ibid.). Others have suggested that the noncommercial nature of fanfic puts it in a category of creative work to which the law grants wider latitude. The claims to authority over reputation here are also quite striking and the practices that must be deployed to secure this kind of control could be fairly pernicious. Tushnet argues that, "Fundamentally, the issue of character integrity is a dispute about how much control companies should exercise over how their images are received. If a line is not drawn at noncommerciality

when it comes to creative re-use of characters, then a fan's daydream is theoretically as illegitimate as the story she posts on the Web" (Tushnet 1997, 22).

Some who watched the unfolding of this story also noted what they saw as
a distinctly hypocritical stance to the company's position. It seemed to them
that *EQ* only allowed role-playing on SOE's terms—that while Mystere's dis-
turbing tale was troublesome and cause for alarm, all the other quite violent
and sexually explicit imagery in the world was permissible because it was
SOE's own content. As Scott Jennings, at the time writing as Lum the Mad and
now an employee at Mythic Entertainment noted,

Regardless, and again, if the side of the story we're hearing is the truth, Verant banned
someone for role-playing incorrectly . . . Everything is happy and perky, and most
importantly, child-safe in Norrath. There is no evil whatsoever. Ignore the mutilated
bodies of dwarves strewn liberally around Feerot. While you're at it, ignore the fact that
while dark elven males default to a fully dressed outfit, dark elven women default to
wearing skimpy bikinis. (Mulligan 2000c)

Eventually the company did decide they had acted severely and apologized
to the author, saying they would not actively pursue monitoring fan fiction
in the future.[10] While SOE expressed some regret about how the issue was
handled, both Mystere and the owner of an *EQ* fanfic site expressed understanding for the company's position and appeared to internalize the reputational argument (though the author never returned to the game . . . at least
under the old account). Goodwin quotes Mystere as saying, "I feel that the
initial response was heavy-handed. While I understand the need to protect a
company's image from social depravity (assuming, of course, a fiction story
could be considered socially depraved), I always like to work things out on an
individual basis." Safka Fairheart, the host of the fanfic site *Safka's Lore,* wrote:
"They [*EQ*] will not pursue authors for breach of intellectual copyright (which
is what we were concerned about), but they will be forced to consider their options should the boundaries of good taste be crossed by any given piece of *EQ*
fiction. That we feel is fair enough, that is their right, they have to act to protect their brand image" (Fairheart 2000). Player communities, rather than re-
futing the claims and domain of the game companies they deal with, more
often than not seem to accept and concede ground in the hopes of remaining
on good terms. This presents a complication to the framing of player culture
as one that presumes oppositional orientations first and foremost. Just as frequently fans are enmeshed in complicated relationships with game companies. Sometimes this is because of their reliance on them. But just as often it

can be tied to a desire to be legitimated by them (even to the extent of eventually being hired by the company) or deeper values about the "rightness" of commercial and market structures. Matt Hills's work points to the "curious co-existence within fan cultures of both *anti-commercial ideologies and commodity-completist practices*" (emphasis his, 2002, 28).

As one user later wrote, the banning reverberated through the community and calls into question not only the relationship users have to fan fiction and *EQ* but some of the broader questions of ownership of identity in this space:

> While it is true that Verant partly enabled me to introduce Nep [the character's name] to *EverQuest* by using the computer code to decide on Nep's looks, her gender, her stats, her race, her class and her religion, that really is only a limited start to developing a character. In order to role-play my character, it is necessary to flesh her out. Beyond the effects given by the software code, it's up to me to figure out what to do with her . . . What the computer will not and cannot do though is create a role for Nep set in the Norrathian history and geography, nor can it give her personality, speech, connections and relationships. I am her creator and it is both through my play and pleasure to develop those aspects for her in game and to more thoroughly solidify her existence through the use of the traditional role-play tools of background stories, current tales of adventures, art, poems, etc. . . . (Nepenthia 2000, 1)

The act of appropriation is but one of many ways media consumers try to creatively work with and through the cultural artifacts they encounter. Indeed their reworkings highlight the ways the bits and pieces of culture are quite malleable, open to multiple interpretations, and "made real" only through engagement with audiences. The idea that one might regulate all aspects of a media product and try to control and contain its meaning runs directly against what sociological and anthropological studies of culture teach us. While the company eventually apologized for the way in which they handled the matter, and even went so far as to suggest that they would not be monitoring fan fiction in the future, the precedent remains and the broader claims to reputational jurisdictions of the game were never challenged.

This renunciation of collaborative ownership is particularly striking when contrasted with *EverQuest*'s own use of common symbolic terrain. Norrath is a world populated by Orcs, large animate trees, Halflings, and other fantasy-derived imagery, all of which are quite familiar to anyone who has encountered J. R. R. Tolkien's stories. That lineage is further complicated by the fact that parts of Tolkien's imagery itself has links back to Celtic myths and other folklore.[11] *EverQuest* is a game filled with images and story lines deeply rooted in various fantasy traditions. The underlying play structures—of leveling, "rolling" for base statistics for characters, and other mechanics—existed prior to *EQ* as common game tropes. Indeed, Marks provides some powerful examples of the ways *EQ* designers have drawn explicitly on their previous gaming experiences. Bill Trost, one of *EQ*'s original designers, for example, even went so far as to incorporate characters and places from one of his *D&D* campaigns into the game. More playfully, he also mentions the way one of the characters in the game "Karg Icebear and his bear, Iceberg, were based on Yukon Cornelius and the Bumble from the '60s film Rudolph the Red-Nosed Reindeer" (Marks 2003, 88). As Marks notes, the result was "a multi-layered game, with references upon references that could be spotted by alert players" (ibid.). This raises the question of how *EQ* squares its own practice of authorship and reappropriation with its otherwise narrow claims of intellectual property.[12]

Quite interestingly, the use of established aesthetics and mechanics goes even deeper, to the very structure of the system. Several astute MUD developers noticed early on that *EQ* appeared strikingly similar to a type of MUD called DIKU. Indeed, even the underlying command structure for emoting is recognizably similar to many MUDs and the link between this newest version of a multiplayer space and its predecessors is readily apparent. After some investigation, sworn affidavits where given substantiating that the game was not explicitly built using DIKU source code. In a move many corporate entities would be well served to learn from, the DIKU community said they saw the similarity not as an infringement on, but a tribute to, their platform, writing that "The DIKU group is proud that 'the DIKU feeling' has found its way into a game as enjoyable and award winning as *EverQuest*" (DIKU MUD Web page 2000).

EverQuest quite reasonably has drawn on existing symbols and conventions, and to try to prohibit such forms of creative reappropriation is absurd.[13] Tushnet quotes Judge Kozinski of the Ninth Circuit on the matter of cultural production, writing that:

Overprotecting intellectual property is as harmful as underprotecting it. Creativity is impossible without a rich public domain. Nothing today, likely nothing since we tamed fire, is genuinely new: Culture, like science and technology, grows by accretion, each new creator building on the works of those who came before. Overprotection stifles the very creative forces it's supposed to nurture. (Tushnet 1997, 9)

Rich gaming traditions typically are not lost on designers who quite often can trace back in detail how a particular game builds on a previous one or how elements from a classic are incorporated as homage into a new environment (Asher 2001; Burka 1995; Damarr 2001; Koster 2002). The hitch in the argument (and in world-management practice) seems to be in extending the notion of collaborative cultural production to the users.

Productive Players and Remapping Ownership

With increasing frequency the notion that user-generated content can be tapped into for commercial products is circulating in development communities. Certainly games like *The Sims* have integrated this aspect into their design explicitly and player-produced content often is noted by the developers themselves as one of the key factors in the games' success (Bradshaw 2005). MMOG designers similarly have batted around the idea, and it often is seen as providing a model for building more interesting and dynamic spaces. But as Dave "Fargo" Kosak, in a 2002 article at the GameSpy Web site anticipates, "sometime in the next five years, expect a couple of legal battles involving user-created content. If you create something spectacular within a game world, is that your property? Or does it belong forever to the game publisher? More importantly, who owns your online persona? Chew on that!" (Kosak 2002).

While in previous chapters I discuss the ways players contribute to the game through their labor on third-party sites, and the ways they foster emergent culture within the game, the notion that players are productive is becoming even more formalized into game systems. Sal Humphreys suggests that *EverQuest* players,

in their passionate, voluntary and willing participation hold particular kinds of power as well. The reliance of Sony and other game developers on player communities for content creation of various forms—both the tangible and the more intangible social forms—means they are subject to the goodwill of these player communities. (2005, 46)

The trend to enlist player communities in the explicit production of the game or additional game content is hitting its stride. John Banks's (2002) fascinating study of the Australian game-development company Auran examines its adaptation to, and success with, actively utilizing the player base for their *Trainz* simulator software. In Stephen Kline, Nick Dyer-Witheford, and Greig DePeuter's valuable book (2003) on the development of the game industry, they trace the long history of enlisting player communities into production processes, resulting in the emergence of the "prosumer." Hector Postigo (2003) similarly explores the contribution "modders" (those who modify and alter games) and player-driven game innovations make to the industry, suggesting companies are benefiting from a sizable amount of unpaid labor. While there are serious questions to be raised about both the avidity and ease with which post-industrial capital seems to have accommodated otherwise unruly audiences, the voluntary "free labor" being produced in these communities cannot be written off easily nor simply deemed alienated. It has become central to the success of these companies and, indeed, enjoyable to many players. Tiziana Terranova suggests that "Rather than capital 'incorporating' from the outside the authentic fruits of the collective imagination, it seems more reasonable to think of cultural flows as originating within a field that is always and already capitalistic" (2000, 38). Whether it is bundling tools to allow players to produce game modifications or providing them mechanisms to share content from their own play experience, players can be formally enrolled as productive agents at multiple levels.[14] Some virtual worlds are relying centrally on user-produced content for their space. Cory Ondrejka, vice president of product development for Linden Research, makers of the popular player-produced virtual world *Second Life,* notes that expansive growth in the market will be possible "if its users are given the power to collaboratively create content within it, if those users receive broad rights to their creations and if they can convert those creations into real world capital and wealth" (2004, 83).

Despite some interesting moves within development communities to reckon with their players as agents within the construction of the product, we continue to have much heavily tilting to the power of corporate authorship claims and little commensurate responsibility required. If indeed companies want to retain all the privileges of being primary owners of these worlds and insist on retaining narrow formulations of how game-space is constituted, do they then have corresponding sets of responsibilities to their user base? In a recent story on *EverQuest,* Robert Pfister, senior producer on the game, noted:

Managing *EverQuest,* we often feel like the mayor of the place, since the game operates a lot like a medium-sized city. It has an infrastructure, a political system, an economic system; it has holidays, geography, and events. It has laws that are enforced, even its own type of health and safety system. And most important of all, it has a population. People live there, they elect representatives, they perform their jobs, they make new friends and stay in touch with old ones. (Humble 2004, 25)

As a technology, a game, and a media product, *EQ* sits along several rails, ranging from the commercial to a more generalized sense of communal space (as we have seen in cases presented in this book and in this quote). Peter Jenkins's article (2004) on virtual worlds as "company towns" intersects here quite nicely. He recounts the U.S. Supreme Court case of *Marsh v. Alabama,* which turned on the status of Chickasaw, a company town owned by Gulf Ship-building in which most of its workers lived. As he points out, like Chickasaw one of the most salient questions facing these games is whether or not they "are more like community associations, clubs, condominiums and other private organizations or do they on the other hand assume a 'public function' which satisfies the requirements of the state action doctrine," in other words, the threshold point for First Amendment rights (2004, 3). An inquiry around participation and accountability is especially provocative if the notion of these environments as lifeworlds—something evidenced repeatedly both in how players understand their involvement with the game and in the company's own framing of the space—is taken seriously. How far exactly can Pfister's mayor comparison be taken? Should users have meaningful rights to, and in, the game world? Or the development of its culture and structure? A voice in its management? Should game companies be meaningfully accountable to their users?

As we have seen on the subject of women and gaming, there is a fair amount of frustration at developers for not addressing user concerns and critiques around representation. Many women express dismay at the way their avatars look and simply must "live with" the avatar images—the bodies—they are given. Must game companies bear a burden in meaningfully responding to their player base? What forms of accountability come with running a game world? While it is an easy path simply to claim full authorship, it is much more challenging to face potential responsibilities that would come from such a claim. I do not want to argue that cooperative ownership of game artifacts lets world developers "off the hook" or that we need virtual environments governed by paternalistic administrators "responsible" for their users. I do, however, want to raise an inquiry about whether or not the systems we see now are ones in which corporate owners want to have their cake and eat it too.

Given the intense ways users are living and embodying themselves in these virtual environments, we need to develop more complex ideas about the life of digital cultural artifacts, joint ownership, and the autonomy of user experience. The current turn toward privileging corporate interests above the creative independent and collaborative work of users is setting up worrisome precedents. While this chapter calls for a broader view of cultural production, to dismiss it as simply impossible given the "fact" of existing copyright law and notions of authorship would be shortsighted. If anything we need clearer representations of the flexible nature of legal understandings and analysis grounded in a recognition that our current property regimes are historically mediated, contextually specific, and not without politics.

James Boyle (1996) provides important historical context to the debate around authorship and property and traces the varied ways formulations come to be in dialogue with legal verdicts and legislation. Ultimately, as Tushnet argues, the intent of copyright is for the promotion of culture and the benefit of the public. She writes that:

> People should be able to participate actively in the creative aspects of the world around them. When most creative output is controlled by large corporations, freedom to modify and elaborate on existing characters is necessary to preserve a participatory element in popular culture. Copyright's purpose, after all, is to encourage creativity for the public interest, not only to ensure monopoly profits. (Tushnet 1997, 29)

Lawrence Lessig further articulates the complications that arise when we enter the terrain of overzealously protecting property rights. He cautions us to consider the implications of the control regimes we currently seem to be setting up by suggesting that "we stand on the edge of an era that demands we make fundamental choices about what life in this space, and therefore life in real space, will be like. These choices will be made; there is no nature here to discover. And when they are made, the values we hold sacred will either influence our choices or be ignored" (Lessig 1999, 220).

EverQuest has boasted the tagline "You're in our world now," and over time many users came to cite this as summing up not simply the experience of virtual-world immersion but a problematic management stance in which the definition of whose world it was actually ended up negating their (often valuable) experience and input. Typically termed "the vision" (as in the meta-vision of gameplay), this phrase also has been reframed by some users into the "Victims of The Vision™" tagline, suggesting that various imperatives—be they legal concerns, marketing strategies, or even game mechanics—often run roughshod over actual players. As Mulligan and Patrovsky note regarding the general "vision thing":

> It does not normally allow for flexibility or change based on the actual play styles of for-pay gamers. No designer or team of designers could possibly hope to close all the holes or find and fix all the flaws in a PW [persistent-world] design; the collective intelligence

of a player base in the thousands or tens of thousands dictates that any design hole or flaw will be found and exploited. On top of that, the collective intelligence of the players also dictates that they will find ways to play your design within the rules you have set and coded, but in ways you never expected. (2003, 161)

The social, political, and design implications such an emergent system suggests is not only one of the most challenging but most exciting aspects of these spaces.

In June 2004, SOE invited seventy players to their offices in San Diego, California, for a Guild Summit. While *EverQuest* designers and community managers long have been meeting the more general player population at Fan Faires, this event was organized with the explicit intent of player input on the game and design decisions. Participants were brought in for several days of socializing, tours, and meetings with the game developers. Following on the heels of the disappointing *Gates of Discord* expansion to the game, the summit provided selected players an opportunity to provide direct feedback and input, though in reading the reports it also seemed just as much an opportunity to let players peek into the everyday work of running the game. Some participants brought prewritten material outlining frustrations with the game, others noted in their online post-event reports how they sometimes tried to get together to present a united voice on a subject. As might be expected, though, there was not always agreement about issues among the players participating. The event was widely reported, and it launched fairly extensive discussions on various Web sites. While there were certainly some skeptical comments or feelings of dissatisfaction within the larger player community, from all the reports I read the event's actual participants felt quite pleased with the outcome. The discussions appear to have been focused on fundamental game-design issues—how can augmentations be improved, is NPC artificial intelligence being worked on, can more dynamic content be introduced—rather than the broader concerns about process, rights, or ownership that fill the minds of researchers and theorists. Several message-board commentators noted how much less attention was given to mid-to-lower or casual player's concerns, and in this regard it is worth being clear about how the subset of players invited— leaders of high-level guilds, fan Web site operators, longtime players—influences its role as a representational mechanism. Of course, such an event serves several purposes in that while the players give feedback, the company also has the opportunity to do a kind of soft PR. Certainly the goodwill generated by the positive write-ups of the event should not be underestimated. Nonetheless, it provides a preliminary attempt at enfranchising the player community, and it will be interesting to see if it is continued regularly in the future.

The introduction of the Guild Summit, and the notion that player representatives might come together with company representatives to discuss (and maybe someday deliberate and design?) puts an interesting spin on the notion of governance. Raph Koster, former chief creative officer at SOE, wrote a piece several years ago entitled "Declaring the Rights of Players" (2000). It is both a playful and provocative imagination of what player rights might look like in virtual environments. As such, it is a fascinating map of the various arguments that surround the debate. In it he prompts designers and those interested in game worlds to imagine what applying something like France's Declaration of the Rights of Man and of the Citizens or the U.S. Constitution's Bill of Rights to avatars. The results of his thought experiment led to proclamations such as "No avatar shall be accused, muzzled, toaded, jailed, banned, or otherwise punished except in the cases and according to the forms prescribed by the code of conduct" (Koster 2000). What is, of course, typically "black-boxed" are codes of conduct, all too often vaguely defined or unspecified notions of "vision" or "essence" ultimately governed and regulated by the game company. What might raise the stakes fruitfully is opening this up to the community—a community broadly defined as made up of designers *and* players? While progressive ideas exist for integrating players in more interesting ways, most designers find themselves operating in organizational contexts that give serious weighting to legal and promotional departments who may see the interests of the product quite differently. Often innovative design choices are mediated by other institutional stakeholders and thus we cannot simply hope for designers to solve this issue alone. Serious attention must be given to the gap that may exist between design desires and corporate interest in the given models of property and authorship. In addition to changes in design practice, there must be a simultaneous move toward more progressive understandings of intellectual property, product identity, and the status of players as active coproducers of the worlds they inhabit. Examining the collective construction of culture—which, it must be said, turns on constant acts of reappropriation by *all* parties—introduces useful provocations for the analysis of games.

6 The Future of Persistent Worlds and Critical Game Studies

We have reached an interesting moment in the development of persistent virtual worlds. Compared to the idiosyncratic MUDs or social-avatar worlds many of us built or studied ten or more years ago, virtual worlds have gone mass market. Games like *EQ* and *World of Warcraft* have popularized virtual reality far beyond any dreams LambdaMOO or head-mounted displays may have produced. The field of MMOG studies seems to me to be both one step ahead and one step behind past virtual environments (VE) and the Internet studies that emerged from that period. It is one step ahead in that practices like eBaying have brought the boundary question—between "real" and "virtual"—to the fore and raised issues around regulation and community status much more quickly than Usenet (the large-scale Internet message board system) or MUDs did. When scholars, developers, and the public see people going online to buy and sell game items for "real money," they are confronted with the notion that sometimes our "virtual" spaces leak over into our "real" worlds, and the nature of concepts like ownership in shared multiuser space are not a given.

I am concerned, however, that there is an emerging notion that we can, or should, reconstitute that boundary—between real and virtual, game and nongame—thereby solving the deeper social and regulatory issues that can nag us. Katie Salen and Eric Zimmerman, well-known game designers, draw on the work of Johan Huizinga in suggesting that there is a space, often termed a "magic circle," bounded off from nonplay space that people step into for the purposes of the game. They argue that "The fact that the magic circle is just that—a circle—is an important feature of this concept. As a closed circle, the space it circumscribes is enclosed and separate from the real world" (Salen and Zimmerman 2004, 95). The language is meant to evoke the special attitude players take when entering the game world, the acceptance of rules that may not have correlates in "real life," the agreement to adhere to a new kind of fictional structure for play. While the notion of a magic circle can be a powerful tool for understanding some aspects of gaming, the language can hide (and even mystify) the much messier relationship that exists between spheres—especially in the realm of MMOGs. Salen and Zimmerman suggest that this boundary is open or closed depending on the approach used to understand the game, that is, whether viewed through the lens of rules, play, or culture. Though they give much attention to the cultural life of games, there remains a somewhat implicit divide at work in their model, that rules can be untangled from the other categories. The idea that somehow—be it to preserve the magic circle and "free play," to tidy up tricky property rights questions, or to ease an anxiety born of the space's indeterminacy—we can shore up the line between the virtual and real world or between game and nongame seems to pop up more frequently in conversation (and sometimes scholarship). It often sounds as if for play to have any authenticity, meaning, freedom, or pleasure, it must be cordoned off from "real life." In this regard, MMOG (and, more generally, game) studies has much to learn from past scholarship. Thinking of either game or nongame space as contained misses the flexibility of both. If we look at online spaces historically, for example, we find people negotiating levels of self-disclosure and performance, multiple forms of embodiment, the integration of dual (or multiple) communities, webs of technologies, and the importing of meaningful offline issues and values into online spaces.

In much the same way there was an exoticism infused in some early Internet research, current discussion around MMOGs at times seems to be drawing on the same motifs. But approaches that rely on "fantastical" stories may prevent a more nuanced understanding of player's relationships with these games as a kind of everyday technology. Our relationships with technological objects are always moving closer to the mundane. In fact, we might even say these objects are *always* mundane. Despite advertising ploys that often seek to create stories of magical technologies, as we have seen in this book actual users are engaged in much more grounded practices with the technologies they encounter. We integrate systems into our everyday lives and, in turn, into our everyday social networks and practices. It is not that new phenomena never (or simply) appear, but that they emerge in relationship to a web of practices, technologies, networks, structures, attitudes, and a range of actors other than ourselves. Rather than adopting the language of advertising (new! best! brightest! fastest!), the challenge ahead involves exploring grounded practices, the structural conditions of production and use, and the real ways players make sense of these spaces. To imagine we can segregate these things—game and nongame, social and game, on- and offline, virtual and real—not only misunderstands our relationship with technology, but our relationship with culture.

My call then is for nondichotomous models. One of the biggest lessons from Internet studies is that the boundary between online and offline life is messy, contested, and constantly under negotiation. Issues around gender or race, for example, do not simply fall away online but get imported into the new space in complicated ways (Kendall 2002; Kolko 2000; McDonough 1999; Nakamura 2002). Economist Edward Castronova has argued for the serious consideration that play is in danger of being overrun by fatal encroachments from the "Earth" world of law, taxes, policing, and the like: "When Earth's culture dominates, the game will be over, the fantasy will be punctured and the illusion will be ended for good [. . .] Living *there* will no longer be any different from living *here,* and a great opportunity to play the game of human life under different, fantastical rules will have been lost" (emphasis his; 2004, 196). I am very sympathetic to the underlying intent here—the maintenance of spaces of experimentation and the invaluable role of play in our lives.[1] I worry, however, that the idea there is a place called "game" that can somehow be separate from "Earth's culture" fails to capture the nature of both. I also am not so sure that kind of division is what necessarily leads to experimentation and innovation. Ultimately, notions that games can become contaminated by the outside world, that they are separate from "real life," or that they are only something with no real consequence seem to lack resonance with the stories like those presented in this book. Of course, we could just choose to move MMOGs out of the "game" category, but I find it much more interesting to see if there are problems with the definition itself. There still seems to me something at stake in whether or not we bestow on MMOGs the label "game."

The competing memes that Castronova proposes ("virtual worlds are play spaces" and "virtual worlds are extensions of the Earth") present a false dichotomy (ibid.). MMOGs are particularly good at simultaneously tapping into what is typically formulated as game/not game, social/instrumental, real/virtual. And this mix is *exactly* what is evocative and hooks many people. The innovations they produce there are a result of MMOGs as vibrant sites of culture, and we inhabit—indeed embody—culture constantly. Rather than seeing that as a detriment or a potential hazard, the process of creating culture is exactly how we perform interesting experimentations. Only when we really acknowledge these spaces as legitimate and powerful sites of production, and acknowledge the diverse agents involved in their creation, can we begin to address the challenges facing them progressively.

When all is said and done though is it just "complicated" and "messy," irreducible to any and all categories? Do we not need to be able to put x in one box and y in another? Does game structure matter at all? Absolutely, structure (and by extension, designers) play an incredible role in shaping culture. But we need a nuanced understanding of the relationship between structure and culture, between the formalizations the designers set up and emergent practices and patterns. Henry Jenkins's caution against oversimplifying poles is instructive. He writes of his own work in examining the "interactive audience" that:

In doing so, I hope to move beyond the either-or logic of traditional audience research—refusing to see media consumers as either totally autonomous from nor totally vulnerable to the culture industries. It would be naive to assume that powerful conglomerates will not protect their own interests as they enter this new media marketplace, but at the same time, audiences are gaining greater power and autonomy as they enter into the new knowledge culture. The interactive audience is more than a marketing concept and less than "semiotic democracy." (Jenkins 2002)

And is there any danger in too much "real world" seeping in? If critical Internet studies (not to mention broader work on technology and culture) can teach us anything, it is that there is no firm line between these multiple worlds we move through. Keeping the real world out is not the battle to be won or lost. That is, I think, held on the terrain of equity, justice, fairness, and innovation. We do not shed culture when we go online and enter game worlds, nor do designers create these incredible spaces in a vacuum. And this is a good thing. Culture is what we are and what we do, and understanding the varying ways *all* participants are productive is one of our best tools in making sense of what emerges.

The cultural often is the unarticulated component hiding below many of the debates we currently see rising to the surface in this field. Rather than thinking narrowly about how property or speech should be regulated, what would it look like to ask how much *culture* should be regulated? Or, even better, how much culture *can* be regulated, and through what forms? This is the framework that has been skipped over, and there remains much work to be done exploring the sometimes unruly nature of culture, its emergent quality in MMOGs, the labor of productive players within distinctly social contexts, modes of control (both formal and informal), and the possibilities for reconciliation in commercial frameworks. I am not suggesting, of course, that everything important emerges solely from players and that developers, or the structures they create, are somehow secondary characters in this story. MMOG designers and developers inform potentialities for play and life in powerful ways. They act as economists, philosophers, political scientists, and sociologists (Callon 1991; Kling 1996; Winner 1980). Beyond the structures they create, the objects that populate these worlds (including avatars, our bodies in virtual spaces) are material to work with and matter deeply. But how might we begin to explore in more depth the relationship between the various actors we find within game culture? How do not only developers but players make up the game space, and how are those very categories undermined to some degree when we begin to take emergent culture seriously? This book has sought to provide some initial findings by taking a close look at *EverQuest*.

Players Are Producers

Consider the range of material productions players are engaged in: the creation of game guides, walk-throughs, answers to frequently asked questions (FAQs), maps, object and monster databases, third-party message boards and mailing lists, play norms, server guidelines, modifications, plug-ins, strategies and strategy guides, auctions/trading, tweaks to user interfaces (UI), macro sharing, fanfic, game movies, counter-narratives, comics, and fan gatherings. The idea of the passive reception of media has been the focus of much critique over the last two decades (Ang 1991; Fiske 1989; Hall, Hobson, Lowe, and Willis 1980; H. Jenkins 1992; Radway 1991), and certainly we see MMOG players actively engaged in creating the game worlds they inhabit. These are worlds in which "gameness" is deeply woven together with the social and the co-constructive work of players. We can tally up everything from the very obvious (the creation of walk-throughs and quest guides) to the less tangible but often quite powerful (local server cultures). Players not only have been enlisted in formal (unpaid) beta testing, but on live servers continue to act as an (unpaid) quality assurance (QA) force. I semi-emphasize "unpaid" here because it is worth noting the incredible amount of labor gamers contribute. Somewhere between America Online volunteer lawsuits and preprofessional modding we need good accounts that help us understand the passionate engagement of players and how to attend to it fairly.

Play Is Diverse and Socially Situated

As we have seen by looking at power gamers, families who play together, and women gamers, there is a diversity of play forms. Quite often the styles are contextually specific such that people choose particular characters in relation to who they want to group up with or what kind of activity they want to do during that gaming session. Bart Simon (2004) lays out one interesting model of the range of ways players may be oriented to the gaming moment: playing with others, playing next to others, playing with others online, playing alone. Rather than simply black-boxing the play moment, he prompts us to think about the multiple and varying contexts that always will be at work when someone sits down to engage with a game. Within this examination of *EQ* alone we can point to exploration, power gaming, socializing, role-playing, griefing, goal(s)-orientation, one-time-only groupings, raids of 50+ people, playing with partners/children/parents/friends, playing alone on a Monday night or at 5 p.m. on a Saturday, playing with a 56k modem or a 256MB graphics card, being a newbie or a former FPS player, multi-boxing, playing in co-located spaces, and guild membership. Using terms like "fun," for example, may not help us understand the diverse pleasures some players find in very instrumental or work-like play, the ways complex social organization can mediate the game experience, or the varying forms of success for a given play session. Also, despite all kinds of "minimum system requirement" disclaimers, players enter game spaces with diverse technological setups and knowledge. Ultimately in any given session a player may cycle through several varieties of orientation—solo, grouping, goal-oriented, free-play and/or be enmeshed in layered technologies and other media of varying type/quality (in addition to the game itself, Web pages, third-party helper applications, high-end PCs to those that nearly go up in flames when more than two avatars come into the field of view) and/or participate in multiple and varying social configurations that extend to offline space.

Play is situational and reliant not simply on abstract rules but also on social networks, attitudes, or events in one's non/game life, technological abilities or limits, structural affordances or limits, local cultures, and personal understandings of leisure. The flexibility at work here moves in several directions. *EQ* as a game is subject to specific contexts but it simultaneously shapes them also. The challenge for those of us interested in studying MMOG spaces is that they often are moving targets, as are their player communities. They seem to resist closure in any overarching way. Rather than being daunted by this, we can find paths into the study of these games by paying close attention to their contextual and provisional natures, as well as the practices in and around them.

Rules Are Often Contextual and Contested

Despite the common notion that computer games lock down modes of play via the system, rules and norms can be, especially in the case of MMOGs, incredibly contextual, socially negotiated, heterogeneous, ambiguous, and quite often contradictory between players. Linda Hughes argues that within traditional games "Game rules can be interpreted and reinterpreted toward preferred meanings and purposes, selectively invoked or ignored, challenged or defended, changed or enforced to suit the collective goals of different groups of players. In short, players can take the same game and collectively make it strikingly different experiences" (1999, 94). It's not that play is either rule or nonrule based but a question of *whose* rules in *which* contexts. Consider aspects like *ShowEQ,* player auctions, camping, pathing and bug exploits, ever increasing level caps, multiple formal play paths, game "enhancing" plug-ins, third-party resources, PvP versus PvE contexts, or role-players confronting power gamers. In MMOGs we see emergent and contingent rule structures, influenced not only via the formal system but by everything from personal gaming histories to local server cultures.

Mulligan and Patrovsky (2003) put out a strong challenge for designers to rethink how they view games. They argue that far too often developers are not able to untangle themselves from the game they have been working on. They argue that players will engage with it on their own terms. This contextual notion of play is important, as it prompts us to consider the ways players and player communities actively shape their own experiences. We need to make sure we recognize the different layers of actors and wide contexts, from the individual player on up to formal groups, as well as the various degrees of freedom any given system provides—these allow us to more accurately think about how these configurations prompt emergent rule sets. This is not to argue that powerful structures, rules, and norms cannot be found in any given MMOG. They can, absolutely. And indeed this is part of the work of culture. Models that rest on emergence or the co-construction of game space should not be equated with "anarchy." Indeed, some of the most powerful norms and rules we see in *EQ* come from the community itself. My call is for more examination of the variety of agents and variables that go into the creation of order in games, the mechanisms of enrollment and sanctioning, the places where they are challenged, and the ways they change over time.

Cocreation and Participatory Culture

Most of my previous points are not unfamiliar to developers and designers. Indeed, I must confess that throughout this work I often have felt in the position of one trailing after hard lessons many designers have learned on the job and as part of their long involvement in the field. As John Law recounts of his early research, "we were often simply rediscovering, or re-articulating, what was already clear in the practice, and not infrequently in the talk, of engineers and systems builders" (2000, 3). Game designers know all too well how unruly player populations can be. The question becomes how do we proceed from that fact? I think there is an emerging tendency to try to retrofit complex social systems into tidy mechanical models, which leads to a preoccupation with creating worlds that can be constantly monitored, tuned, regulated, and controlled. The dream of perfectly balanced game mechanics spreads out to encompass players and the culture of the game. Not only are the formal components of the system imagined to be infinitely regulatable, but the individual players themselves through their location within the system are presumed to be as well. Indeed we might even say this colonization, where hyper-rationalization begins to infiltrate all arenas, follows from the pursuit of system balance since there is, in fact, no clean line between mechanics and players, system and culture.

I can see the appeal this has for working game producers. It certainly would make life much easier if the game could be micromanaged to such a precise degree, if unauthorized behavior just could be "balanced" out of the system. Game researchers are sometimes also drawn to such a dream. Though the language often invokes problems like "cheating," "griefing," or disruption of the "magic circle" or community, I would suggest that the underlying anxiety about unruliness, subversion, and the emergent nature of these spaces needs to be addressed more fully. Rather than simply being frustrated about players who do not play a game "right" or who "mess up" otherwise perfect systems,

I would argue we need to take seriously the range of interventions that occur and why. Players are social laborers and act as central productive agents in game culture—more progressive models are needed for understanding and integrating their work in these spaces. As Sue Morris notes, "While the concept of 'participatory media' is familiar from research into television communities, I would argue that these games are 'co-creative media'; neither developers nor players can be solely responsible for producing the final assemblage regarded as 'the game,' it requires the input of both" (2004, 4). What might it look like to move from models emphasizing (community) "management" to more participatory modes? How can we begin to validate game culture, and what models of governance are in accord with doing so?

Participatory Futures?

The word "participatory" might raise red flags for some designers. The idea that players can act as meaningful agents within the overarching game structure is generally seen as naive.[2] But let me reframe this: players *already are* core actors in the maintenance and life of the game. There is no culture, there is no game, without the labor of the players. Whether designers want to acknowledge it fully or not, MMOGs *already are* participatory sites (if only partially realized) by their very nature as social and cultural spaces. Of all design challenges, of all authorship or ownership challenges to face the field, is this not one of the most interesting?

So what are some of the bumps in the road in pursing radical design approaches? What hinders full recognition (and subsequent considerations) of the participatory nature of MMOGs? Brand identity remains one of the most underexplored aspects of these games and something that deeply intersects this issue. As we have seen, *EverQuest* had some early wrangling with users over the very identity of the game. This is not just a matter of narrative/play control but folded back into everything from age ratings to marketing strategies and imagined demographics. Even if some designers are willing to let go of controlling the identity of the game, can the corporate structures they (and their games) are embedded in turn the game over to the players? As we can see from *EQ*, the meaningful incorporation of players into the very heart of the game remains at times quite contested. What does design look like when it takes seriously the emergent properties of a game, including the very question of what it is? This certainly can twist back into the ownership question but raising it around brand identity may give us another path into considering these games within a larger context.

We also might ask how the size of games like *EQ* shape the question of participatory models. I admit, a number of years ago the notion of the metaverse (à la Neal Stephenson's vision of connected worlds presented in his 1992 novel *Snow Crash*) was compelling to me at some level (and to many virtual world designers). But now I wonder, is massive always good? Does striving for the huge market, the one-game-to-rule-them-all, back designers into a corner when it comes to innovation? Raph Koster has noted the adjustments that come with the switch from smaller MUDs to big products like *Star Wars Galaxies:* "I was used to talking through issues with players and arriving at a consensus on things. That's impossible with a user base as large as the big commercial graphical worlds get. We try anyway—spend lots and lots of time on the boards discussing things, posted philosophical essays explaining why we were doing things, and so on. But it's an uphill battle" (Asher 2001, 1). Might there be ways—structural, economic, organizational—in which smaller game worlds are at an advantage in exploring participatory practices, innovative forms of government, or even radical design challenges more easily?

As MMOGs become key spaces of social life, and as they are simultaneously sites of cultural production, we must reckon with the ways they may at times serve as a form of public space. In much the same way the notion of a "town square" has been displaced onto privatized arenas like malls (even to the extent that mall architectures may try to symbolically tap into that mythos), MMOGs increasingly are acting as prime venues for a configuration of the "public." Yet how that might be reconciled with commercialization raises another set of questions. As several examples in this book show, players often take a much more expansive approach to their play—both in how they think about it and what they actually do when they game. The relationship between game player as consumer and as citizen seems to be another site at which we might fruitfully challenge simple dichotomies. As we can see in *EQ,* gamers never are simply consuming a product they have purchased off the shelf.

As we attend to the productive action of players, those moments when they move beyond the framework of simple consumption, the immense amount of labor they engage in is highlighted. This can range from volunteer game "guide" programs to the creation of much-needed technical interventions (such as UI plug-ins). Some speak of all this work as part of the gift economy, while others (often former volunteers) feel it falls more along the lines of employment.

The legal and design challenges that emerge from the productive engagement of players in the commercial viability of these spaces is not trivial.

While there are important issues to understand around the ways game worlds are governed formally by underlying game structure, designers/corporate practices, or laws, we need much more work on the ways informal systems of control and regulation exist between players, as well as in the complicated relationship developers have with varying members of their communities. Even without a formal "heavy hand," player communities still construct ideas about what is normal and what warrants stigma, they still deploy status and hierarchies, and they often self-regulate based on a kind of internal imagined dialogue with designers and corporations.

Games As Technology and Transmedial Phenomena

And in the end, what of this game that I and thousands of others have been engaged with for so many years? Writing this book has been a bit like trying to describe a moving object, one which, the moment I think I have a handle on it, slightly morphs. When I look back at my first forays into the subject I am struck by how much the game has changed since it began. I briefly considered trying to tally up a list of the significant developments and changes since I began playing and quickly felt daunted. It was clear there were just so many I was bound to overlook something. John Smedley, in the face of the huge *World of Warcraft* launch, released a statement on the *EQ* Web site asking about the future of MMOGs, prompting players to consider some new questions:

What if you could have families in MMO's? Virtual Children . . . What if your characters could have children and pass on the family name . . . What if players could build fantastic dungeons that become part of the worlds we create with tools we give them? (2005).

Even now those who continue the formal development of the game seem themselves to acknowledge its mutable character. I am sure that by the time you hold this book in your hands several points I make will be rendered obsolete by new expansion releases, new player productions, and new practices (both within the design and gamer communities). In the face of its competition the game further changes, with servers being joined together and new features being added. Most striking are the moments when changes to the game are quite at odds with how it previously defined itself.

While I have tried to signal it in various fashions, the artifact of *EverQuest* itself is not only constantly changing but contextually rendered by different actors. The story of *EQ* is simultaneously always about the development of a technology and how it is (re)produced over time among not only its formal developers, but other organizational entities, players, as well as against and in relation to competitor games. The game's first designers involved themselves with one iteration, the Live Team with another, and the legal and marketing departments understand the object in their own ways. The players, who bring with them a diverse set of histories and practices through which they engage with the entity called *EverQuest* then cycle into the picture, as does the fact that the game exists within a much larger market in which alternative designs and practices are instantiated in a competitive market. The simple punch line, you see, is *EverQuest* is not just one thing nor easily contained in the object that came off the shelf in 1999. In some ways we might think of it as a boundary object.[3] Bowker and Star suggest that "Boundary objects are those objects that both inhabit several communities of practice and satisfy the informational requirements of each of them. Boundary objects are thus both plastic enough to adapt to local needs and constraints of the several parties employing them, yet robust enough to main a common identity across sites" (1999, 297). The focus on the ways artifacts circulate in and are created through particular and multiple communities of practice—lending to what Bowker and Star call an ecological understanding of phenomena—is central to the story I want to tell about the game.[4]

The game also has been one of the most energetic in launching itself into transmedial space. On my shelves sit not only the traditional boxed PC version of *EQ* and all its various expansions, but hardbound books detailing the pen-and-paper rule set, *EverQuest Online Adventures* for PS2 (the Sony Playstation 2 console version of the game), *Champions of Norrath* (a PS2 implementation of the game in an action RPG form), and a comic book based on the world of Norrath. If I wanted to, I could go to the SOE Web site and order a version of the game for my mobile phone, and even some ringtones to go along with it. And, of course, there is *EverQuest 2.* With all these versions of the game, the figurines, the spiral-bound *EQ* map book, the puzzle, the published strategy guides, the T-shirts and watches and baseball caps, it is clear this is a world that has a life far beyond the simple product that comes out of the box. Whether it is in the realm of "official" releases and SOE-produced products, the emergent culture generated by the players, or the dynamic space always in between, *EverQuest* is something more than what we typically think when we call it "just a game."

Glossary

Buffing   When a player casts beneficial spells on themselves or another player, result-ing in some statistics (intelligence, mana, hit points, etc.—see below) being raised.

Class   A term within role-playing games (including nondigital tabletop varieties) that refers to various categories of skill and/or profession (for example, Hunter, War-rior, Magician).

HP   Hit points. A statistic which, generally speaking, designates the amount of health you have (when a character reaches 0 HP, it dies).

INT   Intelligence. A statistic used to formulate the amount of mana (see below) pos-sessed and how quickly a character can progress in certain in-game skills.

KoS   Kill on sight. The condition upon which a character will be attacked immedi-ately, even without any provocation, by an NPC (see below).

KS   Kill steal, also kill stealer. The act of jumping into a fight already underway and trying to kill a monster already engaged in battle with another player or group of play-ers. If the person kill stealing does enough damage to the monster they then reap the experience points and any items on the creature.

Levels/leveling (lvl)   Numeric stages of progression signaling advancement in the game the player goes through.

Live team   The group of people (ranging from development to customer support) that takes over the game at launch and manages it once it is online and open to players.

Mana   A depletable, but renewable, component required to cast spells. A kind of "magic reservoir." The supply of mana is based on the amount of intelligence points (see above) a character has.

Mob   Monsters, creatures, or any other nonplayer characters (see below) in the game.

NPC   Nonplayer character. An entity in the world that is not controlled by another player but instead "driven" by the game's artificial intelligence system. NPCs can take the form of anything from a marketplace vendor to the largest and deadliest creature in the game. All mobs (see above) are therefore also NPCs, but this term refers to a more general class while "mob" specifies an object intended for a fight.

Plat   Platinum. The highest denomination of currency in the game.

Port   Instantaneous transportation, either by spell or using the automated system within the game.

Race   A term within role-playing games (including nondigital tabletop varieties) that refers to various species categories (for example, Elf, Human, Troll).

Raid   A large collection of players gathered together generally to undertake a particularly difficult or challenging battle or quest.

.sig   A signature, in either text or picture form, attached by the author to the bottom of e-mail or message-board postings.

SoW   Spirit of Wolf. A beneficial spell that increases the speed at which the character can run.

Stats   Statistics. Numerical formulations of properties like intelligence, mana, hit points, magical qualities, and a wide variety of other attributes attached to artifacts, monsters, and players in the game.

Train   A group of monsters in attack mode, running in a line or close cluster, generally after a fleeing player.

Training   The act, either intentional or deliberate, of starting a train which then overruns other players, often resulting in mass deaths.

XP   Experience, as in accumulating the experience points ("xping") necessary to progress through the levels of the game.

Notes

Chapter 1

1. All participant, server, and guild names in this book (including my own) have been given pseudonyms except in cases of material written where an author clearly intended it to have broader public consumption (as in the case of some message-board postings).

2. In retrospect I can see how my lack of identification with the term "gamer" is not unlike that experienced by many women. As I think back over my history with games, I can recount engagement with everything from board games to arcade machines to PC games, yet somehow I never quite self-identified as a gamer. As I discuss more in the chapter on women and gaming (chapter 4) however, there are many ways women's play is rendered invisible—to others and even to themselves sometimes—and I now see this lack of identification with the term "gamer" as tied to both how the identity is typically formulated and my own relationship to a broader game culture.

3. The number of servers the game runs has grown over time and likely will contract a bit too. Even now, faced with changing numbers in the player base and competition from other MMOGs, some servers are being consolidated.

4. A quick note on language. In past work I felt it was particularly important to remain vigilant about not reifying the boundary distinction between the "real" and the "virtual" by even using these terms. Much of my concern came from a particular historical moment in cyberspace theory during the 1990s in which the battle over "othering" experience by relegating it to the "virtual" took on heightened meaning given the way Internet technology and experience still occupied a kind of marginal form. I think the stakes have changed dramatically with the growing pervasiveness, indeed mundaneness, of things like online communication and Internet-based communities. While I tend to still substitute words like "corporeal" and "digital" for "real" and "virtual" when talking about bodies/avatars, I am less concerned now with the rhetorical power calling these online environments "virtual worlds" presents. We are simply too far along in the integration of these spaces into everyday life for that language to hold the kind of meaning it once did.

5. At the time of this writing I have several, though I have only played two with any real focus.

6. The other options at the time that would do this were the Ogre or the Troll, but I found myself having a difficult time imagining really hooking into these characters in the long run—they were simply too hideous, too alienating in another direction. Mindy Miron Basi (n.d., 4) has interestingly suggested that "The races that are 'ugly,' namely the trolls and ogres (and perhaps bearded dwarf women), are acknowledged as being unattractive in female form, and treated as non-player characters as a contrast to the more attractive races." The methodological implications of this kind of choice would be fascinating to explore in more depth.

Chapter 2

1. The number of subscribers to the game peaked at somewhere around 460,000 in the summer of 2003. For extensive information on subscribers across a number of MMOGs, see Bruce Sterling Woodcock's MMOGChart.com Web site.

2. A client program is an application that mediates between the server and the user's computer. It provides a more easy-to-use interface, and for text-based worlds integrates aspects like separate input lines, word wrap, and often triggers.

3. Many thanks to Richard Bartle for providing me with the opening text.

4. The term "MUD" originally stood for this particular game, not as it generally does now, for a whole class of text-based environments. Except in this first instance, this book uses the term "MUD" to refer to the overall genre of text-based multiuser games.

5. Personal communication via e-mail, June 2005. The quote originally appeared in the interactive version of The MUD Tree online, which was a repository of information about the genre.

6. For those particularly interested in the lineage, a prior version of the software, operated under the name *Club Caribe,* experimented with many of these basic properties. See Farmer, Morningstar, and Crockford (1994) for more on *Habitat.*

7. Its designers sometimes described it as 2 1/2 D, because of its use of perspective.

8. On a side note regarding the institutional structures these worlds were embedded in, eventually *The Palace* and *OnLive!* came to be owned by Communities, Inc., a company eventually run by F. Randall Farmer, one of the key designers for the first world, *Habitat.*

9. For an almost evangelical exploration of virtual worlds during this period see Bruce Damer's *Avatars!* book (1998).

10. Available at http://www.meridien59.com/.

11. The various names that have prefaced "*EverQuest*" can be a bit confusing, so a short history is in order. Essentially the general idea that an online game should be produced

originated within Sony Interactive Studios of America (SISA) under the leadership of John Smedley. In 1998, SISA changed its name to 989 Studios and, when the decision was made that it should focus on console titles, Verant Interactive emerged as a spin-off venture to continue to support online game development. Created in 1999, Verant (with the group still headed up by John Smedley) went on to develop not only *EverQuest* but several other titles. Eventually Sony Online Entertainment (SOE), Verant's primary publisher, acquired the company (in 2000) and continues to develop and manage *EverQuest*.

12. Nick Yee suggests that about half of *EQ* players have at least tried out PvP (Yee 2001).

13. This aspect of the game has changed dramatically over the years—the numbers of players who are completely new to either the genre or the game itself has significantly decreased. Low-level characters now are often longtime players starting up new characters or those migrating over from other MMOGs, and this shift in demographic has had profound changes on the game itself.

14. The reference is to Simone de Beauvoir's famous statement: "One is not born, but rather becomes, a woman" (1989/1949, 267).

15. For more on this idea of communities of practice, see Bowker and Star 1999, Lave and Wenger 1991, and Star 1983.

16. When *EverQuest 2* (*EQ2*) launched, it "locked" encounters such that players were not able to help each other out once combat had begun unless they issued a specific command for help. Many players commented on the ways this "feature" actually undermined a fairly common, and useful, practice in the original game.

17. Unfortunately I do not have data on how this dynamic operates on servers dedicated to direct oppositional play, such as the "race war" server (Humans against Trolls, for example) or PvP. I have heard anecdotally that despite server rules, helping often occurs anyway, so I would certainly not be surprised if there is a more complex mechanism for assistance on these servers.

18. Author unknown, *EverQuest Train Grading Points,* http://www.geocities.com/ rustycat3/TrainGradingPoints.html.

19. The underlying time requirement continues to present one of the biggest challenges to the genre in that it is difficult for the casual player to simply pop in for a brief period of time and accomplish much.

20. Nicolas Ducheneaut and Robert Moore (2004) have done some interesting work regarding how the design of *Star Wars Galaxies* affects various modes of interactivity. They point to not only the ways social interaction has been facilitated through particular game mechanisms, but instances in which "over-design" has also occurred, producing a more rote, instrumental pattern of play. From a slightly different perspective, Jeff Dyck, David Pinelle, Barry Brown, and Carl Gutwin (2003) have examined user-interface design in computer games and the ways various innovations lend to community formation and collaboration.

21. People are not notified when they have been added to a friend list, so it is a fairly private mechanism and does not build on the kinds of mutual signals you see in Web-based networks like Friendster or Orkut (see Donath and Boyd 2004 for more on social networking software like these).

22. Interestingly *EQ2* has developed this even more by providing guilds with Web pages and tools to manage their membership databases. The Web pages, hosted at the official Sony site, provide guilds space to support discussion forums and ways of distributing information.

23. Each *EQ* account is allowed eight characters per server, and many players maintain several characters at once. Indeed, some players have access to multiple accounts (and computers), thus multiplying their number of characters on each server. Given that each player also has her own network of contacts, any given group extends well beyond the six characters in the group list.

24. "Uber" (from the German *über*) is a term that is commonly used by players in reference to these guilds.

25. In a particularly nuanced analysis of the relationship between player action and design, one player suggests that the people who think high-end guilds are somehow ruining the game should "wise up" and recognize that the underlying structure of the game actually *fosters* some of the behavior typically criticized: "Dude your ****ing deaf dumb and blind if you believe that. NONE of them are saints. PERIOD. VI [Verant Interactive] didn't DESIGN this ****ing game for them TO be saints" (Satan Goat 2002).

26. In Nick Yee's dataset he finds 69.5% of women playing with their romantic partners (versus 16.4% of men playing with theirs), 8.1% playing with a parent or child, and 15.9% with a sibling (Yee 2001). Contrary to more negative findings typically reported in the press, a study out of the Pew Internet and American Life Project also suggests that some American college students use gaming as a way to spend time with friends, stating that 20% "felt moderately or strongly that gaming helped them make new friends as well as improve existing friendships," and 65% of respondents did not feel that gaming had taken any time away from what they might spend with family and friends (Jones 2003).

27. Among pen-and-paper players this kind of importation of character and identity is not uncommon, at least for a player's first character. It points in part to the powerful ways game histories travel across play spaces and how people approach and make sense of a game based on their past experiences.

28. One of the more entertaining examples I found of this was the baseball player Doug Glanville of the Philadelphia Phillies explaining two recent home runs against former teammate Curt Schilling. He playfully recounted the way his home runs acted as retribution for the death of his character while playing with Schilling: "I vowed to revenge on the soul of Bingbong [his character] for the negligent actions of Cylc [Schilling's Dwarf Cleric]. . . . Not enough attention is paid to the off-the-field moti-

vators that create nasty on-fiend grudges. I believe video atrocities top the list. Curt Schilling assassinated my lovable Dwarf Paladin in EverQuest, happily smiling as his character stood in the safety of the town guards" (Stark 2003).

29. "Power leveling" is when a high-level character helps a low-level character progress through the game at an accelerated rate, typically by helping kill tough monsters. While this type of play is not explicitly prohibited, it is seen by some as going against the spirit of the game. Nonetheless many players rely on it as a technique for integrating new friends into the game and feel that it is a central aspect of the social networking and bonding between players.

30. The line between these two is not completely clear, however. On more than one occasion I have been surprised to learn that a character I was playing with was the child of a fellow player—a revelation frequently revealed when the parent says something to the child in the game about doing homework or lapsed bedtimes.

31. Nick Yee (2001) has found that nearly half of *EQ* players would be interested in meeting their game friends offline (though 40% answered they had "mixed feelings" about doing so). Similarly, almost half of the *EQ* players responding to his survey found "their *EQ* friendships are comparable to their real-life friendships," with 15% feeling they were better and 37.7% feeling they "do not come close to their real-life relationships" (2001, 27). This trend is also mirrored in Axelsson and Regan's (2002) work on the MMOG *Asheron's Call*.

32. She later noted that "I got her hooked. And then she got her boyfriend, who she met on *ICQ,* so they play."

33. Available at http://www.eqatlas.com/.

34. Available at http://www.allakhazam.com/.

35. Available at http://graffe.com/.

36. The original no longer exists, but some of the community eventually moved over to a new site sponsored by a major gaming portal.

37. I should note that at the time of this writing a new expansion has been recently introduced and none of those new zones support the automatic porters. Not surprisingly, there has been some resurgence in people requesting the help of those with transport spells.

38. For example, Edward Castronova, in a landmark work, detailed how much trade was occurring around game items outside of the game world. His 2001 study of the economy of Norrath proposed that the "labors of the people [players] produce a GNP per capita somewhere between that of Russia and Bulgaria" (Castronova 2001). This phenomenon is discussed more in chapter 5.

39. There were, not surprisingly, innovative attempts by the player community to manage and regulate the markets within the game even before the implementation of

the Bazaar. Third-party Web sites hosted items' sales data where buyers and sellers could input their recent purchase prices. When someone then wanted to buy or sell an item in the game, he could look it up at the site and see what it had most recently been going for on a particular server.

40. There is a companion discussion I am not covering here on the development of "instanced zones" in the game. These are spontaneously created replicas of specific areas for fixed sets of players. They are one way designers try to work around the difficulty produced when many people want access to the same monsters or areas simultaneously. Instead of people competing, negotiating, and generally finding a way to handle access (something they have historically done remarkably well in a self-organized fashion in the game) instanced zones solve the competition problem by providing multiple copies of the same thing. As Mikael Jakobsson (forthcoming) notes, while this is a design choice that breaks basic virtual-world models, *EQ* provides an interesting "test bed" for design concepts.

Chapter 3

1. Bartle (2004) makes an excellent point when he remarks that what is particularly important is not simply knowing about different play styles, but how they interact with one another. While that issue falls outside of the scoop of this chapter, the *relational* nature of play styles is absolutely an important topic and one I certainly hope other researchers pick up on. See Appelcline (2003) for a slight modification of Bartle along social lines.

2. The founder of one of the longest running raiding guilds on my server said, for example:

I think there are two kinds of power gamers: [A] power gamer is a gamer who knows the system and plays for the goal. Doesn't play to explore. He plays to reach some goals and that's why he's a power gamer cause he goes straight in for the goal. Level fast, goes very fast for that goal. People around him fall behind and that's why they think he's a power gamer cause he knows the game system, knows all the stuff and just wants to get to his goal. So that's one power gamer. The other power gamer is how much time you spend. The common power gamer spends a lot of time as well. What is a casual gamer that plays like a power gamer? Is he a power gamer or a casual gamer? The guy who logs on and knows exactly what to do but doesn't log on everyday. I don't know what to call that guy. I still think he's a power gamer. I mean, the time invested isn't really about power gaming but really about . . . uber gaming maybe. [So he's an] uber gamer maybe [laughter about this distinction].

I have been struck by how many casual gamers play for an equal number of hours with very different results. Despite hours of play, they do not level as fast, gain (as many) rare items, or accomplish other high-end activities of note. This seems to suggest that it is not simply a matter of time but orientation and opportunity (often afforded by things like guilds).

3. Chris echoes something I have heard from professional gamers as well. He feels that the dedication, focus, and attention to competition he learned in soccer transferred

over to his computer-game playing. He went so far as to make comparisons about evaluating the best way to move across the soccer field to the kind of efficiency calculations he makes in gaming. In conversations with professional *CounterStrike* and *WarCraft* players I have heard similar comparisons, where players would draw on their athletic or chess experience to inform strategic stances within the computer game.

4. In some preliminary interviews with professional, competitive computer-game players I have heard similar comments. Top players often remark that nonprofessional players can think they are cheating because their skills and intuition about the game simply seem to defy reasonable expectations. Several players I have interviewed talked about feeling they now have a kind of sixth sense while playing but to an opponent, of course, such language can sound more like an attempt to hide cheating.

5. And in an interesting twist, Bob, the player who felt a significant amount of frustration with power gamers, actually used *ShowEQ* as a way of competing with them: "It allowed me to do something sort of passively that allowed me to level the playing field. It's such a good tool, everybody would love to be running it I think."

6. Mikael Jakobsson, personal communication via e-mail, 18 September 2003.

7. As is probably quite obvious, the line between the style of play power gamers engage in and that of professional gamers is not very distinct. After some preliminary work in the area, I find that the instrumental and rigorous approach to gaming among professionals is not unique. In fact, professional gamers (who often play FPS and strategy games) probably would be more at home discussing what it means to play with some of the *EQ* power gamers than a casual gamer in their own genre. Some of the suspicion or skepticism with which power and professional gamers are viewed does not do justice to the general approach as a legitimate gaming style.

Chapter 4

1. It does not help that within game culture some notion of what "real games" are seems to predominate, often seeing only huge commercial games or first person shooters as "hardcore" enough to warrant being called a "real" game.

2. Available at http://games.yahoo.com.

3. They no longer collect this information upon registration so the figures are based on past data (Daniel James, personal communication via e-mail, 13 February 2005). An interesting comparison remains with the numbers of women in the non-online gaming and console market. Kathryn Wright (2001a) cites a 1998 survey putting women at 43% of computer gamers and 35% of console users. Women often are "lost" in typical surveys on play because the query is formulated in such a way that ownership is the major marker for denoting the player. But it is often the case that women play on consoles owned by someone else in the household, so changing questions to measure for "secondary users" can produce different results.

4. For some important critiques on the notion of fluid identities and the utopic possibilities often purported, see Lori Kendall (2002), Beth Kolko (2000), and Lisa Nakamura (1995, 2002).

5. Game guides (volunteer player assistants) can only act in their formal helper capacity on a server other than the one they play on.

6. See Bates (2004) for a fairly classic example of the kind historical-physical-psychological difference story that circulates as an explanatory model. I have also posed some critiques of this (Taylor 2004a).

7. We might simultaneously see this as a challenge to the typical ways masculinity is framed. How are common stereotypes of what men like to do challenged by their *EQ* chatting, or customizing their avatar's appearance?

8. Personal correspondence via e-mail, 1 October 2002.

9. Christina Lindsay complicates the picture a bit more by suggesting that, in fact, there are multiple representations located across various actors and differing over time, such that "there is much more to these imagined users than a static image constructed by one group sometime during the development phase of a technology's life history" (Lindsay 2003, 32). The designers may have one image, marketing another, etc., throughout the organization. The notion of the imagined user need not necessarily be construed as a "negative" orientation. As Jessica Mulligan and Bridgette Patrovsky (2003), longtime game developers and consultants, have argued, knowing the target audience is key in MMOG projects, which can suffer from feature-bloat and development problems when developers lack an understanding who their actual players might be. At the same time, they also provide a wonderfully insightful analysis of the complicated, and often ambivalent, relationship designers have with players, especially when those "real" players conflict with the designers' notions of a good game.

10. Personal communication via e-mail, 1 October 2002.

11. Something also can be said here about how even *that* market is not fully tailored to. Certainly not all heterosexual men find the stereotypical images of women we find in computer games their idealized image of beauty. Mia Consalvo (2003) adds additional nuance to the argument by exploring the nature of sexuality and hetero-normativity often at work in computer games.

12. Here I am only addressing the issue of avatars. As others have documented, the production of race in online environments extends to a much broader range of practices, regulations, and norms and is always present even when visual representations are not (Bailey 1996; Burkhalter 1999; Kolko 2000; McPherson 2000; Silver 2000; Sterne 2000).

13. Nick Yee's (2001) data suggests similar usage. His figures put Erudites at 5.8%, with Wood Elfs the highest at 16.3%, and Ogres the lowest at 2.0%.

14. The issue of how to handle race and the design of digital spaces is something explored in greater detail by Jerry Kang (2000) in his article "Cyber-race." He proposes we

might think of three possible strategies for how racial identities might be handled online, "abolition, which disrupts racial mapping by promoting racial anonymity; integration, which reforms racial meanings by promoting social interaction; or transmutation, which disrupts racial categories by promoting racial pseudonymity" (Kang 2000, 1153). Kang is interested in showing how one might deploy different design choices strategically and also in prompting consideration of how each might orient not only the individual user, but the online community in which they exist. The notion of "race swapping" that *EQ* players might undertake could sit in both the integrationist and transmutation camps Kang discusses though, as he notes, neither position is any sure pedagogic guarantee and may rest on highly contentious assumptions. Indeed, as Nakamura (1995, 2002) has shown in her previous work, quite often racial and ethnic identities are only permitted and deemed legitimate by the community when they fit stereotypes and signal they are "not real."

15. Beth Kolko's work (2000) on how MUD interfaces and formal (coded) structures regulate racial performance and identities provides an interesting example of the ways such categories can be encoded, even through omissions, within systems.

16. They also circulate in a market economy with the advent of game items and account auctioning. Castronova (2003) has written an interesting paper that takes up the issue of the pricing of male and female *EQ* avatars at eBay and argues that, with all other factors held constant, female avatars are discounted from $40–55 U.S. from their equivalent male counterparts (with average avatar price at $333 U.S.). While some in the player community strongly rebutted the significance of the findings, it nonetheless warrants further consideration in light of the frequency of gender swapping that does take place in the game.

17. Nintendo's twist has been to offer a pink *Game Boy Advance SP,* an amazingly clueless attempt at addressing the issue. Despite this kind of disenfranchisement in marketing, I continually see young girls and women go back to the platform again and again. Such observations seem to me a testament to the commitment women and girls can have to play. They are by no means a tenuous market.

18. Personal communication via e-mail, 1 October 2002.

19. His suggestion is also about refiguring how we think about masculinity, noting, "Boys may need to play in secret gardens or toy towns just as much as girls need to explore adventure islands" (Jenkins 1998a, 292).

Chapter 5

1. Though NCSoft allows noncommercial use (via creations like fan fiction), in a fascinating twist their *City of Heroes* EULA provides fairly wide latitude for *their own* claims against reappropriation:

For clarification purposes only, "derivative works based upon" Game Content are works which are substantially similar, both in ideas and expression, to the Game Content. Similarity of ideas in the

Game Content and derivative works concern similarities between things such as plot, theme, mood, setting, appearance, and character traits. Similarity of expression concerns the total concept and the feel of the Game Content and the derivative works. (NCSoft 2005)

As we will see, such approaches are typical of MMOG companies, who seem to want to play both sides of the IP field.

2. See the Web site Chillingeffects.org for an impressive collection of both such letters and various legal FAQs on the subject.

3. See the *New York Law School Law Review* special issue on games (49, no. 1, 2004–2005) for a fairly representative sample of the way IP and related issues are framed.

4. While I am focusing here on individual player's auctions, there are now several companies that specialize in the buying and selling of in-game items, which can be purchased by players for "real world" cash. While there has not yet been a formal legal battle over *EQ* game auctions, the matter was cursorily raised via an incident around another MMOG, *Dark Age of Camelot*. In 2002 a lawsuit was filed against Mythic Entertainment, the owners of *DAoC*, by Blacksnow Interactive (BSI), an auction clearinghouse. After their accounts were closed by Mythic, BSI contended that the company was trying to overextend its copyright by disallowing the sale of characters and objects (including money). In much the same way as *EQ* framed the issue as one not only of property but reputation, the *DAoC* EULA noted that "In addition to violating our agreement, selling items and/or coin violates our legal rights and may constitute misappropriate, and/or tortuous interference with our business and tarnishes the goodwill in the *Dark Age of Camelot*™ name" (http://support.darkageofcamelot.com, 26 September 2001). In response to being banned from the game world BSI filed suit, claiming that Mythic's attempts to block their auctions represented an infringement on their legitimate commercial activity and that such attempts represent unlawful business practices and unfair advantage. Using rhetoric not unlike the "time" justifications from some who auction, BSI's own "legal disclaimer and buyer's agreement" stated that "Seller is only providing a service to the buyer. No goods or property are being sold to buyer by seller. Seller claims no title to any intellectual property interests held by Mythic Entertainment Corporation (Mythic)" (originally at http://www.camelotexchange.com/DAOC.asp). The case never made it to court as BSI, apparently operating under questionable conditions, simply closed and the owners were unable to be tracked down. Though BSI marked one of the first coordinated third-party retailers for in-game goods, the practice has been picked up by companies like IGE (Internet Gaming Entertainment) who specialize in buying and selling items for the majority of MMOGs currently on the market, including *EverQuest, City of Heroes, The Sims Online,* and *World of Warcraft.* IGE has done quite a bit of PR online and at industry events in an attempt to legitimize their practice. It is not unusual to see them attending conferences right alongside the representatives of the game companies who goods they deal in, though it remains to be seen whether the game industry reconciles itself with companies like this or continues to view them as illegitimate encroachers.

5. One of the earliest pieces was Jennifer Mnookin's "Virtual(ly) Law: The Emergence of Law in LambdaMOO" (1996). See also, for example, the ongoing State of Play conference sponsored by the New York Law School and their most recent edited collection in the *New York Law School Law Review* 49, no. 1 (2004), http://www.nyls.edu/pages/3176.asp.

6. Early on the company also ran a program that would "monitor the programs running on the player's computer, searching for cheat programs. If one was found, the user's account would be banned" (Marks 2003, 49; see also Mulligan 2000b). Ultimately this practice was dropped because of privacy concerns, though the loss of that kind of tool has proven disappointing for some. Marks quotes Smedley as saying,

"Early on, somebody found this out [the use of the program], and we very quickly had to change our stance on that—now we're privacy advocates. It bothers me still to this day, though, that we have easy means of catching people who are cheating, but now it's tough because we can't use them. So now we have to do it the hard way—we have to look at what they're doing on the server, seeing if they're trying to cheat, and we catch 30 people or so every day. It bothers me that we are trying to protect the game from cheaters, and we are using methods that are less than adequate." (Marks 2003, 49)

The use of, and strong debate around, such monitoring programs continues, most notably with the revelation that *World of Warcraft* was implementing such a device.

7. Available at http://www.uorobot.com.

8. Robert X. Cringley (2002), in a short article on the software, notes one of the original authors now works at Sony. Such movements from independent developer/player to formal employee highlight an increasingly common move in the game industry.

9. This kind of collective database-building now also is seen in the Thottbot program for *World of Warcraft* (http://www.thottbot.com/). Players can set up third-party software that interfaces with the game to automatically report back to the main system all monsters, items, and quests they have encountered and thus build a vast database about the world, which then can be searched by other users. In many ways this automates the kind of work now collected in spaces like Allakhazam, and it will be interesting to see what community implications it has.

10. It is worth noting, however, that Marks quotes John Smedley as saying, "We now have more caution in terms of looking at things a little deeper. However, I would absolutely not change the end result one bit. In fact, I have refused to put out policies on fanfiction, even though it was suggested by a lot of people that we do that" (Marks 2003, 108).

11. On previous versions of their Web site, Tolkien Enterprises listed a variety of "fanciful names" which included "Orcs." Anyone wishing to use one or more terms was requested to submit a written "proposal" to the director of licensing. I recently sought clarification from the Tolkien estate on whether or not they own the term "orc" but have been unable to get a clear answer thus far, though in one e-mail exchange they misunderstood my question and thought I was asking for permission to use the word in this book. They granted it, and that alone may say something about their position.

They have, however, recently sought to bar the owner of Shiremail.com from using the word "shire" in the URL, arguing that "The incorporation of the SHIRE name into a domain name by you is a misrepresentation to the public that the domain is connected to the *Lord of the Rings* books and/or films" (McCarthy 2004). The loops of IP claims seem to be unending.

12. In an example of how we should deploy the term *"EverQuest* designer" cautiously, such that it appears to reflect any singular sensibility, Marks notes the difference in the team that took over once the game went "live":

As the new blood in the *EverQuest* Live team took on the responsibility for balancing the game and designing new levels for upcoming expansions, they brought a new design philosophy to the game. The original design team had included numerous in-jokes and references to the design. The *EverQuest* Live team, however, wanted nothing to with that—their own design style was straight-laced, with a focus on keeping the world self-contained and without outside references. Rather than drawing off literary or cinematic inspiration, they wanted to create in each zone an experience for the players, one that would reflect the reality of Norrath. (Marks 2003, 93)

13. As Lessig suggests in his latest book, *Free Culture,* often Walt Disney's "great genius, his spark of creativity, was built on the upon the work of others" (Lessig 2004, 22).

14. One area in which more work is necessary is the ways these bundled tools and centralized distribution mechanisms limit and afford particular developments and configure player-player, player-designer, and player-company relations.

Chapter 6

1. In a language intentionally similar to that of John Perry Barlow's "A Declaration of the Independence of Cyberspace" (1996) Castronova writes, "The recent appearance of massively immersive play spaces, where the ordinary rules of Earth do not apply, is a tremendous gift to us all, a great moment of liberation, and a dramatically powerful re-connection between human beings and the artists who sustain us" (2004).

2. Kurt Squire (2001) examines a kind of participatory design that *Star Wars Galaxies* used in developing their game. While some see this process as more about community building or using future players as sounding boards (versus stronger models that actually integrate them fundamentally into the process), his examples on their use of discussion forums to consider actual game-play issues (such as who should be a Jedi, or if Stormtroopers should be playable characters) is interesting.

3. It is important to note here that I am not using the term "boundary" in the same way Juul (2005) does when describing MMOGs. For him, they are boundary objects in that they are outside of a formal (and, to my reading, systemically privileged) definition of "game." Star and Bowker are working with a very different conception that I want to draw on.

4. I also find the work of Annemarie Mol (2002) instructive on this notion of how phenomena are enacted within different contexts and by different actors, often with the intent of "speaking to" the same artifact or phenomenon but at times with incommensurate models.

References

Aarseth, Espen J. 1997. *Cybertext: Perspectives on ergodic literature.* Baltimore: The Johns Hopkins University Press, 1997.

Adams, Ernest. 2003. Not just rappers and athletes: Minorities in video games. Gamasutra (27 August). http://www.gamasutra.com/features/20030827/adams_01.shtml.

Aihoshi, Richard. 2002. Brad McQuaid interview. RPG Vault (6 April) http://rpgvault.ign.com/.

Akrich, Madeleine. 1995. User representations: Practices, methods, and sociology. In *Managing technology in society: The approach of constructive technology assessment,* ed. Arie Rip, Thomas J. Misa, and Johan Schot, 167–184. London: Pinter Publishers.

Anablepophobia [pseudo.]. 2003. Just say no to power gamers. GameGrene (23 May). http://www.gamegrene.com/game_material/just_say_no_to_powergamers.shtml.

Ang, Ien. 1991. *Desperately Seeking the Audience.* New York: Routledge.

Appelcline, Shannon. 2003. Social gaming interactions. Skotos (20 November). http://www.skotos.net/.

Asher, Mark. 2001. Massive (multiplayer) entertainment: Playing together online—yesterday. Computer Games Online (17 July). http://www.cgonline.com/.

Axelsson, Ann-Sofie, and Tim Regan. 2002. How belonging to an online group affects social behavior: A case study of *Asheron's Call.* Microsoft Research Technical Report MSR-TR-2002-7, Redmond, WA.

Bailey, Cameron. 1996. Virtual skin: Articulating race in cyberspace. In *Immersed in technology: Art and virtual environments,* ed. Mary Anne Moser with Douglas MacLeod, 29–49. Cambridge, MA: The MIT Press.

Banks, John. 2002. Gamers as co-creators: Enlisting the virtual audience—A report from the Net face. In *Mobilising the audience,* ed. Mark Balnaves, Tom O'Regan, and Jason Sternberg, 188–212. St. Lucia, Queensland: University of Queensland Press.

Barlow, John Perry. 1996. A declaration of the independence of cyberspace. http://homes.eff.org/~barlow/Declaration-Final.html.

Bartle, Richard. 1990a. Early MUD history. http://www.ludd.luth.se/mud/aber/mud-history.html.

———. 1990b. Interactive multi-user computer games. Commissioned report for British Telecom. http://www.mud.co.uk/richard/imucg.html.

———. 1996. Hearts, clubs, diamonds, spades: Players who suit MUDs. *Journal of MUD research* 1 (1, June). http://www.mud.co.uk/richard/hcds.htm.

———. 2004. *Designing virtual worlds.* Indianapolis, IN: New Riders.

Basi, Mindy Miron. n.d. The construction of gender in a massively multiplayer on-line role playing game. (Provided to author via e-mail.)

Bates, Jess. 2004. Soapbox: On girls and video games. Gamasutra (30 November). http://www.gamasutra.com.

Baym, Nancy. 1999. *Tune in, log on: Soaps, fandom, and online community.* New York: Sage.

Becker, Howard S. 1998. *Tricks of the trade: How to think about your research while you're doing it.* Chicago: University of Chicago Press.

Bhabha, Homi K. 1999. The other question: The stereotype and colonial discourse. In *Visual Culture: The Reader,* ed. Jessica Evans and Stuart Hall, 370–378. London: Sage.

Bolin, Anne, and Jane Granskog, eds. 2003. *Athletic intruders: Ethnographic research on women, culture, and exercise.* Albany, NY: State University of New York.

Bourdieu, Pierre. 1984. *Distinction: A social critique of the judgment of taste.* Cambridge, MA: Harvard University Press.

Bowker, Geoffrey C., and Susan Leigh Star. 1999. *Sorting things out: Classification and its consequences.* Cambridge, MA: The MIT Press.

Boyle, James. 1996. *Shamans, software, and spleens: Law and the construction of the information society.* Cambridge, MA: Harvard University Press.

Bradshaw, Lucy. 2005. Avoiding sequelitis in *The Sims 2. Game Developer* 12 (1, January): 38–43, 63.

Bruckman, Amy. 1993. Identity Workshop: Emergent Social and Psychological Phenomena in Text-Based Virtual Reality. http://www.cc.gatech.edu/~asb/papers/old-papers.html.

Brunner, Cornelia, Dorthy Bennett, and Margaret Honey. 1998. Girl games and technological desire. In *From Barbie to Mortal Kombat: Gender and computer games,* ed. Justine Cassell and Henry Jenkins, 72–87. Cambridge, MA: The MIT Press.

Bryce, Jo, and Jason Rutter. 2003. The gendering of computer gaming: Experience and space. In *Leisure cultures: Investigations in sport, media, and technology,* ed. S. Fleming and I. Jones. Leisure Studies Association.

Burka, Lauren P. 1995. The MUDline. http://www.linnaean.org/~lpb/muddex/mudline .html.

Burkhalter, Byron. 1999. Reading race online: Discovering racial identity in Usenet discussions. In *Communities in Cyberspace,* ed. Marc A. Smith and Peter Kollock. London: Routledge.

Butler, Judith. 1990. *Gender trouble: Feminism and the subversion of identity.* New York: Routledge.

Caillois, Roger. 2001. *Man, play, and games,* trans. Meyer Barash. Urbana, University of Illinois Press. (Orig. pub. 1958.)

Callon, Michel. 1991. Techno-economic networks and irreversibility. In *A sociology of monsters: Essays on power, technology and domination,* ed. John Law. London: Routledge.

Carr, Diane. 2005. Contexts, pleasures, and preferences: Girls playing computer games. Paper presented at the Digital Games Research Association Conference, Vancouver.

Cassell, Justine. 1998. Storytelling as a nexus of change in the relationship between gender and technology: A feminist approach to software design. In *From Barbie to Mortal Kombat: Gender and computer games,* ed. Justine Cassell and Henry Jenkins, 298–326. Cambridge, MA: The MIT Press.

Cassell, Justine, and Henry Jenkins, eds. 1998. *From Barbie to Mortal Kombat: Gender and computer games.* Cambridge, MA: The MIT Press.

Castronova, Edward. 2001. Virtual worlds: A first-hand account of market and society on the cyberian frontier. The Gruter Institute Working Papers on Law, Economics, and Evolutionary Biology 2 (1). http://papers.ssrn.com/sol3/papers.cfm?abstract_id=294828.

———. 2003. The price of "man" and "woman": A hedonic pricing model of avatar attributes in a synthetic world. CESifo Working Paper 957. http://papers.ssrn.com/sol3/ papers.cfm?abstract_id=415043.

———. 2004. The right to play. *New York Law School Law Review* 49 (1). http://www .nyls.edu/pages/3176.asp.

———. 2005. Synthetic statehood and the right to assemble. TerraNova (1 February). http://terranova.blogs.com/terra_nova/2005/02/the_right_to_as.html.

Cherny, Lynn. 1999. Conversation and community: Discourse in a social MUD. Palo Alto: Center for the Study of Language and Information, Stanford University.

Chodorow, Nancy. 1978. *The reproduction of mothering: Psychoanalysis and the sociology of gender.* Berkeley: University of California.

Club FU. 2003. Club FU recruitment (24 January). http://www.clubfu.com/.

Collins, Patricia Hill. 2000. *Black feminist thought: Knowledge, consciousness, and the politics of empowerment.* New York: Routledge.

Consalvo, Mia. 2003. Hot dates and fairy-tale romances: Studying sexuality in video games. In *The video game theory reader,* ed. Mark J. P. Wolf and Bernard Perron. New York: Routledge.

Coombe, Rosemary J. 1998. *The cultural life of intellectual properties: Authorship, appropriation, and the law.* Durham: Duke University Press.

Coombe, Rosemary J., and Andrew Herman. 2001. Culture wars on the net: Trademarks, consumer politics, and corporate accountability on the World Wide Web. *The South Atlantic Quarterly* 100 (4): 919–947.

Cringely, Robert X. 2002. Get a life (which one?): A real battle is brewing in the world of *Everquest. I,* Cringely: The Pulpit (14 November). http://www.pbs.org/cringely/pulpit/pulpit20021114.html.

Csikszentmihalyi, Mihaly. 2002. *Flow: The classic work on how to achieve happiness.* London: Rider.

Cunningham, Helen. 2000. *Mortal Kombat* and computer game girls. In *Electronic media and technoculture,* ed. John Thornton Caldwell. New Brunswick: Rutgers.

Damarr [pseudo.]. 2001. The history of the MMOG. Stratics (8 October). http://www.stratics.com/.

Damer, Bruce. 1998. *Avatars!* Berkeley: Peach Pit Press.

Danet, Brenda. 2001. *Cyberpl@y: Communicating online.* Oxford: Berg Publishers.

de Beauvoir, Simone. 1989. *The second sex,* trans. and ed. H. M. Parshley. New York: Vintage Books. (Orig. pub. 1949.)

de Castell, Suzanne, and Mary Bryson. 1998. Retooling play: Dystopia, dysphoria, and difference. In *From Barbie to Mortal Kombat: Gender and computer games,* ed. Justine Cassell and Henry Jenkins. Cambridge, MA: The MIT Press.

Denzin, Norman K., and Yvonna S. Lincoln. 2003. The discipline and practice of qualitative research. In *The landscape of qualitative research: Theories and issues,* ed. Norman K. Denzin and Yvonna S. Lincoln. Thousand Oaks: Sage.

Dibbell, Julian. 1998. *My tiny life: Crime and passion in a virtual world.* New York: Owl Books.

———. 2004. Ludified: On work and play at the dawn of the game age. Paper presented at the State of Play: Reloaded conference, New York Law School. http://www.juliandibbell.com/texts/state_of_play_2.html.

———. 2006. *Play Money.* New York: Basic Books.

DIKU MUD. 2000. Statement on *EverQuest.* http://www.dikumund.com/everquest.aspx.

Dines, Gail, and Jean M. Humez, eds. 1995. *Gender, race, and class in media.* Thousand Oaks: Sage.

Donath, Judith. 1999. Identity and deception in the virtual community. In *Communities in cyberspace,* ed. Marc Smith and Peter Kollack. London: Routledge.

Donath, Judith, and Danah Boyd. 2004. Public displays of connection. *BT Technology Journal* 22 (4, October): 71–82.

Dragonmist, Valorin [pseudo.]. 2002. Bristlebane serverwide first—Tashakhi slain in Inner Acrylia. Post on EQStratics Bristlebane Web forum (15 May). http://boards.stratics.com/php-bin/eq/postlist.php?Cat=2&Board=eqsrvbristle.

Ducheneaut, Nicholas, and Robert J. Moore. 2004. The social side of gaming: A study of interaction patterns in a massively multiplayer online game. Paper presented at the annual Computer Supported Cooperative Work conference, Chicago.

Dugger, Karen. 1991. Social location and gender-role attitudes: A comparison of black and white women. In *The social construction of gender,* ed. Judith Lorber and Susan A. Farrell. Newbury Park: Sage.

DuVal Smith, Anna. 1999. Problems of conflict management in virtual communities. In *Communities in cyberspace,* ed. Marc Smith and Peter Kollack. London: Routledge.

Dyck, Jeff, David Pinelle, Barry Brown, and Carl Gutwin. 2003. Learning from games: HCI design innovations in entertainment software. Paper presented at the GI conference on human-computer interaction and computer graphics, Halifax, Nova Scotia.

Edmonds, Lisa. 1998. A joystick of one's own. *Herizons* 12 (2): 20–23.

Entman, Robert, and Andrew Rojecki. 2001. *The black image in the white mind: Media and race in America.* Chicago: University of Chicago Press.

Fairheart, Safka [pseudo.]. 2000. Safka's Lore re-opens! *EverQuest* Vault (11 October). http://www.eqvault.com/.

Farmer, F. Randall. 2004. KidTrade: A design for an eBay-resistant virtual economy. Paper presented at the State of Play II Reloaded conference, New York. http://www.fudco.com/habitat/archives/KidTrade.pdf.

Farmer, F. Randall, Chip Morningstar, and Douglas Crockford. 1994. From *Habitat* to global cyberspace. Paper presented at CompCon, the IEEE Computer Society meeting, San Francisco.

Featherstone, Mike, Mike Hepworth, and Bryan Turner, eds. 1991. *The body: Social processes and cultural theory.* London: Sage.

Fiske, John. 1989. *Understanding popular culture.* New York: Routledge.

Foo, Chek Yang, and Elina M. Koivisto. 2004. Grief player motivations. Paper presented at the Other Players conference, Copenhagen, Denmark. http://www.itu.dk/op/proceedings.htm.

Foucault, Michael. 1979. *Discipline and punish: The birth of the prison.* New York: Vintage Books.

Fuller, Mary, and Henry Jenkins. 1995. Nintendo and new world travel writing: A dialogue. In *Cybersociety: Computer-mediated communication and community,* ed. Steven G. Jones. Thousand Oaks: Sage.

Funk, Jeanne B. 2001. Girls just want to have fun. Paper presented at Playing by the Rules: The cultural policy challenges of video games conference, Chicago. http://culturalpolicy.uchicago.edu/conf2001/papers/funk2.html.

Gilligan, Carol. 1982. *In a different voice: Psychological theory and women's development.* Cambridge, MA: Harvard University Press.

Goffman, Erving. 1959. *The presentation of self in everyday life.* Garden City: Anchor.

Goodwin, Jon. 2001. Follow the bouncing breasts. Joystick101 (31 January). http://www.joystick101.org/.

———. 2000. Banned for roleplaying: An interview with Mystere. Joystick101 (9 November). http://www.joystick101.org/.

Gorman, James. 2001. The family that slays demons together. *The New York Times,* 15 November. http://www.nytimes.com/.

Graner Ray, Sheri. 2004. *Gender inclusive game design: Expanding the market.* Hingham: Charles River Media.

Gray, Herman. 2004. *Watching race: Television and the struggle for blackness.* Minneapolis: University of Minnesota.

Grimmelmann, James. 2003. The state of play: On the *Second Life* tax revolt. *LawMeme,* 21 September. http://research.yale.edu/lawmeme/.

Grosz, Elizabeth. 1994. *Volatile bodies: Toward a corporeal feminism.* Bloomington: Indiana University Press.

Guernsey, Lisa. 2001. Women play games online in larger numbers than men. *The New York Times,* 4 January. http://www.nytimes.com/.

Halberstam, Judith. 1998. *Female masculinity.* Durham: Duke University Press.

Hall, Stuart, ed. 1997. *Representation: Cultural representations and signifying practices.* London: Sage.

Hall, Stuart, Dorothy Hobson, Andrew Lowe, and Paul Willis, eds. 1980. *Culture, media, language*. London: Routledge.

Hargreaves, Jennifer. 1994. *Sporting females: Critical issues in the history and sociology of women's sports*. London: Routledge.

Harmon, Amy. 2004. A real-life debate on free expression in a cyberspace city. *The New York Times*, 15 January. http://www.nytimes.com.

Hayot, Eric, and Edward Wesp. 2004. Style: Strategy and mimesis in ergodic literature. *Comparative Literature Studies* 41 (3): 404–423.

Hills, Matt. 2002. *Fan cultures*. London: Routledge.

Hine, Christine. 2000. *Virtual ethnography*. London: Sage.

hooks, bell. 1981. *Ain't I a woman? Black women and feminism*. Boston: South End Press.

———. 1996. *Reel to real: Race, sex, and class at the movies*. New York: Routledge.

Hughes, Justin. 1999. "Recoding" intellectual property and overlooked audience interests. *77 Texas Law Review*, 923.

Hughes, Linda A. 1999. Children's games and gaming. In *Children's folklore: A source book*, ed. Brian Sutton-Smith, Jay Mechling, Thomas W. Johnson, and Felicia R. McMahon. Logan: Utah State University Press.

Huizinga, Johan. 1955. *Homo ludens: A study of the play element in culture*. Boston: The Beacon Press.

Humble, Rod. 2004. Inside *EverQuest*. *Game Developer* 11 (5): 18–26.

Humphreys, Sal. 2005. Productive players: Online computer games' challenge to conventional media forms. *Communication and Critical/Cultural Studies* 2 (1): 36–50.

Jakobsson, Mikael. 2002. Rest in peace, Bill the bot: Death and life in virtual worlds. In *The social life of avatars: Presence and interaction in shared virtual environments*, ed. Ralph Schroeder. London: Springer-Verlag.

———. Forthcoming. Questing for knowledge: Virtual worlds as dynamic processes. In *Avatars at work and play*, ed. Ralph Schroeder. London: Springer-Verlag.

Jakobsson, Mikael, and T. L. Taylor. 2003. The *Sopranos* meets *EverQuest:* Socialization processes in massively multi-user games. *FineArt Forum* 17 (8, August). http://www.fineartforum.org/Backissues/Vol_17/faf_v17_n08/reviews/jakobsson.html.

Jenkins, Henry. 1992. *Textual poachers: Television fans and participatory culture*. Routledge: New York.

———. 1998a. Complete freedom of movement: Video games as gendered play spaces. In *From Barbie to Mortal Kombat: Gender and computer games,* ed. Justine Cassell and Henry Jenkins. Cambridge, MA: The MIT Press.

———. 1998b. Voices from the combat zone: Game grrlz talk back. In *From Barbie to Mortal Kombat: Gender and computer games,* ed. Justine Cassell and Henry Jenkins. Cambridge, MA: The MIT Press.

———. 2002. Interactive audiences? The "collective intelligence" of media fans. In *The new media book,* ed. Dan Harries. London: British Film Institute. http://web.mit.edu/21fms/www/faculty/henry3/collective7.20intelligence.html.

Jenkins, Peter S. 2004. The virtual world as a company town: Freedom of speech in massively multiple on-line role playing games. *Journal of Internet Law* 8 (1, July): 1–20. http://papers.ssrn.com/sol3/papers.cfm?abstract_id=565181.

Jones, Steve. 2003. Let the games begin: Gaming technology and entertainment among college students. Pew Internet and American life project. http://www.pewinternet.org/PPF/r/93/report_display.asp.

Juul, Jesper. 2003. Just what is it that makes computer games so different, so appealing? The Ivory Tower (April). http://www.igda.org/columns/ivorytower/ivory_Apr03.php.

———. 2005. *Half-real: Video games between real rules and fictional worlds.* Cambridge, MA: The MIT Press.

Kafai, Yasmin B. 1996. Gender differences in children's constructions of video games. In *Interacting with Video,* ed. P. M. Greenfield and R. R. Cocking. Norwood: Ablex Publishing.

———. 1998. Video game designs by girls and boys: Variability and consistency of gender differences. In *From Barbie to Mortal Kombat: Gender and computer games,* ed. Justine Cassell and Henry Jenkins. Cambridge, MA: The MIT Press.

Kang, Jerry. 2000. Cyber-race. *Harvard law review* 113: 1131–1208. http://ssrn.com/abstract=631725.

Kay, Tess. 2003. Sport and gender. In *Sport and society,* ed. Barrie Houlihan. London: Sage.

Keegan, Martin. 1997. A classification of MUDs. *Journal of MUD Research* 2 (2, July). http://www.brandeis.edu/pubs/jove/HTML/v2/kegan.html.

Kendall, Lori. 2002. *Hanging out in the virtual pub: Masculinities and relationships online.* Berkeley: University of California Press.

Kennedy, Helen. 2002. Lara Croft: Feminist icon or cyberbimbo? On the limits of textual analysis. *Game Studies* 2 (2). http://www.gamestudies.org/0202/kennedy/.

———. Forthcoming. Illegitimate, monstrous, and out there: Female *Quake* players and inappropriate pleasures. In *Feminism in popular culture,* ed. Joanne Hollows and Rachel Moseley. London: Berg.

Kerber, Linda K., Catherine G. Greeno, Eleanor E. Maccoby, Zella Luria, Carol B. Stack, and Carol Gilligan. 1986. On *In a different voice:* An interdisciplinary forum. *Signs: Journal of Women in Culture and Society* 11 (21): 304–333.

Kerr, Aphra. 2003. ~~Girls~~ Women just want to have fun. In *Level Up Conference Proceedings,* ed. Marika Copier and Joost Raessens. Utrecht: Utrecht University.

Kinder, Marsha. 1991. *Playing with power in movies, television, and video games: From Muppet Babies to Teenage Mutant Ninja Turtles.* Berkeley: University of California Press.

King, Brad, and John Borland. 2003. *Dungeons and dreamers: The rise of computer game culture from geek to chic.* New York: McGraw Hill/Osborne.

Klein, Naomi. 1999. *No logo.* New York: Picador.

Kline, Stephen, Nick Dyer-Witheford, and Greig De Peuter. 2003. *Digital play: The interaction of technology, culture, and marketing.* Montreal: McGill-Queen's University Press.

Kling, Rob. 1996. Information and computer scientists as moral philosophers and social analysts. In *Computerization and controversy: Value conflicts and social choices,* ed. Rob Kling. 2nd ed. San Diego: Academic Press.

Kolbert, Elizabeth. 2001. Pimps and dragons. *The New Yorker* (28 May): 88–98.

Kolko, Beth, and Elizabeth Reid. 1998. Dissolution and fragmentation: Problems in online communities. In *Cybersociety 2.0: Revisiting computer-mediated communication and community,* ed. Steven G. Jones. Thousand Oaks: Sage.

Kolko, Beth. 2000. Erasing @race: Going white in the (inter)face. In *Race in cyberspace,* ed. Beth Kolko, Lisa Nakamura, and Gil B. Rodman. Routledge: New York.

Kollock, Peter. 1999. The economies of online cooperation: Gifts and public goods in cyberspace. In *Communities in cyberspace,* ed. Marc Smith and Peter Kollack. London: Routledge.

Kordama, Kiaora. 2001. Swords and bikinis: The portrayal of women in *EverQuest.* EQWomen. http://fp.kiaora.plus.com/reviews/bikinis.htm.

Kosak, Dave. 2002. What's this world coming to? The future of massively multiplayer games. Gamespy (17 April). http://www.gamespy.com/.

Koster, Raph. 2000. Declaring the rights of players (27 August). http://www.legendmud.org/raph/gaming/playerrights/html.

———. 2002. Online world timeline. http://www.legendmud.org/raph/gaming/mudtimeline.html.

———. 2005. *A theory of fun for game design.* Scotsdale, AZ: Paraglyph Press.

Krotoski, Aleks. 2004. Chicks and joysticks: An exploration of women and gaming. Entertainment and Leisure Software Publishers Association (ELSPA) White Paper. http://www.elspa.com/about/pr/elspawhitepaper3.pdf.

Kuecklich, Julian. 2004. Other playings: Cheating in computer games. Paper presented at the Other Players conference, Copenhagen, Denmark. http://www.itu.dk/op/proceedings.htm.

Laber, Emily. 2001. Men are from *Quake,* women are from *Ultima. The New York Times,* 11 January. http://www.nytimes.com/.

Lastowka, F. Gregory, and Dan Hunter. 2004. The laws of the virtual worlds. *California Law Review* 92 (1): 18–26.

Laurel, Brenda. 2001. *Utopian entrepreneur.* Cambridge, MA: The MIT Press.

Lave, Jean, and Etienne Wenger. 1991. *Situated learning: Legitimate peripheral participation.* Cambridge: Cambridge University Press.

Law, John. 2000. Networks, relations, cyborgs: On the social study of technology. Published by the Centre for Science Studies, Lancaster University. http://www.comp.lancs.ac.uk/sociology/papers/Law-Networks-Relations-Cyborgs.pdf.

Legion of Valor. 2003. Recruit information (27 January). http://eqlov.com/.

Lessig, Lawrence. 1999. *Code and other laws of cyberspace.* Basic Books: New York.

———. 2004. *Free culture: How big media uses technology and the law to lock down culture and control creativity.* New York: The Penguin Press.

LeValley, Janet. 1999. CyberEmbodiment: Personalizing the transpersonal. In *The multiple and mutable subject,* ed. Vera Lemecha and Reva Stone. Manitoba: St. Norbert Arts Centre.

Levy, Pierre. 1997. *Collective intelligence: Mankind's emerging world in cyberspace.* Cambridge: Perseus.

Lindsay, Christina. 2003. From the shadows: Users as designers, producers, marketers, distributors, and technical support. In *How users matter: The co-construction of users and technology,* ed. Nelly Oudshoorn and Trevor Pinch. Cambridge, MA: The MIT Press.

Lorber, Judith. 1991. Dismantling Noah's ark. In *The social construction of gender,* ed. Judith Lorber and Susan A. Farrell. Newbury Park: Sage.

Madow, Michael. 1993. Private ownership of public image: Popular culture and publicity rights. *California Law Review* 81: 125–142.

Marks, Robert B. 2003. *EverQuest companion: The inside lore of the game world.* New York: McGraw-Hill/Osborne.

Marvel. 2004. Complaint against NCSoft and Cryptic Studios (11 November). http://eff.org/IP/Marvel_v_NCSoft/.

Mauss, Marcel. 1950. *Sociology and psychology: Essays.* London: Routledge.

McCarthy, Kieren. 2004. *Lord of the Rings* domain fight enters realms of fantasy. *The Register,* 14 July. http://www.theregister.co.uk/.

McChesney, Robert W. 1999. *Rich media, poor democracy: Communication politics in dubious times.* New York: The New Press.

McDonough, Jerome. 1999. Designer selves: Construction of technologically mediated identity within graphical, multi-user virtual environments. *Journal of the American Society for Information Science* 50 (10): 855–869.

McPherson, Tara. 2000. I'll take my stand in Dixie-Net: White guys, the South, and cyberspace. In *Race in Cyberspace,* ed. Beth E. Kolko, Lisa Nakamura, and Gilbert B. Rodman. New York: Routledge.

Mnookin, Jennifer L. 1996. Virtual(ly) law: The emergence of law in *LambdaMOO. Journal of Computer-Mediated Communication* 2 (1). http://www.ascusc.org/jcmc/vol2/issue1/lambda.html.

Mol, Annemarie. 2002. *The body multiple: Ontology in medical practice.* Durham: Duke University Press.

Morningstar, Chip, and F. Randall Farmer. 1991. The lessons of Lucasfilm's *Habitat.* In *Cyberspace: First steps,* ed. Michael Benedikt. Cambridge, MA: The MIT Press.

Morris, Sue. 2003. Make new friends and kill them: Online multiplayer computer game culture. Paper presented at the Ludic Moments Seminar, Sydney, Australia.

———. 2004. Co-creative media: Online multiplayer computer game culture. *Scan* 1 (1, January). http://www.scan.net.au/scan/journal/.

Morrison, Jim. 2001. Homeward bound. *Context* (June). http://www.contextmag.com/.

Mortensen, Torill. 2003. Pleasures of the player: Flow and control in online games. PhD diss., University of Bergen, Norway.

———. 2004. Flow, seduction, and mutual pleasures. Paper presented at the Other Players conference, Copenhagen, Denmark. http://www.itu.dk/op/proceedings.htm.

Mulligan, Jessica. 2000a. EULAquest: Part 1. *HappyPuppy* 9 (11). http://www.happypuppy.com/.

———. 2000b. EULAquest: Part 2. *HappyPuppy* 9 (12). http://www.happypuppy.com/.

———. 2000c. Mommy, she talked dirty! *HappyPuppy* 9 (28). http://www.happypuppy.com/.

———. 2002. I own yoo, dOOd. Skotos (19 February). http://www.skotos.net/.

Mulligan, Jessica, and Bridgette Patrovsky. 2003. *Developing online games: An insider's guide.* Boston: New Riders.

Nakamura, Lisa. 1995. Race in/for cyberspace: Identity tourism and racial passing on the internet. *Works and days* 13 (1–2): 181–193.

———. 2002. *Cybertypes: Race, ethnicity, and identity on the Internet.* New York: Routledge.

NCSoft. 2005. *City of Heroes* user agreement (February). http://www.plaync.com/help/eula_coh.html.

Nepenthia [pseudo.]. 2000. Roleplay and intellectual property. *Stratics* 144 (Oct. 7–13). http://express.stratics.com/.

Ondrejka, Cory. 2004. Escaping the gilded cage: User created content and building the metaverse. *New York Law School Law Review* 49 (1): 81–101. http://www.nyls.edu/pages/3176.asp.

Oudshoorn, Nelly, Els Rommes, and Marcelle Stienstra. 2004. Configuring the user as everybody: Gender and design cultures in information and communication technologies. *Science, Technology, and Human Values* 29 (1, Winter): 30–63.

Pargman, Daniel. 2000. *Code begets community: On social and technical aspects of managing a virtual community.* PhD diss, Linköpings University, Sweden.

Parker, Sam. 2000. Verant Q & A. GameSpot (10 October). http://gamespot.com/.

Polsky, Allyson D. 2001. Skins, patches, and plug-ins: Becoming women in the new gaming culture. *Genders* 34 (Fall). http://www.genders.org/g34/g34_polsky.html.

Postigo, Hector. 2003. From *Pong* to *Planet Quake:* Post-industrial transitions from leisure to work. *Information, Communication, and Society* 6 (4): 593–607.

Radway, Janice. 1991. *Reading the romance.* Chapel Hill: University of North Carolina Press.

Reid, Elizabeth. 1996. Text-based virtual realities: Identity and the cyborg body. In *High Noon on the Electronic Frontier,* ed. Peter Ludlow. Cambridge, MA: The MIT Press.

———. 1999. Hierarchy and power: Social control in cyberspace. In *Communities in cyberspace,* ed. Marc Smith and Peter Kollack. London: Routledge.

Ring of Valor. 2003. What it means to be ROV (24 January). http://pub146.ezboard.com/fringofvalor44669frm2.showMessage?topicID=393.topic.

Romero, Mary. 1992. *Maid in the U.S.A.* New York: Routledge.

Salen, Katie, and Eric Zimmerman. 2004. *Rules of play: Game design fundamentals.* Cambridge, MA: The MIT Press.

Sandoval, Greg. 2001. eBay, Yahoo crack down on fantasy sales. *CNet News* (26 January). http://news.cnet.com/.

Satan Goat [pseudo.]. 2002. RoV force play nice policy. EQStratics message board (27 June). http://www.stratics.com/.

Schaap, Frank. 2002. *The words that took us there: Ethnography in a virtual reality.* Amsterdam: Aksant Academic Publishers.

Schott, Gareth. 2004. "For men": Examining female reactions to Nintendo's marketing for GameBoy Advance SP. Paper presented at the New Zealand Game Developers Conference. http://www.gameslab.co.nz/Docs/schott_NZGDA.pdf.

Schott, Gareth R., and Kirsty R. Horrell. 2000. Girl gamers and their relationship with the gaming culture. *Convergence* 6 (4): 36–53.

Schroeder, Ralph, Noel Heather, and Raymond M. Lee. 1998. The sacred and the virtual: Religion in multi-user virtual reality. *Journal of Computer-Mediated Communication* 4 (2). http://www.ascusc.org/jcmc/vol4/issue2/schroeder.html.

Schroeder, Ralph, ed. 2002. *The social life of avatars: Presence and interaction in shared virtual environments.* London: Springer-Verlag.

Scraton, Sheila, and Anne Flintoff. 2002. *Gender and sport: A reader.* New York: Routledge.

Sherman, Sharon R. 1997. Perils of the princess: Gender and genre in video games. *Western Folklore* 56 (Summer/Fall): 243–258.

Shilling, Chris. 1993. *The body and social theory.* London, Sage.

Silver, David. 2000. Margins in the wires: Looking for race, gender, and sexuality in the Blacksburg Electronic Village. In *Race in Cyberspace,* ed. Beth E. Kolko, Lisa Nakamura, and Gilbert B. Rodman. New York: Routledge.

Simon, Bart. 2004. Toward a sociology of players: Looking at digital game play as a social encounter. Lecture presented at the Montreal International Game Developers Association meeting.

Smedley, John. 2005. Towards the future. EverQuestLive.com (February). http://eqlive .station.sony.com/news_section/newsview.jsp?story=49987.

Smith, Jonas Heide. 2004. Playing dirty: Understanding conflicts in multiplayer games. Paper presented at the Association of Internet Researchers conference, Brighton, England.

Sony Online Entertainment (SOE). 2001. Fippy's facts (29 August). http://everquest .station.sony.com/featured_content/fippyfacts/082901.jsp.

———. 2005. EverQuest end user license agreement (February). http://eqlive.station .sony.com/support/customer_services/cs_EULA.jsp11.

Squire, Kurt. 2001. Star Wars Galaxies: A case study in participatory design. Joystick101 (20 July). http://www.joystick101.org.

Stald, Gitte. 2001. Meeting in the combat zone: Online multi-player computer games as spaces for social and cultural encounters. Paper presented at the Association of Internet Researchers conference, Minneapolis, MN.

Star, Susan Leigh. 1983. Simplification in scientific work: An example from neuroscience research. *Social Studies of Science* 13: 205–228.

Stark, Jayson. 2003. Wild pitches. ESPN baseball (18 May). http://espn.go.com/mlb/columns/star_jayson/1201283.html.

Stephenson, Neil. 1992. *Snow Crash.* New York: Bantam Books.

Steiner, Peter. 1993. On the Internet, nobody knows you're a dog. *The New Yorker,* 5 July.

Steinkuehler, Constance A. 2004. Learning in massively multiplayer online games. In *Proceedings of the Sixth International Conference of the Learning Sciences,* ed. Y. B. Kafai, W. A. Sandoval, N. Enyedy, A. S. Nixon, and F. Herrera. Mahwah, NJ: Erlbaum.

Sterne, Jonathan. 2000. The computer race goes to class: How computers in schools helped shape the racial topography of the Internet. In *Race in Cyberspace,* ed. Beth E. Kolko, Lisa Nakamura, and Gilbert B. Rodman. New York: Routledge.

Subrahmanyam, Kaveri, and Patricia M. Greenfield. 1998. Computer games for girls: What makes them play? In *From Barbie to Mortal Kombat: Gender and computer games,* ed. Justine Cassell and Henry Jenkins. Cambridge, MA: The MIT Press.

Suler, John. 1996. The Psychology of Cyberspace. http://www.rider.edu/~suler/psycyber/psycyber.html.

Sun, Chuen-Tsai, Holin Lin, and Cheng-Hong Ho. 2003. Game tips as gifts: Social interactions and rational calculations in computer gaming. In *Level Up Conference Proceedings,* ed. Marika Copier and Joost Raessens. Utrecht: Utrecht University.

Sundén, Jenny. 2003. *Material virtualities: Approaching online textual embodiment.* New York: Peter Lang.

Sutton-Smith, Brian. 1997. *The ambiguity of play.* Cambridge, MA: Harvard University Press.

Synnott, Anthony. 1993. *The body social: Symbolism, self, and society.* London: Routledge.

Taylor, T. L. 2002. Living digitally: Embodiment in virtual worlds. In *The Social Life of Avatars: Presence and Interaction in Shared Virtual Environments,* ed. Ralph Schroeder. Springer-Verlag, London.

———. 2003. Intentional bodies: Virtual environments and the designers who shape them. *International Journal of Engineering Education* 19 (1): 25–34.

————. 2004a. Review of *Gender inclusive game design: Expanding the market* by Sheri Graner Ray. Game-Research (October). http://www.game-research.com/art_review_granerray.asp.

————. 2004b. The social design of virtual worlds: Constructing the user and community through code. In *Internet research annual volume 1: Selected papers from the Association of Internet Researchers conferences 2000–2002*, ed. Mia Consalvo, Nancy Baym, Jeremy Hunsinger, Klaus Bruhn Jensen, John Logie, Monica Munero, and Leslie Regan Shade. New York: Peter Lang.

Tedeschi, Bob. 2001. Expansion sought for online games. *The New York Times*, 31 December. http://www.nytimes.com/.

Terranova, Tiziana. 2000. Free labor: Producing culture for the digital economy. *Social Text* 18 (2).

Thomas, Shannon. n.d. Gems? What about naked *Tetris?* Tweetyrants. http://tweety.bowlofmice.com/tweety/gems.html.

Tryne [pseudo.]. 2001. EQWomen. http://eqwomen.co.uk.

Turkle, Sherry. 1995. *Life on the screen: Identity in the age of the Internet*. New York: Simon & Schuster.

Turner, Bryan. 1996. *The body and society*. London: Sage.

Tushnet, Rebecca. 1997. Legal fictions: Copyright, fan fiction, and a new common law. *Loyola of Los Angeles Entertainment Law Journal* 17 (3): 651–686.

Tussey, Deborah. 2001. From fan sites to filesharing: Personal use in cyberspace. *Georgia Law Review* 35: 1129–1171.

U.S. Department of Education. 1997. Title IX: Twenty five years of progress. http://www.ed.gov/pubs/TitleIX/.

Wajcman, Judy. 1991. *Feminism confronts technology*. University Park: Pennsylvania State University.

Walker, Trey. 2002. Brad McQuaid interview. GameSpot (14 January). http://gamespot.com/.

Wearing, Betsy. 1998. *Leisure and feminist theory*. London: Sage.

Weber, Max. 1958. *The Protestant ethic and the spirit of capitalism*. New York: Charles Scribner's Sons.

Wellman, Barry, and Milena Gulia. 1999. Virtual communities as communities: Net surfers don't ride alone. In *Communities in cyberspace*, ed. Marc Smith and Peter Kollack. London: Routledge.

Williams, Patricia. 1997. *Seeing a color-blind future: The paradox of race*. New York: The Noonday Press.

Williams, Simon J., and Gillian Bendelow. 1998. *The lived body: Sociological themes, embodied issues.* London: Routledge.

Winner, Langdon. 1980. Do artifacts have politics? *Daedalus* 9 (1): 121–136.

Woodcock, Bruce Sterling. 2005. An analysis of MMOG subscription growth. MMOG Chart 14.0 (11 February). http://www.mmogchart.com.

Woolgar, Steve. 1991a. The turn to technology in social studies of science. *Science, Technology, and Human Values* 1 (1, Winter): 20–50.

———. 1991b. Configuring the user: The case of usability trials. In *A sociology of monsters: Essays on power, technology, and domination,* ed. John Law. London: Routledge.

Wright, Kathryn. 2001a. Video gaming: Myths and facts. http://www.womengamers.com/articles/myths.html.

———. 2001b. GDC 2000: Race and gender in games. http://www.womengamers.com/articles/racegender.html.

Wright, Talmadge, Eric Boria, and Paul Breidenbach. 2002. Creative player actions in FPS online video games: Playing *Counter-Strike. Game Studies* 2 (2). http://www.gamestudies.org/0202/wright/.

Yates, Simeon J., and Karen Littleton. 1999. Understanding computer game cultures: A situated approach. *Information, Communication, and Society* 2 (4): 566–583.

Yee, Nick. 2001. The Norrathian scrolls: A study of *EverQuest* (version 2.5). http://www.nickyee.com/eqt/report.html.

Index